The Knowledge Capital of Nations

CESifo Book Series

Hans-Werner Sinn, editor

The Knowledge Capital of Nations: Education and the Economics of Growth

Eric A. Hanushek and Ludger Woessmann

The MIT Press
Cambridge, Massachusetts
London, England

This book was set in Sabon by Toppan Best-set Premedia Limited.

Library of Congress Cataloging-in-Publication Data
Hanushek, Eric A. (Eric Alan), 1943-
  The knowledge capital of nations : education and the economics of growth / Eric A. Hanushek and Ludger Woessmann.
      pages cm. -- (CESifo book series)
  Includes bibliographical references and index.
  ISBN 978-0-262-02917-9 (hardcover : alk. paper)
  ISBN 978-0-262-54895-3 (paperback)
  1. Economic development--Effect of education on. 2. Education--Economic aspects.
I. Woessmann, Ludger. II. Title.
  HD75.7.H366 2015
  338.9'26--dc23
                                      2014039904

Contents

CESifo Book Series Foreword

This volume is part of the CESifo Book Series. Each book in the series aims to cover a topical policy issue in economics. The monographs reflect the research agenda of the Ifo Institute for Economic Research and they are typically "tandem projects" where internationally renowned economists from the CESifo network cooperate with Ifo researchers. The monographs have been anonymously refereed and revised after being presented and discussed at several workshops hosted by the Ifo Institute.

Preface

This book has been long in the making. Perhaps that is only fitting for a book that takes a long-term perspective, inquiring into the foundations of human prosperity. But we are still somewhat chagrined that we signed the contract to write it more than ten years ago. The problem is that the contract said we would finish it by the end of 2006. But only after we signed it did we realize many unanswered questions needed to be addressed before we could produce a coherent understanding of long-run economic growth. We now feel that we understand enough about international differences in growth to put together our facts—facts that have looked increasingly consistent across different specific inquiries.

Work on such a long-term project involves taking one step at a time. Thus many pieces that come together in this book have previously been published as articles in academic journals, in particular, the *Journal of Economic Literature*, the *Journal of Economic Growth*, the *Journal of Development Economics*, the *Handbook of the Economics of Education*, *Economic Policy*, and *Economics Letters*. We are grateful to the publishers of these outlets—the American Economic Association, Elsevier, Springer, and Wiley—for allowing us to draw heavily on those works here.

At various stages of our research on the topics of this book, we benefited from helpful comments from many colleagues, including Martha Ainsworth, Gary Becker, Luis Benveniste, Mark Bils, François Bourguignon, Deon Filmer, Paul Gertler, Dennis Kimko, Manny Jimenez, Chad Jones, Ruth Kagia, Beth King, Pete Klenow, Harry Patrinos, Giovanni Peri, Luigi Pistaferri, Lant Pritchett, Paul Romer, Fabiano Schivardi, Emiliana Vegas, several anonymous referees, and seminar participants at two book workshops at CESifo in Munich, as well as at countless paper presentations. On different parts, Jason Grissom, Lukas Haffert, and Trey Miller provided capable research assistance. At the finishing line, Lisa Ferraro

Parmelee provided a deft editorial touch in improving the readability of the book.

We are grateful to CESifo for supporting this project throughout. Special thanks go to our respective home institutions—the Hoover Institution at Stanford University and the Ifo Institute at the University of Munich—not least for their hospitality when hosting our mutual visits to work together. At various stages, additional support has come from the Pact for Research and Innovation of the Leibniz Association, the Packard Humanities Institute, the World Bank, the Inter-American Development Bank, and the Program on Education Policy and Governance of Harvard University.

1

Introduction

This book has a simple theme built on the long-run growth experience of nations: knowledge is the key to economic development. Nations that ignore this fact suffer, while those that recognize it flourish.

Around the world, people in virtually every country repeat the mantra that developing human capital is important, that we need to invest in youth, and that schools have a central role. This idea is actually centuries old. In the seventeenth century Sir William Petty, a British economist, suggested that to account properly for the wealth of a nation, one must assess the skills of its labor force.[1] This theme entered into Adam Smith's classic eighteenth-century treatise, *The Wealth of Nations*, although it was overshadowed by the issues of division of labor and the invisible hand of the market that received more historical attention. To Smith,

A man educated at the expence of much labor and time to any of those employments which require extraordinary dexterity and skill, may be compared to [an] expensive machin[e]. The work which he learns to perform, it must be expected, over and above the usual wages of common labor, will replace to him the whole expence of his education, with at least the ordinary profits of an equally valuable capital. (Smith [1776] 1979: 118)

Over two centuries later, we more than ever think that in today's knowledge economy, education equips people with the skills that make them more productive in their work. Perhaps even more important, education conveys the knowledge and competencies that enable a nation's people to generate and adopt the new ideas that spur innovation and technological progress and thereby ensure future prosperity.

But the common refrain about investing in human capital, translated worldwide into numerous languages across the cities and villages and borne across time, has become a cacophony of voices that modify and distort the message such that it has lost much of its substance and force. Even with the best intentions, both policy makers and researchers have concentrated their attention not on valued skills but on proxies related to school attainment levels. In developed countries, this is secondary school completion and, more recently, access to colleges and universities. In developing countries, led by the World Bank's Education for All initiative and the United Nation's Millennium Development Goals, it is access to schooling and completion of lower secondary schooling. When issues pertaining to quality are raised, attention has turned to school inputs—spending, class size, and the like.

As the world has moved forward on this implied consensus investment plan, disappointments have mounted. Economic development has failed to follow many of the human capital policies that have been pursued,[2] and policy advice has moved away from human capital to other investments and institutions.[3]

The conclusion of the analysis we develop in this book is that Adam Smith was right: human capital, as we now call it, is extraordinarily important for a nation's economic development. The significance of education, however, has been obscured by measurement issues. Time in school is a very bad measure of what is learned and of what skills are developed, particularly in an international context. With better measures, the fundamental importance of human capital becomes clear.

Although many factors enter into a nation's economic growth, we conclude that the cognitive skills of the population are the most essential to long-run prosperity. These skills, which in the aggregate we call the "knowledge capital" of a nation, explain in large part the differences in long-run growth we have seen around the world in the past half century. Moreover, in the presence of measures of cognitive skills, school attainment does not even have a significant independent relationship with growth. This finding corroborates the stylized fact that just keeping children in school and lengthening aggregate years of schooling is largely inconsistent with growth performance. When we consider acquired skills rather than time in school, we find a clear explanation for this inconsistency.

1.1   The World as Seen from Latin America in 1960

World policy attention today focuses on the lagging fortunes of sub-Saharan Africa, South Asia, and Latin America.[4] Considerably less attention goes to East Asia; if anything, it is proposed as a role model for the lagging regions. Yet to an economist contemplating development policy in the 1960s, this perspective would not have been so obvious, and the plight of Latin America today provides a simple illustration of the central theme of this book.

In 1960 the average income in Latin America exceeded that in the sub-Saharan and Middle East and North Africa (MENA) regions, and both the Latin American and the African averages exceeded that in East Asia.[5] In those days Latin America had schooling levels higher than those of the MENA and East Asia regions, whose levels were roughly equal. Thus, on the basis of observed human capital investments, one might have expected Latin America to pull even farther ahead while having no strong convictions about the prospects of the other regions.

The unmistakable failure of Latin America's meeting its expectations is central to many current policy discussions. Today East Asia has moved far ahead of Latin America in growth and income. The MENA region has also jumped ahead, if not as much, leaving only Latin America and sub-Saharan Africa at the bottom with very low long-term growth rates and commensurate low income per capita.[6] This outcome remains puzzling by conventional thinking. Why was Latin America's growth performance so much poorer than that of East Asia and even MENA, given its high schooling level in 1960? While institutional and financial factors have drawn more attention as explanations,[7] we suggest that imperfect measurement of human capital investments rather than any empirical reality has led to skepticism about using human capital policies to foster development.

The measurement issues become apparent when we introduce into the growth picture direct measures of cognitive skills from international tests of math and science (the exact derivation of which we will describe in the next chapter). The entire picture changes. Figure 1.1 plots regional growth in real per-capita gross domestic product (GDP) for the period 1960 to 2009 against average test scores after conditioning on initial GDP per capita in 1960.[8] Regional annual growth rates, which vary from 0.8 percent in sub-Saharan Africa to 4.5 percent in East Asia, fall on a straight line.[9] But school attainment, when added to this analysis, is unrelated to growth rate differences. As the figure shows, conditional on initial income levels, regional growth over the past half century is completely circumscribed by differences in knowledge capital.

In simplest terms, while Latin America has had reasonable levels of school attainment, the skills of students remain relatively poor. In terms of student achievement on international tests, both Latin America and sub-Saharan Africa are near the bottom of the international rankings, while MENA and, especially, East Asia rank much higher. The evidence, as

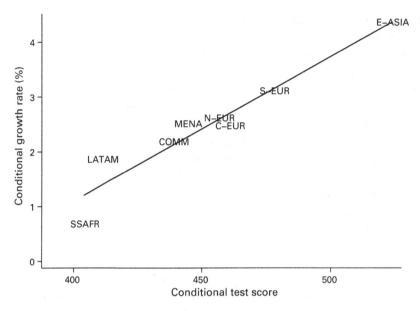

Figure 1.1

Knowledge capital and economic growth rates in regions across the world

Notes: Knowledge capital is measured by international test scores. The added-variable plot shows a regression of the average annual rate of growth (in percent) of real GDP per capita in 1960 to 2009 on average test scores on international student achievement tests and initial level of real GDP per capita in 1960 (mean of unconditional variables added to each axis). Authors' calculations. See table 1A.1 in appendix 1A for a list of countries contained in each region. Region codes: Central Europe (C-EUR), Commonwealth OECD members (COMM), East Asia (E-ASIA), Latin America (LATAM), Middle East and North Africa (MENA), Northern Europe (N-EUR), Southern Europe (S-EUR), sub-Saharan Africa (SSAFR). The Commonwealth OECD countries are Australia, Canada, New Zealand, and United States.

figure 1.1 reveals, of the population's low level of cognitive skills appears sufficient to reconcile the poor growth performance of Latin America with outcomes in the rest of the world over the past five decades. We conclude that knowledge capital is the crucial missing link in explaining why Latin America went from reasonably rich in the early postwar period to relatively poor today. Indeed Latin America's future appears to be closely connected to the progress that can be made in building up the knowledge capital of the region.

Table 1.1
Long-term growth and the impact of compound interest

Annual growth rate▶ ▼ Years from start	0%	0.5%	1%	2%	3%	4%	5%	6%
0	100	100	100	100	100	100	100	100
10	100	105	110	122	134	148	163	179
25	100	113	128	164	209	267	339	429
50	100	128	164	269	438	711	1,147	1,842

Notes: The value of $100 after growing at $X\%$ for Y years = $100 * (1 + X\%)^Y$.

1.2   The Focus on Growth

What does it mean for people's average prosperity if, for fifty years, a region grows by over 4 percent a year (e.g., East Asia) as opposed to less than 1 percent a year (e.g., sub-Saharan Africa) or less than 2 percent a year (e.g., Latin America)? The power of compound interest when accrued over a long period of time is something most people fail to realize. Indeed, while difficult to verify, Albert Einstein is reputed to have said that compound interest is the most powerful force in the universe. In table 1.1 we show how much an initial $100 would be worth after growing at a given rate for a given period of time. If the $100 grows at 1 percent, it will be worth $164 in fifty years. But if it grows at 4 percent, it will be worth $711 in fifty years. Note that without considering the compound interest, one might have guessed that the people in the country whose growth rate is 4 percent would in fifty years be roughly three times as prosperous (an increase of 50 * 4% = 200%). But the truth is, people in East Asia are more than seven times as prosperous as they were less than two generations ago, whereas people in Latin America are only about two and a half times as prosperous, and those in sub-Saharan Africa only one and a half times.[10]

In general, a government's economic policies that deal with current aggregate demand conditions and business cycles take priority over longer run policy considerations. Perhaps this has never been as true as today in the aftermath of the 2008 worldwide recession. However, in this book, we argue that issues of longer run economic growth are more critical to the welfare of nations. In a statement that we identify with, Nobel laureate Robert Lucas concluded in his 2003 presidential address to the

American Economic Association that "taking US performance over the past 50 years as a benchmark, the potential for welfare gains from better long-run, supply-side policies exceeds *by far* the potential from further improvements in short-run demand management" (Lucas 2003: 1). One way to see the importance of long-run growth is to contrast the potential gains from growth improvements with the losses from the 2008 recession—the largest growth slump since the Great Depression of the 1930s. For the United States, the Congressional Budget Office (2013) has estimated cumulative losses from 2008 to 2012 to fall in the neighborhood of $4 trillion. But an increase in the US growth rate of just one-half percentage point over the next fifty years has a present value of $67 trillion.[11] Indeed such an increase would alleviate most, if not all, of the concerns about the fiscal imbalances of the US government that have dominated public policy discussions in recent years.

Our interest is in understanding the systematic underpinnings of long-run growth differences. We can see instances in which a nation begins with very bad economic institutions and experiences substantial growth that is sustained for some time when it eliminates the distortions caused by the bad structure.[12] The case of China comes to mind here. China has experienced close to double-digit growth rates over a quarter century that might be largely attributed to having reduced economic distortions. But even in China, human capital has undoubtedly played a role,[13] and that role can only expand. Eventually the growth from the fixing of institutions disappears as the economic structures approach in soundness those of the best in advanced countries. At that point it is natural for such countries to look to other sources of growth—and here we conclude that to be successful they must turn to their knowledge capital.

1.3   Outline of the Book

The next chapter provides a model of human capital and economic growth that we use in developing our empirical work. It also describes how we measure the knowledge capital of different countries, basing our measurement on international assessments of mathematics and science skills.

The main results from the estimation of empirical growth models that test our hypotheses are found in chapter 3. Here we provide the primary estimates of the relationship between cognitive skills and economic growth. We also provide a series of robustness tests exploring alternative specifications, different subsets of countries, alternative ways to measure cognitive skills, and different time periods. In all these analyses the main results prove amazingly robust.

While estimation of cross-country growth regressions was quite popular in the 1990s and early 2000s, it has receded because of concerns about sensitivity to model specification and the identification of causal structure. Chapter 4 provides a variety of alternative econometric tests designed to investigate causal interpretations within our growth models. While addressing all possibilities is difficult, we show that our results are impervious to a wide range of commonly expressed threats to identifying a causal relationship between skills and growth. In a complementary analysis to our overall focus on growth relationships, we further show that knowledge capital also accounts for significant portions of the observed variation in world income levels.

We then investigate the implications of our growth models for both developing (chapter 5) and developed countries (chapter 6). We explore in more detail the reliability of our analysis for explaining observed income and growth differences within the developing world and the countries of the Organisation for Economic Co-operation and Development (OECD). In these specialized investigations, we find the overall conclusions hold equally well in developing and developed countries.

The final two chapters turn to the policy implications of the work. Chapter 7 estimates the economic value of alternative programs that enhance student achievement, showing the huge benefits to nations that solve the puzzle of improving cognitive skills. Chapter 8 discusses current knowledge about ways to improve skills. The overall framework is one in which, in the absence of any obvious panaceas or cure-alls that would bring about general improvements, we can describe various institutional changes related to performance. Existing evidence indicates that it is possible to improve and further that policy approaches supporting improvement can be identified.

Appendix 1A: Regional Education, Income, and Growth Statistics

Table 1A.1
Income, education, and economic growth across world regions

Region[a]	GDP per capita 1960 (US$)	Growth of GDP per capita 1960–2000 (%)	GDP per capita 2000 (US$)	Years of schooling 1960	Test score	Number of countries[b]	All Penn World Tables Countries	
							Number of countries[c]	GDP per capita 1960 (US$)
Asia	1,891	4.5	13,571	4.0	479.8	11	15	1,642
Sub-Saharan Africa	2,304	1.4	3,792	3.3	360.0	3	40	1,482
Middle East and North Africa	2,599	2.7	8,415	2.7	412.4	8	10	2,487
Southern Europe	4,030	3.4	14,943	5.6	466.4	5	5	4,030
Latin America	4,152	1.8	8,063	4.7	388.3	7	24	3,276
Central Europe	8,859	2.6	24,163	8.3	505.3	7	7	8,859
Northern Europe	8,962	2.6	25,185	8.0	497.3	5	5	8,962
Commonwealth OECD	11,251	2.1	26,147	9.5	500.3	4	4	11,251
Note: Asia w/o Japan	1,614	4.5	12,460	3.5	474.7	10	14	1,427

Sources: GDP: own calculations based on Penn World Tables (Heston, Summers, and Aten 2002); years of schooling: own calculations based on Cohen and Soto (2007); test score: own calculations based on international student achievement tests; see appendix 2A for details.

a. Country observations in the eight regions are: Asia (11): China, Hong Kong, India, Indonesia, Japan, Rep. of Korea, Malaysia, Philippines, Singapore, Taiwan, Thailand; sub-Saharan Africa (3): Ghana, South Africa, Zimbabwe; Middle East and North Africa (8): Cyprus, Egypt, Iran, Israel, Jordan, Morocco, Tunisia, Turkey; Southern Europe (5): Greece, Italy, Portugal, Romania, Spain; Latin America (7): Argentina, Brazil, Chile, Colombia, Mexico, Peru, Uruguay; Central Europe (7): Austria, Belgium, France, Ireland, Netherlands, Switzerland, United Kingdom; Northern Europe (5): Denmark, Finland, Iceland, Norway, Sweden; Commonwealth OECD members (4): Australia, Canada, New Zealand, United States.

b. Sample of all countries by region with internationally comparable data on GDP that ever participated in an international student achievement test; see appendix 2A for details.

c. Sample of all countries in Penn World Tables with data on GDP per capita in 1960 by region.

2

A Structure for Understanding Growth

Recognizing the importance of growth is different than understanding the driving forces behind it. Measuring which countries have succeeded and which have not in terms of long-run growth is easy; much less easy is to understand the factors that lead to success.

To develop an understanding of the structure of growth, economists have followed two tracks that are largely separated but sometimes intersect. On one track are the theoretical models that identify specific features and mechanisms of economies and trace their implications for growth over time. On the other are empirical exercises designed to extract regularities in growth based on the observed differences in outcomes. At times, specific theoretical models drive a particular empirical analysis. At other times, the empirical work is more loosely connected to any specific model and driven more by data and statistical forces.

Invariably both strands of modern work on growth recognize the importance of human capital. This recognition partly incorporates the insight from the work of Theodore Schultz (1961), Gary Becker (1964), Jacob Mincer (1974), and others since the late 1950s that human capital is important for individual productivity and earnings. But, even more, productivity improvements, while possibly differing in the underlying details, are known to have been fundamentally guided by the underlying inventions of people, which in turn flow from the knowledge and skills of a population. Nevertheless, the link between human capital and growth is open to a number of questions.

Our work builds on the existing growth research, but it largely differs in emphasis from the developments of the past two decades. We focus our attention on the measurement of human capital and show how improved measurement alters our views about some fundamental economic issues. We begin with classic school attainment measures of human capital and proceed to broader measures that revolve around cognitive skills, which we often refer to in the aggregate as knowledge capital.

In this chapter, section 2.1 provides an overview of the conceptual underpinnings of our analysis of economic growth. Section 2.2 presents the empirical analysis, largely based on measuring human capital with school attainment, that precedes our work. Section 2.3 identifies the shortcomings of measuring human capital with school attainment and indicates the conceptual appeal of relying on measures of cognitive skills. Section 2.4 shows how available international assessments of achievement can be combined to construct measures of human capital that more reliably indicate skill differences across nations. These new measures, representing the knowledge capital of nations, are employed throughout the analysis of economic growth in the subsequent chapters of this book.

2.1   A Conceptual Framework for Knowledge and Growth

Economists have devoted enormous time and effort to developing and studying alternative mechanisms that might underlie the growth of nations. Indeed entire books have been devoted to models of economic growth and their implications.[1] We cannot do justice to the richness of this work in a short section. Our aim is simply to provide the outlines of competing approaches because they will have implications regarding not only how to proceed in the empirical work but also how to interpret any subsequent analyses.

Theoretical models have emphasized different mechanisms through which education may affect economic growth. Generally speaking, three types of models have been applied to economic growth: augmented neoclassical growth theories, endogenous growth theories, and technological diffusion theories. While each has been supported by data, comparing the models empirically and choosing among them based on the available data has been difficult.

The most straightforward modeling follows a standard characterization of an aggregate production function where the output of the macroeconomy is a direct function of the capital and labor in the economy (but not human capital). The basic growth model of Solow (1956) began with such a description and then added an element of technological change to trace the movement of the economy over time. The source or determinants of this technological change, although central to understanding economic growth, were not integral to the analysis.

So-called augmented neoclassical growth theories, developed by Mankiw, Romer, and Weil (1992), extended this analysis to incorporate human capital, stressing the role of education as a factor of production. Education can be accumulated, increasing the human capital of the labor force and thus the steady-state level of aggregate income. The human capital component of growth comes through accumulation of more education that implies the economy moves from one steady-state level to another because of the added input to production. Once at the new level, education exerts no further influence on growth. The common approach to estimating the neoclassical growth model focuses on the level of income and relates *changes* in GDP per worker to *changes* in education (and in capital). This view implies a fairly limited role for human capital, because the amount of schooling in which a society will invest is naturally constrained. It also fails to explain patterns of education expansion and growth for many developing countries (Pritchett 2006).

A very different view comes from the so-called endogenous growth literature that has developed over the past quarter century, partly building on the early insight of Schumpeter ([1912] 2006) that growth is ultimately driven by innovation. In this school of thought, a variety of researchers—importantly, Lucas (1988), Romer (1990a), and Aghion and Howitt (1998)—stressed the role of human capital in increasing the innovative capacity of the economy through the development of new ideas and technologies. These are called endogenous growth models because technological change is determined by forces within an economy. By these models, a given level of education can produce a continuing stream of new ideas, making it possible for education to affect long-run growth rates even when no additional education is added to the economy. The common way to estimate these models focuses on growth in income and relates *changes* in GDP per worker (or per capita) to the *level* of education.

A final view of human capital in production and growth centers on the diffusion of technologies. If new technologies increase firm productivity, countries can grow by adopting them more broadly. Theories of technological diffusion, such as those developed by Nelson and Phelps (1966), Welch (1970), and Benhabib and Spiegel (2005), stress the ability of education to facilitate the transmission of knowledge needed to implement new technologies.

All these approaches have in common a view of human capital as an ingredient vital to growth. The latter two stress its impact on long-run growth trajectories. This is the notion we build on.

2.2   A Canonical Growth Model with School Attainment

The following equation provides a very simple but convenient growth model: a country's rate of economic growth (g) is a function of the skills of workers (H) and other factors (X) that include initial levels of income and technology, economic institutions, and other systematic factors, as well as a stochastic term (ε):[2]

$$g = \gamma H + \beta X + \varepsilon. \tag{2.1}$$

Worker skills are best thought of simply as the stock of workers' human capital. For expositional purposes, we assume that H is a one-dimensional index and that growth rates are linear in these inputs, although these assumptions are not really important for our purposes.[3]

Human capital is nevertheless a latent variable that is not directly observed. For it to be useful and verifiable, we need to specify the measurement of H. The vast majority of existing theoretical and empirical work on growth has begun—frequently without discussion—by taking the quantity of workers' schooling (S) as a direct measure of H. This choice was largely a pragmatic one related to the availability of data, but it also had support from the empirical labor economics literature. Mincer (1974), in looking at the determinants of wages, demonstrated that years of schooling provided an informative empirical measure of differences in individual skills.[4]

In what might be called the standard approach, empirical growth modeling has quite consistently relied on school attainment averaged across the labor force as the measure of aggregate human capital.[5] Early work used readily available cross-country data on school enrollment rates, which essentially were interpreted as capturing changes in school attainment.[6] These studies were followed by attempts to measure average years of schooling based on perpetual inventory methods.[7] An important contribution by Barro and Lee (1993) was the development of internationally comparable data on average years of schooling for a large sample of countries and years, using a combination of census or survey data on educational attainment wherever possible and literacy and enrollment data to fill gaps in the census data.[8]

Following seminal works by Barro (1991, 1997) and Mankiw, Romer, and Weil (1992),[9] a vast early literature of cross-country growth regressions tended to find a significant positive association between quantitative measures of schooling and economic growth.[10] The idea of the reliability of this approach was furthered by the extensive robustness analyses of

Sala-i-Martin, Doppelhofer, and Miller (2004) who explored the impact of sixty-seven explanatory variables in growth regressions on a sample of eighty-eight countries. Primary schooling, as it turned out, was the most robust influence factor (after an East Asian dummy) on growth in GDP per capita in 1960 to 1996.

To frame the subsequent discussion, we produce our own estimates of common models that incorporate school attainment, using improved school attainment data and an extended observation period for economic growth through 2000. We use a modified version of the education data produced by Cohen and Soto (2007), representing the average years of schooling of the population aged fifteen to sixty-four.[11] Data on real GDP per capita in 1960 to 2000 come from the Penn World Tables by Heston, Summers, and Aten (2002).[12]

Figure 2.1 plots the average annual rate of growth in GDP per capita over the forty-year period against years of schooling at the beginning of

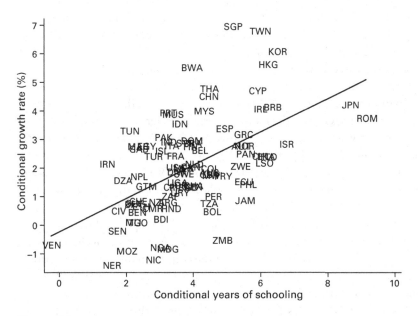

Figure 2.1

Years of schooling and economic growth rates without knowledge capital

Notes: Added-variable plot of a regression of the average annual rate of growth (in percent) of real GDP per capita in 1960 to 2000 on average years of schooling in 1960 and initial level of real GDP per capita in 1960 (mean of unconditional variables added to each axis). Authors' calculations. See table 2A.1 in appendix 2A for country letter codes.

the period for a sample of ninety-two countries. Both growth and education are expressed conditional on the initial level of per-capita GDP, to
account for a significant conditional convergence effect.[13] The regression
results depicted by the figure imply a statistically and substantively significant association with a long-run annual growth rate that is 0.6 percentage points higher for an additional year of school. The association
is somewhat lower (at 0.3) but still significant when regional variation
is taken out of the analysis (by regional fixed effects). The positive association is substantially larger in the sample of non-OECD countries (at
0.6) than in the sample of OECD countries (at 0.3). Alternatively, results
based on the samples of countries below and above the median of initial
output are in line with the pattern of larger returns to education in developing countries.

After we control for institutional differences reflected in the openness
of each economy and the security of property rights, however (a subject
to which we return in chapter 3), the association with school attainment
becomes substantially smaller and turns statistically insignificant. It is
close to zero when the total fertility rate is additionally controlled for.
Thus, while a positive association between years of schooling and growth
is clear in these data, it is sensitive to the model specification—which
raises questions about the precise role of human capital.

In our discussion of conceptual models, we noted the considerable controversy about which is the more important driver of economic growth—
the level of years of schooling (as would be predicted by several models
of endogenous growth) or the change in years of schooling (as would be
predicted in basic neoclassical frameworks). When we add the change
in years of schooling over 1960 to 2000 to the specification depicted in
figure 2.1 and similar specifications, the change in schooling never is a
significant explanation of growth with the sole exception of the sample of
OECD countries, and there it is sensitive to the inclusion of the Republic
of Korea. Because mismeasurement in the education data may be substantial, though, the estimates based on changes in education may well suffer,
and we hesitate to make any strong conclusions from these models.[14]

Two skeptical studies have presented noteworthy caveats. First, there
is the issue of causality. Bils and Klenow (2000) raised this issue, suggesting that reverse causation, running from higher economic growth to
additional education, may be at least as important as the causal effect of
education on growth in the cross-country association. Second, there is the
issue of the fragility of the evidence. Among other conclusions Pritchett
(2001, 2006) drew from the fragility of the evidence linking changes in
education to economic growth was the importance to economic growth

of getting other things right, as well—in particular, the institutional framework of the economy. Easterly (2001) has reinforced this general theme. We return to both issues and address them in the context of our expanded analysis below.

2.3   An Extended View of the Measurement of Human Capital

Measuring human capital by average years of schooling implicitly assumes a year of schooling delivers the same increase in knowledge and skills regardless of the education system. For example, a year of schooling in Papua New Guinea is assumed to create the same increase in productive human capital as a year of schooling in Japan. Additionally this measure assumes that formal schooling is the primary, or sole, source of skills and that variations in nonschool factors have a negligible effect on education outcomes.[15] This disregard of cross-country differences in the quality of education and the strength of family, health, and other influences is a major drawback of using a quantitative measure of school attainment to proxy for skills of the labor force in cross-country analyses.[16]

The larger issues can be better understood if we consider the source of the skills (H). As discussed in the extensive educational production function literature (Hanushek 2002), it has been very generally shown that skills are affected by a range of factors, including family inputs (F), the quantity and quality of inputs provided by schools (qS), individual ability (A), and other relevant factors (Z), which include labor market experience, health, and so forth, as in

$$H = \lambda F + \phi(qS) + \eta A + \alpha Z + v. \tag{2.2}$$

The schooling term combines school attainment (S) and its quality (q). Indeed a broad research base documents each of these components.

Obviously, if equation (2.2) describes the formation of skills, simply relying on school attainment (S) to measure skills (H) in the growth modeling of equation (2.1) is unlikely to provide reasonable estimates of the role of human capital. The estimates will undoubtedly be biased, and they will be sensitive to the exact model specification and the inclusion of other country measures—exactly as we saw in our limited analysis above.

The complications from the multiple inputs into skills suggest the alternative of measuring H directly—a compelling alternative that we pursue here. We focus directly on the cognitive skills component of human capital and measure H using scores from international tests of mathematics, science, and reading achievement.[17] This use of measures of educational achievement, which builds on prior research on both educational production functions and models of economic returns, has three potential advantages. First, achievement measures capture variations in the knowledge and skills schools strive to produce and thus relate the putative outputs of schooling to subsequent economic success. Second, by emphasizing total outcomes of education, such measures incorporate skills from all sources—families, schools, and ability. And third, by allowing for differences in performance among students whose quality of schooling differs (but whose quantity of schooling may not), they open the investigation of the importance of different policies designed to affect the quality aspects of schools (as will be discussed in chapter 8).[18]

2.4   Measuring Knowledge

A key element of this work is developing a measure that can equate knowledge of people across countries. In many ways, this is an extension of notions of human capital that have been developed over the past half century. But it is a specific refinement that, while important in a variety of applications within nations, becomes a necessity when comparing different countries.[19]

The remainder of this chapter focuses on developing a consistent measure of the knowledge capital of nations. It turns out that this measure is quite different from the school attainment measure used standardly as a proxy for the aggregate human capital of a nation. In the remaining chapters of this book, we show that knowledge capital is the key ingredient into economic growth and that differences in knowledge capital explain a wide range of "development puzzles" that have previously resisted explanation.

To develop a common measure of skills across countries, we turn to international assessments of student achievement. These provide a consistent measure of skills in math, science, and reading across countries, but—as discussed below—they also present some analytical challenges. In the remainder of this chapter, we describe the tests and how we combine them into measures of country differences in skills. (We further discuss their application and interpretation in chapters 3 and 4.)

Although we discuss the full range of currently available international assessments, our primary focus is on developing measures that will relate to economic growth over the 1960 to 2000 period. Thus the actual construction of human capital measures will not include information on recent students, who were not members of the labor force during the relevant period.

Overview of Available International Testing and Participation

Until recent publicity raised awareness of it, most people did not know about the international testing that could provide direct comparisons of student knowledge across countries. In fact international assessment of student achievement, focused largely on math and science, began a half century ago. Although national participation has been voluntary, recent expansions to all OECD countries and others have led to increasingly valid and reliable indicators of cognitive skills.

In the late 1950s and early 1960s international testing began with a series of meetings of academics, who came together to design a program for testing mathematics, reading comprehension, geography, science, and nonverbal ability skills.[20] An exploratory study for this purpose was conducted in 1959 to 1962 (see Foshay 1962), leading to the First International Mathematics Study (FIMS) in 1964, in which twelve countries voluntarily participated. A series of assessments for an expanding group of countries followed this first major test through a cooperative venture developed by the International Association for the Evaluation of Educational Achievement (IEA). Continuing IEA efforts were more recently complemented by an ongoing testing program run by the OECD.[21]

These international testing programs have some common elements. Each involves a group of voluntarily participating countries. These countries pay for participation and administer their own assessments according to agreed-upon protocols and sampling schemes. Since their involvement depends on individual policy decisions, the set of participating countries has differed over time and even across subparts of specific testing occasions. The tests have also differed somewhat in their focus and intended subject matter. For example, the IEA tests, of which the most recent version is the Trends in International Mathematics and Science Study (TIMSS), are developed by international panels but related to common elements of primary and secondary school curricula, while the OECD tests (in particular, the Programme for International Student Assessment, or PISA) are designed to measure more applied knowledge and skills.[22] The range of subjects tested varies over time, with assessments in math and science supplemented by reading tests.[23] Until recently little effort has been made to equate test scores over time. Furthermore the testing has been almost exclusively cross-sectional in nature, not following individual students' change in achievement.[24]

The IEA and OECD, whose tests have the broadest coverage, have adopted regular testing cycles. Table 2.1 provides an account of their major international tests, indicating age (or grade level) of students tested,

Table 2.1
History of international student achievement tests

	Abbreviation	Study	Year	Subject	Age[a,b]	Countries[c]	Organization[d]	Scale[e]
1	FIMS	First International Mathematics Study	1964	Math	13,FS	11	IEA	PC
2	FISS	First International Science Study	1970–71	Science	10,14,FS	14,16,16	IEA	PC
3	FIRS	First International Reading Study	1970–72	Reading	13	12	IEA	PC
4	SIMS	Second International Mathematics Study	1980–82	Math	13,FS	17,12	IEA	PC
5	SISS	Second International Science Study	1983–84	Science	10,13,FS	15,17,13	IEA	PC
6	SIRS	Second International Reading Study	1990–91	Reading	9,13	26,30	IEA	IRT
7	TIMSS	Third International Mathematics and Science Study	1994–95	Math/Science	9(3+4), 13(7+8),FS	25,39,21	IEA	IRT
8	TIMSS-Repeat	TIMSS-Repeat	1999	Math/Science	13(8)	38	IEA	IRT
9	PISA 2000/02[f]	Programme for International Student Assessment	2000+02	Math/Science/ Reading	15	31+10	OECD	IRT
10	PIRLS	Progress in International Reading Literacy Study	2001	Reading	9(4)	34	IEA	IRT

11	TIMSS 2003	Trends in International Mathematics and Science Study	2003	Math/Science	9(4),13(8)	24,45	IEA	IRT
12	PISA 2003	Programme for International Student Assessment	2003	Math/Science/Reading	15	40	OECD	IRT
13	PIRLS 2006	Progress in International Reading Literacy Study	2006	Reading	>9.5(4)	39	IEA	IRT
14	PISA 2006	Programme for International Student Assessment	2006	Math/Science/Reading	15	57	OECD	IRT
15	TIMSS 2007	Trends in International Mathematics and Science Study	2007	Math/Science	>9.5(4), >13.5(8)	35,48	IEA	IRT
16	PISA 2009	Programme for International Student Assessment	2009	Math/Science/Reading	15	65	OECD	IRT
17	PIRLS 2011	Progress in International Reading Literacy Study	2011	Reading	9(4)	48	IEA	IRT
18	TIMSS 2011	Trends in International Mathematics and Science Study	2011	Math/Science	9(4),13(8)	52,45	IEA	IRT
19	PISA 2012	Programme for International Student Assessment	2012	Math/Science/Reading	15	65	OECD	IRT

a. Grade in parentheses where grade level was target population.

b. FS = final year of secondary education (differs across countries).

c. Number of participating countries that yielded internationally comparable performance data.

d. Conducting organization: International Association for the Evaluation of Educational Achievement (IEA); Organisation for Economic Co-operation and Development (OECD).

e. Test scale: percent-correct format (PC); item-response-theory proficiency scale (IRT).

f. The same PISA tests administered in 2000 to 31 countries were subsequently administered to an additional 10 countries in 2002; we consider this a single test administration.

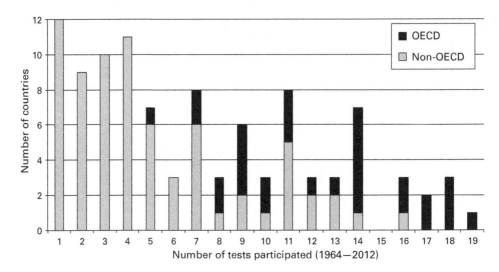

Figure 2.2

Country participation in international student achievement tests

Notes: Number of tests in which a country has participated in the following 19 IEA and OECD tests: FIMS, FISS, FIRS, SIMS, SISS, SIRS; TIMSS 1995, 1999, 2003, 2007, and 2011; PISA 2000/02, 2003, 2006, 2009, and 2012; PIRLS 2001, 2006, and 2011. Total number of participating countries: 102.

subject matter, and number of participating countries. By 2012 nineteen testing occasions had taken place, with most including subparts based on subject and grade level.[25]

The major IEA and OECD testing programs have expanded dramatically in terms of participating countries. While only 29 countries participated in these programs through 1990, the total rose to 102 by 2012. Only the United States participated on all nineteen testing occasions, but 32 other countries participated in ten or more different assessments. Figure 2.2 presents participation in the IEA and OECD tests between 1964 and 2012, divided by OECD and other countries. As the figure shows, coverage has been much greater for developed than for developing countries. Furthermore much of the participation in one or two different test administrations occurred after 2000 (which excludes them from most of our growth analysis). Importantly, those countries participating ten or more times have now accumulated information on intertemporal patterns of performance, with testing going back to the early 1990s or before, and we make use of this intertemporal information at various times below.

We address two questions in this regard: Given the different test designs, can results be compared across countries? And can the different tests be aggregated for individual countries? Although the various tests have different focuses and perspectives, they are highly related to each other, suggesting that they measure a common dimension of skills.[26] In particular, the TIMSS tests, with their curricular focus, and the PISA tests, with their focus on real-world application of knowledge, are highly correlated at the country level. For example, the correlation coefficients between the TIMSS 2003 test of eighth-graders and the PISA 2003 test of fifteen-year-olds across the nineteen countries participating in both tests are 0.87 in math and 0.97 in science, and they are 0.86 in both math and science across the twenty-one countries participating in both the TIMSS 1999 test and the PISA 2000/02 test.[27]

As discussed below, these correlations lend support to our aggregation of different student tests for each country to develop comparable achievement measures. They also support our interpretation of the tests as identifying fundamental skills comprising the knowledge capital of nations.

Time-Consistent International Measures of Cognitive Skills

Our analysis starts with the development of new aggregate measures of international differences in cognitive skills.[28] Ideally we would have measures of the skills of workers in the labor force, but ours come from data on testing of students who are still in school and who will not be in the labor force until sometime after the testing. This creates a trade-off: incorporating more recent testing has the potential advantage of improved assessments and observations on more countries, but it also weights any country measures more toward students and less toward workers.[29] In the growth analysis that follows, we begin with an expansive inclusion of tests through 2003 and subsequently investigate the impact of this choice through extended robustness checks based on more restrictive choices.[30]

Between 1964 and 2003, twelve different international tests of math, science, and reading were administered (see table 2.1). These produced thirty-six possible scores for year–age–test combinations (e.g., science scores of eighth-grade students in 1972 as part of the First International Science Study and math scores of fifteen-year-olds in the 2000 PISA cycle). The assessments were designed to identify a common set of expected skills, which were then tested in the local language. As doing this is easier in math and science than in reading, most of the testing focused on these subjects. Each test was newly constructed, with no effort until recently to link to any of the previous tests.

We want to construct consistent measures at the national level that will allow us to compare, say, the math performance of thirteen-year-olds in 1972 to that of thirteen-year-olds in 2003.[31] We also want to compare performance across countries, even when some countries did not participate in a specific assessment. Finally, we want to be able to aggregate students' performance across different years, ages, and even subjects as appropriate. The details of construction of such measures, along with the final data, are presented in appendix 2A. Here we simply sketch the methodology we use.

Because the test distribution is normal within the OECD sample, our approach to construction of aggregate country scores focuses on transformations of the means and variances of the original scores to put each into a common distribution of outcomes. The levels of difficulty of the tests can be compared across time because the United States participated in all assessments and because external information exists on the absolute level of performance of US students of different ages and across subjects at different times. The United States began consistent testing of a random sample of students at different ages and subjects in 1969 through the National Assessment of Educational Progress (NAEP) program. From the pattern of these NAEP scores over time, we can consistently map the level of US performance on each of the disparate international tests onto a common metric.

The comparison of other countries' performance to that of the United States also requires developing a common scale for each test. As country participation and test construction vary for each assessment, the variance of scores for each test cannot be assumed to be the same, that is, a ten-point difference in scores might not mean the same thing on any pair of tests. Our approach is built on the observed variations of country means for a group of countries whose educational systems are well developed and relatively stable over the time periods.[32] We created our OECD Standardization Group (OSG) by including the thirteen OECD countries in which half or more of the relevant population attained a secondary education in the 1960s (the time of the first tests). For each assessment we calibrated the variance in country mean scores for the subset of the OSG participating in the specific assessment to the variance observed on the 2000 PISA test (in which all OSG countries participated) among the same subset. The key assumption of this approach is that the *variance* in the mean performance among a group of relatively stable education systems does not change substantially over time.

By combining the adjustments in levels (based on the US NAEP scores) and the adjustment in variances (based on the OSG), we can directly calculate standardized scores that reflect comparable performance for all countries on all assessments. Each age group and subject is normalized to the PISA standard of a mean score of 500 and an individual standard deviation of 100 across OECD countries in 2000. We then aggregate scores across time, ages, and subjects as desired.

We are able to produce aggregate values for skills for the seventy-seven countries that have participated in any of the international assessments between 1964 and 2003 (see appendix table 2A.1). In our growth analysis in the subsequent chapters, however, we rely almost exclusively on the fifty countries that also have consistent economic data.

The international testing protocols have evolved over time so that recent assessments employ careful sampling rules, restrictions on the extent of any student exclusions, and modern psychometric testing procedures. Earlier testing met current standards less consistently, however. This variation in testing quality potentially affects parts of our analyses because the earlier (but poorer) tests relate to relevant members of the labor force during our period of observation for economic growth, while the more recent testing involves students not observed to be in the labor force. As a result most of our estimation relies on an assumption that the average scores for a country tend to be relatively stable over time, and that the differences among countries are a good index of the relative skill differences of the work forces.

This assumption is partially tested below, and, while some changes in scores are observed, the overall rankings of countries show considerable stability. For the 693 separate test observations in the fifty countries employed in our growth analyses, 73 percent of the variance falls between countries. The remaining 27 percent includes changes over time in countries' scores and random noise from the testing. With our averaging procedure, we can minimize the noise component but at the cost of obscuring differences over time for each country. In chapter 4 we will use the intertemporal variation in scores for the subset of countries whose observations over time are sufficient to estimate systematic changes as opposed to test noise. For the fifteen countries employed in the analysis of score trends there, 85 percent of the variance lies between countries, and the remaining 15 percent within countries is more a reflection of systematic trends in the scores.

Finally, since the assessments give cognitive skill measures for tested students, exclusion rates (e.g., for handicapped children) or differential student enrollment and attendance could affect the estimation. Direct investigation of these issues, at least for tests since 1995 when reporting is sufficient, indicates however that the growth analysis is not affected by such variations in testing.[33] As described in appendix 3B, the greater exclusions and higher enrollment rates are correlated with higher average scores, but the variations caused by these factors are orthogonal to growth rates, so they do not bias the estimated skill parameters in our growth models.

The Pattern of Knowledge Capital across the World

The average performance over the 1964 to 2003 period on the standardized tests is shown in Figure 2.3 for the seventy-seven countries that have ever participated in one of the international tests, and additionally the nine Latin American countries that participated in a regional test (on the latter, see section 5.2 below). Some clear patterns emerge when our measures of knowledge capital are arrayed region by region.

Average achievement varies strongly both among and within regions. Notably, within our sample, a wide performance gap can be observed between the best-performing country in sub-Saharan Africa and Latin America and the worst-performing country in Western Europe and the commonwealth OECD group.[34] Even Uruguay, the best-performing Latin American country on a worldwide test, performs on average a full 0.70 standard deviations below the OECD mean—implying that the average Uruguayan performs at the twenty-fifth percentile of the OECD distribution. Students in Peru, the worst-performing of the tested countries in Latin America on a worldwide test, on average are nearly two standard deviations below the OECD mean, putting Peru's average student at the fourth percentile of the OECD distribution.

One striking aspect of these regional comparisons is that differences in knowledge capital are not directly related to common findings about the individual returns to additional schooling. For example, Psacharopoulus and Patrinos (2004) estimate that the added income from an additional year of schooling on average is highest for countries in Latin America and sub-Saharan Africa even though the achievement levels in these regions are lowest in the world. As spelled out in appendix 2B, however, individual wage returns to years of schooling may be quite independent of the average quality of a country's schools. Under common assumptions, school quality enters overall earnings at all levels of schooling so that the

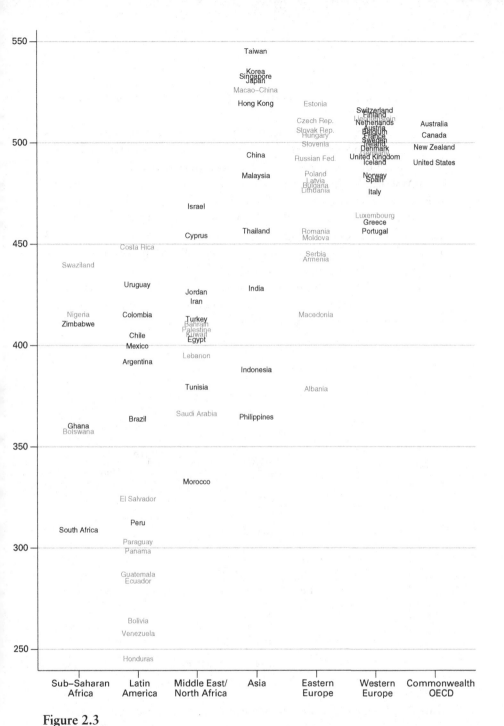

Figure 2.3

Average performance on international student achievement tests by region

Notes: Average score on all international tests 1964 to 2003 in math and science, primary through end of secondary school, using re-scaled data that puts performance at different international tests on a common scale. Countries in growth analysis in black; other tested countries in gray; gray countries in Latin America extended from regional tests.

earnings gradient with respect to years of schooling is not directly related to achievement.

The differences in achievement within regions, though, are worth noting. The difference between Uruguay and Peru means a gap in average performance of more than a full standard deviation exists even within Latin America. Within Western Europe, the gap between top-performing Switzerland and worst-performing Portugal amounts to more than half a standard deviation. And while we are accustomed to thinking of East Asian countries as performing near the top of the assessments, figure 2.3 shows Indonesia and the Philippines actually fall within the range of African and Latin American participants.

Moreover this distribution is not merely a reflection of country differences in years of schooling, the measure used in most previous research. As seen in figure 2.4, while school attainment (the average years of schooling in 1960 and 2000) is positively related to test scores, the spread of

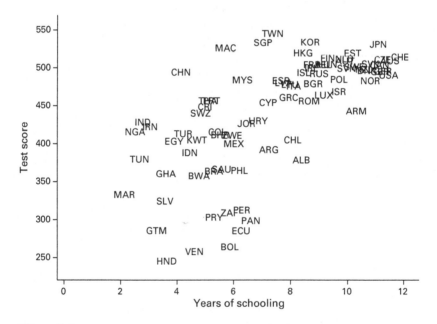

Figure 2.4

Years of schooling and educational achievement across countries

Notes: Average years of schooling (average of 1960 and 2000) plotted against average scores on international student achievement tests (extended with Latin American regional test measures). Authors' calculations; see text for details. See tables 2A.1 and 5A.1 for country letter codes.

results is impressive.[35] The correlation between years of schooling and test scores across the eighty countries in the figure is 0.67. But much of this correlation comes from simply drawing a line from the developing countries (in the lower left) to the developed countries (in the upper right). Within these clusters by development level, the correlations of school attainment and achievement are much lower. Moreover, as we will show below, the variations in achievement within these clusters are important for explaining differences in individual country growth rates. Contrary to the implicit presumption of much past work, school attainment is not a very good proxy for knowledge.

The simple takeaway from these depictions is that knowledge capital is very unevenly distributed around the world. This variation holds even within regions, implying that many simple categorizations of countries of the world would be quite inappropriate.

2.5   Conclusions on Human Capital and Growth

Nobody doubts that human capital is central to economic growth and development. Regardless of the underlying economic model of growth, its centrality remains invariable.

At the same time, few have not been at least somewhat disappointed by the results of the time, energy, and resources that have been devoted to improving human capital. Development simply has not proceeded at the pace many expected, given the sizable expansion of schooling in the depressed countries and regions of the world.

In our view, the problem of failed expectations derives largely from an inappropriate assessment of the progress made in human capital improvements. In particular, the ready availability of school attendance and attainment data, coupled with a long history of productive use in modeling individual skill differences, has obscured the conceptual and empirical shortcomings of such measures of skill levels.

When moving to international comparisons or assessing a country's progress, too little attention has been given to one key point: the amount of learning per year of schooling varies dramatically across countries. If directly asked, nobody would assert that what is learned in a typical year of schooling in Japan is the same as what is learned in a year of schooling in Peru. But that is what is assumed when international organizations assess progress simply by the numbers of students completing lower secondary school, or when economists estimate a common impact of school attainment on economic outcomes across countries.

Indeed a substantial body of research, largely unrelated to work on aggregate income and growth, focuses on formal schooling as just one of a series of inputs determining a student's knowledge and skills. This broader research, which is central to our discussions in chapter 8, leads us to look for other measures of worker skills. Importantly, the availability of international assessments of math and science achievement provides just such a means of comparing workers in different countries according to their skills. If there is one underlying idea of this book, it is that direct measures of cognitive skills offer a superior approach to understanding how human capital affects the economic fortunes of nations.

We take the aggregate historical math and science scores for students from each nation to be a direct measure of the knowledge capital of the nation. The chapters that follow show the utility of this measure for reconciling a wide range of unresolved puzzles in the economic literature and policy discussions: Why has Latin America done so poorly over the past half century? What explains the miraculous growth of East Asian countries? What economic benefits would accrue to a country that moved its students to the achievement levels of those in top-performing countries?

As described in this chapter, using international assessments that involve a varying number of countries across four decades to create a common measure of knowledge capital requires some effort. Once compiled on a consistent basis, though, these test results provide extraordinarily useful comparisons.

Finally, although we began the chapter by describing alternative formal models of growth, our empirical modeling is not linked directly to one or the other of these. Our interpretation is based on our own view of what schooling does for individuals and, by implication, for nations. Our measures focus on the development of general skills, which we see as key to how individuals adapt to new situations and how new ideas and approaches are developed.[36] Countries whose people have more knowledge skills can keep improving their economic performance over time through new technologies, improved production processes, and enhanced economic operations.

While this interpretation is close to that of endogenous growth models, its ramifications for the basic empirical analysis are few. This interpretation does affect our investigations in chapter 7 of how improved knowledge capital will affect future economic outcomes for a nation, but we do not impose this conceptual model on the reader. We show how different views would modify our evaluation of future economic well-being—with, as will be seen, a surprisingly modest impact on our results.

Appendix 2A: Methodology of Data Construction

To derive a common measure that equates the knowledge of people across countries, we aggregate the information from the different international student achievement tests (ISATs) between 1964 and 2003, described in table 2.1, into one measure per country. The general idea behind our approach to aggregation is empirical calibration—that is, we rely on information about the overall distribution of scores on each ISAT to compare national responses. This contrasts with the psychometric approach to scaling, which calibrates tests through introducing common elements into each. In reality, the international testing situations are separate events, with no general attempt having been made to provide common scaling across tests and across the full time period.[37]

The inability to equate scales across tests has been a major drawback in comparative uses of the various ISATs. The tests do not use the same questions, nor even the same technique or scale for mapping answers onto scores.[38] The early tests mainly used aggregate scores in "percent correct" format, but with questions varying in difficulty in the different tests, these scores are not comparable across tests. The later tests have used a more sophisticated scale, constructed using item response theory (IRT), which, among other things, weights different questions by their revealed difficulty and then maps answers onto a preset scale set to yield a given international mean and standard deviation among the participating countries. The questions on which the mapping is based are not the same in the different tests, however. Complicating matters even more, the set of participating countries varies considerably across tests, making the separately developed scales incomparable.

Therefore, to compare performance on the ISATs across tests and over time, we have to project the performance of different countries on different tests onto a common metric, which involves equating both the *level* and the *variation* of performance on different tests.

Comparable Level

To make the level of ISATs comparable, we need information on what levels of test scores imply the same underlying knowledge level across the different tests. Such information can be derived for the United States. Since 1969 the test results from the National Assessment of Educational Progress (NAEP) provide intertemporally comparable scores for math, science, and reading performance levels of nationally representative samples of nine-, thirteen-, and seventeen-year-old US students. While this

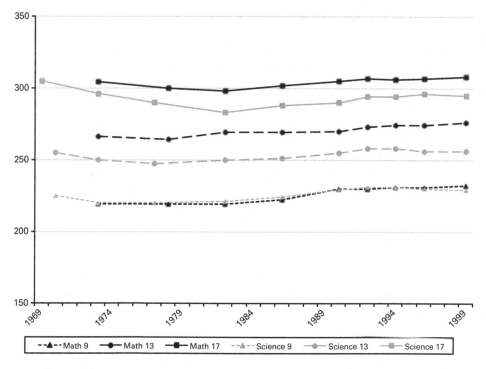

Figure 2A.1

Student achievement (NAEP) in the United States, 1969 to 1999

Notes: Student achievement in math and science at ages 9, 13, and 17, respectively, on the National Assessment of Educational Progress (NAEP). Source: US Department of Education (2008).

is the only international information on educational performance consistently available for comparisons over long periods of time, it is ideal for our purposes because the United States is also the only country that has participated in every ISAT. Given the time-series evidence on the performance of US students, we can thus scale the level of each ISAT relative to the known intertemporally comparable NAEP test performance of the United States. Figure 2A.1 shows the available NAEP results in math and science in the three age groups.[39] Despite some notable changes, the performance of US students was relatively flat over the period 1969 to 1999.

We start by calculating the difference in US performance between 1999 and any earlier point in time and express it in standard deviations (*SD*) of the international PISA 2000 study:

$$U_{a,s,t}^{US} = \left(NAEP_{a,s,t}^{US} - NAEP_{a,s,1999}^{US}\right)\frac{SD_s^{US,PISA}}{SD_{a,s}^{US,NAEP}},\tag{2A.1}$$

where U is the standardized performance difference of US students at age a in subject s at time t relative to 1999, $NAEP$ is the age-, subject-, and time-specific NAEP test score, $SD^{US,PISA}$ is the subject-specific SD of US students on the PISA test, and $SD^{US,NAEP}$ is the age- and subject-specific SD of the US NAEP test.[40] NAEP scores are available at two- to four-year intervals over the period, and values for non-NAEP years are obtained by linear interpolation between available years.

This alone does not yet yield a common scale for all the countries on the different tests. While we know whether each participating country performed above or below the respective US performance on each specific test, we need to make the international variation in test scores comparable across the different ISATs to determine "how much" above or below.

Comparable Variation

Developing a common metric for the variation of test scores in the different ISATs is harder to achieve than it is for the level of test performance. No explicit external information is available on trends in the cross-country performance variation, and the diversity of original tests and participating countries precludes a direct comparison across tests. One way to achieve comparability, though, would be to have a group of countries across which we may reasonably assume relative constancy in the size of the cross-country variation in test scores and whose members participated in sufficient numbers in the different tests. This group could only include relatively stable countries with relatively stable education systems over time, which should not have experienced major changes in overall enrollment across the ISATs.

Thus we apply two criteria for a group of countries to serve as a standardization benchmark for performance variation over time. First, the countries had to have been among the relatively homogenous and economically advanced group of OECD countries during the whole period of ISAT observations—that is, since 1964. Second, the countries' enrollment in secondary education had to have already been substantial in 1964. Given data constraints, we apply these criteria by dropping all countries where more than half of the 2001 population ages forty-five to fifty-four (the cohort roughly in secondary school in the first ISAT) did not attain upper secondary education (Organisation for Economic Co-operation and Development 2003a). Thirteen countries meet both these measures of stability, and we term them the "OECD Standardization Group" (OSG) of countries.[41]

Assuming the cross-country variation among the OSG countries did not vary substantially after 1964, we can use them to develop a comparable scale for the variation on the different ISATs. We use the standard deviation among those of the OSG countries that participated in any particular ISAT to determine the appropriate subject-specific variance, and we transform the original test score O of country i (specific for each age a and subject s) at time t into a transformed test score X according to:

$$X^i_{a,s,t} = \left(O^i_{a,s,t} - \overline{O^{OSG}_{a,s,t}}\right) \frac{SD^{OSG}_{s,PISA}}{SD^{OSG}_{a,s,t}}. \tag{2A.2}$$

The test score X has the following distributional characteristics for each ISAT. First, it has a mean of zero among the OSG (attained by subtracting the OSG mean $\overline{O^{OSG}}$ from each country's original test score). Second, it has a between-country SD among the OSG that is the same as the SD of the very same countries on the PISA test in the specific subject (attained by dividing through the SD among the OSG countries in the specific test and multiplying by the SD of these same countries in the relevant PISA test). This rescaled test score now has in effect a metric whose variation is comparable across tests.

Performance on a Common Metric

Finally, we use the time series evidence on educational performance in the United States derived above to adjust the levels of the different ISATs so that they are comparable over time. This is achieved in the standardized test score I:

$$I^i_{a,s,t} = X^i_{a,s,t} - X^{US}_{a,s,t} + O^{US}_{s,PISA} + U^{US}_{a,s,t}, \tag{2A.3}$$

which adjusts the variation-adjusted test score X so that the US performance level on each test equals the US score on the PISA test in the specific subject plus the age- and subject-specific adjustment factor U based on NAEP, as derived in equation (2A.1).

Equation (2A.3) yields measures of the participating countries' performance on each ISAT on a common scale that is comparable across ISATs. This way the internationally and intertemporally standardized test score I projects the PISA scale onto all other tests.

We are reasonably confident about the comparisons of the standardized scores within the OECD countries, all of which participated in assessments in recent years that were constructed explicitly to assess skills of

OECD students. We are less certain about countries whose results are far from the measured OECD performance. In particular, countries far off the scale of the original test scores—two *SD*s below the mean, for example—may not be well represented because the tests may be too hard and thus not very informative for them. Our linear transformations are susceptible to considerable noise for these countries.

Our main measure of cognitive skills is a simple average of all standardized math and science test scores of the ISATs in which a country participated. Table 2A.1 reports the basic combined measure for the seventy-seven countries that ever participated in any of the math and science tests.[42] The sample for our growth regressions contains the fifty countries shown in panel A of the table.[43]

Table 2A.1

Comprehensive country achievement data, 1964–2003

Panel A: Countries in growth analysis[a]

		Comprehensive achievement		Share of students	
Code	Country	All primary and secondary[b]	Just lower secondary[c]	At basic level[d]	At advanced level[e]
ARG	Argentina	3.920	3.920	0.492	0.027
AUS	Australia	5.094	5.138	0.938	0.112
AUT	Austria	5.089	5.090	0.931	0.097
BEL	Belgium	5.041	5.072	0.931	0.094
BRA	Brazil	3.638	3.638	0.338	0.011
CAN	Canada	5.038	5.125	0.948	0.083
CHE	Switzerland	5.142	5.102	0.919	0.134
CHL	Chile	4.049	3.945	0.625	0.013
CHN	China	4.939	4.939	0.935	0.083
COL	Colombia	4.152	4.152	0.644	0.000
CYP	Cyprus	4.542	4.413	0.825	0.011
DNK	Denmark	4.962	4.869	0.888	0.088
EGY	Egypt	4.030	4.030	0.577	0.010
ESP	Spain	4.829	4.829	0.859	0.079
FIN	Finland	5.126	5.173	0.958	0.124
FRA	France	5.040	4.972	0.926	0.085

Table 2A.1 (continued)

Code	Country	Comprehensive achievement		Share of students	
		All primary and secondary[b]	Just lower secondary[c]	At basic level[d]	At advanced level[e]
GBR	United Kingdom	4.950	4.995	0.929	0.088
GHA	Ghana	3.603	3.252	0.403	0.010
GRC	Greece	4.608	4.618	0.798	0.042
HKG	Hong Kong	5.195	5.265	0.944	0.123
IDN	Indonesia	3.880	3.880	0.467	0.008
IND	India	4.281	4.165	0.922	0.013
IRL	Ireland	4.995	5.040	0.914	0.094
IRN	Iran	4.219	4.262	0.727	0.006
ISL	Iceland	4.936	4.945	0.908	0.074
ISR	Israel	4.686	4.660	0.826	0.053
ITA	Italy	4.758	4.693	0.875	0.054
JOR	Jordan	4.264	4.264	0.662	0.044
JPN	Japan	5.310	5.398	0.967	0.168
KOR	Korea, Rep.	5.338	5.401	0.962	0.178
MAR	Morocco	3.327	3.243	0.344	0.001
MEX	Mexico	3.998	3.998	0.489	0.009
MYS	Malaysia	4.838	4.838	0.864	0.065
NLD	Netherlands	5.115	5.149	0.965	0.092
NOR	Norway	4.830	4.855	0.894	0.056
NZL	New Zealand	4.978	5.009	0.910	0.106
PER	Peru	3.125	3.125	0.182	0.002
PHL	Philippines	3.647	3.502	0.485	0.006
PRT	Portugal	4.564	4.592	0.803	0.032
ROM	Romania	4.562	4.562	0.780	0.046
SGP	Singapore	5.330	5.512	0.945	0.177
SWE	Sweden	5.013	4.948	0.939	0.088
THA	Thailand	4.565	4.556	0.851	0.019
TUN	Tunisia	3.795	3.889	0.458	0.003
TUR	Turkey	4.128	4.128	0.582	0.039
TWN	Taiwan (Chinese Taipei)	5.452	5.599	0.958	0.219

Table 2A.1 (continued)

Code	Country	Comprehensive achievement		Share of students	
		All primary and secondary[b]	Just lower secondary[c]	At basic level[d]	At advanced level[e]
URY	Uruguay	4.300	4.300	0.615	0.049
USA	United States	4.903	4.911	0.918	0.073
ZAF	South Africa	3.089	2.683	0.353	0.005
ZWE	Zimbabwe	4.107	4.107	0.684	0.010

Table 2A.1 (continued)
Panel B: Other tested countries

Code	Country	Comprehensive achievement		Share of students	
		All primary and secondary[b]	Just lower secondary[c]	At basic level[d]	At advanced level[e]
ALB	Albania	3.785	3.785	0.424	0.013
ARM	Armenia	4.429	4.490	0.745	0.008
BGR	Bulgaria	4.789	4.789	0.765	0.083
BHR	Bahrain	4.114	4.114	0.608	0.003
BWA	Botswana	3.575	3.575	0.374	0.000
CZE	Czech Rep.	5.108	5.177	0.931	0.122
EST	Estonia	5.192	5.192	0.973	0.095
GER	Germany	4.956	4.959	0.906	0.105
HUN	Hungary	5.045	5.134	0.941	0.103
KWT	Kuwait	4.046	4.223	0.575	0.000
LBN	Lebanon	3.950	3.950	0.595	0.002
LIE	Liechtenstein	5.128	5.128	0.860	0.198
LTU	Lithuania	4.779	4.694	0.891	0.030
LUX	Luxembourg	4.641	4.641	0.776	0.067
LVA	Latvia	4.803	4.779	0.869	0.050
MAC	Macao-China	5.260	5.260	0.919	0.204
MDA	Moldova	4.530	4.419	0.787	0.029

Table 2A.1 (continued)

Code	Country	Comprehensive achievement		Share of students	
		All primary and secondary[b]	Just lower secondary[c]	At basic level[d]	At advanced level[e]
MKD	Macedonia	4.151	4.151	0.609	0.028
NGA	Nigeria	4.154	4.163	0.671	0.001
POL	Poland	4.846	4.861	0.838	0.099
PSE	Palestine	4.062	4.062	0.571	0.008
RUS	Russian Fed.	4.922	4.906	0.884	0.081
SAU	Saudi Arabia	3.663	3.663	0.331	0.000
SRB	Serbia	4.447	4.447	0.718	0.024
SVK	Slovak Rep.	5.052	5.052	0.906	0.112
SVN	Slovenia	4.993	5.076	0.939	0.061
SWZ	Swaziland	4.398	4.398	0.801	0.004

Notes: A data file is available at www.cesifo.de/woessmann/data.
a. Main sample of 50 countries contained in the growth regressions, for which internationally comparable GDP data are available.
b. Average score on all international tests 1964 to 2003 in math and science, primary through end of secondary school (scaled to PISA scale divided by 100).
c. Average score on all international tests 1964 to 2003 in math and science, only lower secondary school (scaled to PISA scale divided by 100).
d. Share of students reaching basic literacy (based on average score on all international tests 1964 to 2003 in math and science, primary through end of secondary school).
e. Share of top-performing students (based on average score on all international tests 1964 to 2003 in math and science, primary through end of secondary school).

One possible concern with combining the different tests into a single measure is that enrollment shares have changed to different extents, especially at the secondary level. To test how much this affects our cognitive skill measures, we calculate the correlation between our measure of trends in test scores derived in chapter 4 below and changes in enrollment rates. It turns out the two are orthogonal to each other, diluting concerns that differential changes in enrollment bias the results reported here.[44]

The measure of cognitive skills previously developed and employed by Hanushek and Kimko (2000) fails to account for the unequal variances of the tests over time but instead assumes a constant variance.[45]

Our measure is highly correlated with the Hanushek–Kimko measure ($r = 0.83$), but the important question is the relationship with growth. For the thirty countries the two data sets have in common, we estimate the growth models of chapter 3 using the alternative measures of cognitive skills. While both versions of the test score measure enter the model strongly and significantly, statistical precision is considerably higher with the new one ($t = 7.43$ versus $t = 4.02$), as is the explanatory power of the model (adj. $R^2 = 0.80$ versus adj. $R^2 = 0.61$). The content of signal relative to noise in the test score measure thus seems considerably raised in the new measure.

Appendix 2B: Country-Level School Quality and Mincer Returns

In the literature a variety of approaches has been used to estimate rates of return to years of schooling for different countries. The most common approach is a simple Mincer earnings function, but at times direct calculations have been made for internal rates of return (e.g., see the discussions in Psacharopoulos and Patrinos (2004) and in chapter 4 below). In all such cases what is really estimated is the schooling gradient of earnings, and interpretation of this gradient as a rate of return depends on a number of assumptions (as partially detailed by Heckman, Lochner, and Todd 2006). While the basic assumption is that the cost of schooling comprises entirely the forgone earnings from being out of the labor market, assumptions about the length of working life, the constancy of rates of return, the separability of schooling and on-the-job training investments, and the independence from ability differences also enter in. Here we ignore such complications and concentrate on the importance of school quality.

The simplest version of an earnings model employs a basic investment model in which the return r on the investment of spending one more year in school (rather than in the labor market) is the parameter that equates the following investment identity:

$$Y_S(\phi^c) = Y_{S-1}(\phi^c) + r_S I_S, \tag{2B.1}$$

where $Y_\tau(\phi^c)$ is earnings with τ years of schooling, ϕ^c is school quality in country c, I_S is the investment in the Sth year of schooling, and r_S is the return to investment in that year.

The standard simplification is that the cost of investing in another year of schooling is just forgone earnings, so $I_S = Y_{S-1}(\phi^c)$. With this we have

$$Y_S(\phi^c) = Y_{S-1}(\phi^c)(1 + r_S). \tag{2B.2}$$

Then by recursion and assuming we can treat the return, r_t, as a constant:

$$Y_S(\phi^c) = Y_0(\phi^c)\prod\nolimits_0^S (1+r) = Y_0(\phi^c)(1+r)^S, \tag{2B.3}$$

where S is years of schooling.[46] By taking logs, we have

$$\begin{aligned}\ln Y_S(\phi^c) &= \ln Y_0(\phi^c) + \ln(1+r)S \\ &\approx \ln Y_0(\phi^c) + rS\end{aligned} \tag{2B.4}$$

(where the approximation holds for small r).

This is the standard log-linear human capital earnings function. After we allow for experience, it becomes the "Mincer" earnings model most frequently used in empirical analysis. Note that the return to years of schooling r is independent of the average quality of schooling ϕ^c in a country.

What this says is simply that the micro estimates of the returns to a year of schooling are a function of the proportional differences in earnings at different levels of schooling. Those earnings can be a direct function of ϕ^c, the school quality in country c, but the Mincer earnings function in equation (2B.4) still holds as a representation of earnings at different levels of schooling in any country.

An even easier way to see this is to presume that school quality in country c has a constant impact across schooling levels with the simple functional form of $Y_t(\phi^c) = \phi^c Y_t$. Then, rearranging equation (2B.2), we can see the rate of return to one additional year of schooling can be expressed as

$$r = \frac{\phi^c Y_S - \phi^c Y_{S-1}}{\phi^c Y_{S-1}} = \frac{Y_S - Y_{S-1}}{Y_{S-1}}. \tag{2B.5}$$

In other words, the rate of return, r, is simply the proportionate increase in earnings when going from $S-1$ to S years of schooling, and the quality of schooling, ϕ^c, drops out.

To estimate the standard Mincer equation (2B.4) with a pooled, cross-country sample, it would be necessary to adjust the earnings in each country for ϕ^c, but this term within a country is subsumed in the base level of income (the constant) in each country's earnings function. Another way of saying this is that earnings before and after getting additional schooling can be lower or higher in one country or another, but the parameter estimated (r) just provides the gradient of earnings across schooling levels.

3

Knowledge Capital and Growth: The Main Results

We now concentrate directly on the role of knowledge capital in determining the long-run economic fortunes of nations. We present a basic description of the stylized facts of knowledge capital and differences in growth rates across countries and consider how this basic picture is affected by alternative formulations, measures, and samples. This chapter on the facts of growth is intimately linked to the next, which considers whether this description can plausibly be thought of as a causal relationship—that is, one in which a country's improvement in knowledge capital might reasonably be expected to produce higher growth rates.

Our knowledge capital measure turns out to be very closely related to economic growth rates in cross-country growth regressions. Simple growth models considering knowledge capital (in addition to years of schooling and initial income levels) account for three-quarters of the international variation in long-run growth rates—a stark contrast to models excluding cognitive skills that can account for just one-quarter of the variation. And, as was not the case with prior empirical growth studies, our clearest result is the consistency of alternative estimates of the skills–growth relationship, both in terms of quantitative impacts and statistical significance.[1] The remarkable stability of the models in the face of alternative specifications, varying samples, and alternative measures of cognitive skills (section 3.1) implies a robustness uncommon to most cross-country growth modeling. In terms of previous questions about the fragility of any estimates of years of schooling and growth, these estimates underscore a simple finding that prior results suffered from critical measurement issues.

As a preview, it is useful to indicate here the magnitude of the estimated impact of knowledge capital on growth. Following a general convention, we often refer to skill differences in terms of standard deviations, where one standard deviation is, for example, the difference between the median student and the student at the eighty-fourth percentile of the international (OECD) distribution. Almost all of the alternative specifications and modeling approaches suggest a rise of one standard deviation in the cognitive skills of a country's workforce is associated with approximately *two percentage points higher annual growth in per-capita GDP.*

The interpretation and implications of our estimates, to which we devote considerable attention in later chapters, are central to the subsequent policy discussions. While the magnitude of associated growth is clearly substantial, particularly compared to regional rates that average between 1.4 and 4.5 percent over the 1960 to 2000 period (see table 1A.1), expecting the cognitive skills of a country's workforce to improve by one standard deviation—bringing, say, Mexico up to the OECD average—over any reasonable time horizon is implausible. Improving schooling sufficiently to lift a country's average by one-quarter standard deviation (twenty-five points on a PISA scale) is, however, quite plausible. This kind of improvement has, for example, been observed in Germany, Mexico, Poland, and Turkey during the past decade and in Finland over the two to three decades before.[2]

Perhaps a leading competitor as a fundamental explanation of growth differences is the role of societal institutions, including the basic economic and legal structures of nations. This perspective, pursued importantly by Stanley Engerman and Kenneth Sokoloff and by Daron Acemoglu and his collaborators, links growth to some of the overall policies of countries.[3] As we show below, this perspective is actually quite complementary to our own perspective (section 3.2).

Finally, the simple average of skills may not be sufficiently sensitive to the policy options typically facing a nation. Should one institute policies chiefly directed to the lower end of the cognitive distribution, such as the Education for All initiative, or aim more at the top end, such as through the focused technological colleges of India? Using the detailed country-specific distributional dimension of our skill measures, we go beyond simple mean differences in scores to provide estimates of how growth is affected by the distribution of skills within countries and how that might interact with a nation's technology (section 3.3). We find improving both ends of the distribution beneficial and complementary. Perhaps surprisingly, the highly skilled are even more important to developing countries that have scope for imitation than to developed countries that are innovating. In other words, both providing broad basic education—education for all—*and* pushing significant numbers of people to very high achievement levels have economic payoffs.

3.1   Stylized Facts about Knowledge Capital and Growth

While in the previous chapter we sketched the results of "classic" modeling of growth with human capital measured by school attainment, in this chapter we show the importance of measurement issues.[4] We begin with the simplest models of growth using the knowledge capital estimates we have created. This investigation of the role of skills was initiated by Hanushek and Kimko (2000), who related a measure of cognitive skills derived from the international student achievement tests through 1991 to economic growth in 1960 to 1990 in a sample of thirty-one countries with available data. They found the association of economic growth with cognitive skills dwarfs its association with years of schooling and raises the explanatory power of growth models substantially. Their general pattern of results has since been duplicated by a series of other studies that have pursued different tests and specifications along with variations of skills measurement.[5]

Here we estimate the basic growth model of equation (2.1) for the fifty countries with cognitive skill and economic data over the period 1960 to 2000. To avoid the 2008 global recession, its aftermath, and any potential bubbles building up beforehand, our main growth analysis stops at 2000, but this cutoff is not important to our conclusions. Cognitive skills are measured by taking the simple average of all observed math and science scores between 1964 and 2003 for each country, although we test the results for sensitivity to inclusion of varying time periods and subsets of tests. As in the previous chapter, the income data come from version 6.1 of the Penn World Tables (Heston, Summers, and Aten 2002), and the data on years of schooling are an extended version of the Cohen and Soto (2007) data.[6]

While we concentrate on issues surrounding the measurement of cognitive skills here, other questions have recently been raised about the accuracy and reliability of both economic and schooling data. In appendix 3A, we investigate the impact of using the latest Barro and Lee (2013) data on school attainment and of substituting the updated Penn World Table data (version 7.0), which provide additional evidence confirming our basic results through the period up to 2009. This extension of the period of analysis also allows us to separate cleanly the period of test observations from the period of observed growth, which we do in two separate cuts: test scores observed until 1984 are linked to growth since 1985 for a sample of twenty-five countries and tests scores before 1995 are linked to subsequent growth for thirty-seven countries. Because none of these alternatives materially affects our results, we simply combine these sensitivity studies in the appendix.

Basic Results

The central finding of the statistical analysis is the importance of cognitive skills in explaining international differences in long-run growth rates. As a comparison to previous cross-country analyses, however, the first column of table 3.1 presents estimates of a simple growth model with school attainment—the model underlying figure 2.1, above, estimated on our fifty-country sample.[7] While this model explains one-quarter of the variance in growth rates, adding cognitive skills increases this to three-quarters of the variance. The estimated impact of test scores is strongly significant, with a magnitude unchanged by either the exclusion (column 2 in table 3.1) or inclusion (column 3) of initial school attainment in 1960.[8]

Figures 3.1 and 3.2 provide graphical depictions (which are essentially unchanged by the subsequent investigations of alternative specifications) of the basic results. Figure 3.1 plots the independent impact of knowledge capital on growth, based on column 3 of table 3.1. In contrast to the earlier picture of the impact of school attainment on growth in figure 2.1, countries are now seen lying quite close to the overall regression line, indicating a very strong association between educational achievement and economic growth.

Also instructive is plotting the impact of school attainment on growth *after considering cognitive skills*. As seen in figure 3.2, the relationship is now flat: school attainment bears no relationship to long run growth and is not statistically significant in the presence of the direct cognitive skill measure of human capital. This does not change when attainment is measured as the average between 1960 and 2000 (column 4 of table 3.1), rather than at the beginning of the period.

The insignificance of school attainment does not, of course, mean schooling is irrelevant. Measured skills are closely related to schooling—a point we emphasize below—but the accumulation of skills throughout the life cycle depends on learning earlier in life. We measure achievement at various points during primary and secondary education. Even if the added learning with tertiary education were simply additive, knowledge at these earlier points would strongly influence the ultimate skill accumulated by entry into the labor force. As James Heckman and his colleagues have emphasized, however, dynamic complementarity of investments implies a greater impact of further schooling on skills if it builds on a larger

Table 3.1
Cognitive skills and years of schooling in growth regressions

	(1)	(2)	(3)	(4)	(5)a	(6)	(7)
Cognitive skills		2.015***	1.980***	1.975***	1.933***	1.666***	1.985***
		(10.68)	(9.12)	(8.28)	(8.29)	(5.09)	(7.83)
Initial years of schooling (1960)	0.369***		0.026		0.025	0.047	-0.090
	(3.23)		(0.34)		(0.29)	(0.54)	(1.02)
Initial GDP per capita (1960)	-0.379***	-0.287***	-0.302***	-0.298***	-0.298***	-0.255***	
	(4.24)	(9.15)	(5.54)	(6.02)	(5.04)	(3.12)	
Average years of schooling (1960, 2000)				0.024			
				(0.78)			
log (initial GDP per capita (1960))							-0.879***
							(3.39)
Indicators for 8 world regions						yes	
Constant	2.785***	-4.827***	-4.737***	-4.764***	-4.536***	-3.185**	-4.491***
	(7.41)	(6.00)	(5.54)	(5.66)	(4.97)	(2.16)	(4.48)
Number of countries	50	50	50	50	52	50	50
R^2 (adj.)	0.252	0.733	0.728	0.728	0.706	0.706	0.637

Notes: Dependent variable: average annual growth rate in GDP per capita, 1960 to 2000. Cognitive skill measure refers to average score on all international tests 1964 to 2003 in math and science, primary through end of secondary school. t-Statistics in parentheses: statistical significance at * 10 percent, ** 5 percent, *** 1 percent.
a. Robust regression including the two outliers of Botswana and Nigeria (using *rreg* robust estimation command implemented in Stata).

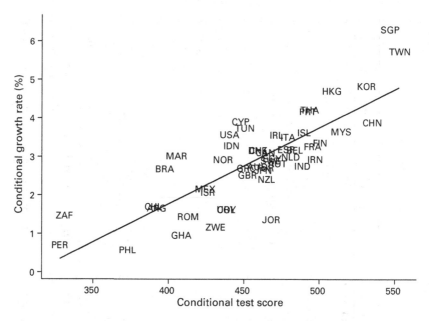

Figure 3.1

Knowledge capital and economic growth rates across countries

Notes: Added-variable plot of a regression of the average annual rate of growth (in percent) of real GDP per capita in 1960 to 2000 on average test scores on international student achievement tests, average years of schooling in 1960, and initial level of real GDP per capita in 1960 (mean of unconditional variables added to each axis). Authors' calculations; see table 3.1, column 3. See table 2A.1 for country letter codes.

base developed earlier (Cunha and Heckman 2007); the simple point is that "skill begets skill through a multiplier process" (Cunha et al. 2006: 698). Conversely, the impact of additional attainment is less if it is built upon lower basic skills.[9] The insignificance of school attainment suggests that simply investing in further schooling without ensuring commensurate improvements in cognitive skills does not lead to economic returns.

With respect to magnitude, one standard deviation in test scores (measured at the OECD student level) is associated with an average annual growth rate in GDP per capita two percentage points higher over the forty years that we observe.[10] As already indicated in the calculations of table 1.1, such impacts are clearly large in substantive economic terms, and in subsequent chapters we provide alternative perspectives on their magnitude.

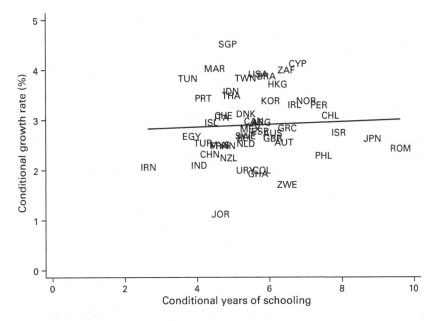

Figure 3.2

Years of schooling and economic growth rates after considering knowledge capital

Notes: Added-variable plot of a regression of the average annual rate of growth (in percent) of real GDP per capita in 1960 to 2000 on average years of schooling in 1960, average test scores on international student achievement tests, and initial level of real GDP per capita in 1960 (mean of unconditional variables added to each axis). Authors' calculations; see table 3.1, column 3. See table 2A.1 for country letter codes.

The remaining columns of table 3.1 provide additional analyses of these basic results. Estimating the model with regression techniques robust to outliers yields coefficient estimates virtually identical to those excluding two significant outlier countries—Nigeria and Botswana— from the growth equation (column 5).[11] Because the robust model assigns essentially zero weight to these two observations, they are dropped from the remaining models.

Perhaps, however, a simpler explanation of the results builds on the rapid growth rates of the "Asian tigers" over the past half century. As figure 2.3 shows, the East Asian countries have had very high test performance, so the regression might just be seen as drawing a line between the high growth there and the low growth in the rest of the world; but including fixed effects for the eight world regions depicted in figure 1.1 (so no between-region variation in test scores is used in the estimation) reduces the estimated test effect just slightly, to 1.7 (column 6). The reduction, at the same time, is consistent with the interpretation that high knowledge capital has been important in East Asia, an interpretation supported by direct analysis in chapter 5.

Finally, the precise specification of the growth model is the subject of considerable debate within macroeconomics. While the argument has many nuances, it can be framed as a simple contrast based on the different growth models introduced in section 2.1. The endogenous growth model indicates increases in human capital can lead to permanent differences in growth rates because a better-educated workforce generates a larger stream of new ideas that produces technological progress faster.[12] By contrast, in the augmented neoclassical growth model, changes in human capital lead to higher steady-state levels of income but do not affect the long-run growth path.[13] Our estimates, which include the level of initial GDP per capita, allow for conditional convergence, but distinguishing between temporary "catch-up" growth and long-run differences in growth in the empirical model is difficult. Those who favor the neoclassical model favor estimation that includes the log (rather than level) of initial income. Column 7 shows these results, where the impact of cognitive skills on growth is little changed from the linear alternative. Thus the results do not appear to depend on the specific empirical model that is estimated. We return to the implications of the different growth models in chapter 7.

While the estimated effect of test scores varies across these different specifications, the cognitive skill coefficients are always very significant, and the variation is quite limited: other things equal, a move of one standard deviation of individual student performance translates into a difference of 1.7 to 2.0 percentage points in annual growth rates. How much is one standard deviation in performance? The difference between the US average and the top performers on the PISA tests is approximately 0.4 standard deviations, while that between the average Mexican student and the OECD average is approximately one standard deviation.

Estimation in Different Samples
Two other important questions—or sets of issues—arise related to interpretation. The first is whether the sample of countries or years of observation heavily influence the results, which would imply the results are potentially driven by other, unmeasured factors. The second is whether the specific measure of cognitive skills drives the estimates.

Tables 3.2 and 3.3 provide the matrix of estimated cognitive skill coefficients across different samples of observations. The columns consider sample sensitivity and concentrate on whether the overall results are driven by specific subsets of countries or years, which might indicate that the cognitive skill measures simply proxy for other facets of the economies or times. In each table the top row is focused on the average of all observed math and science scores—as presented previously—while, as explained below, the second row relies on just lower–secondary school scores, which may be a more reliable measure of differences in skills. Each entry comes from a separate regression that includes GDP per capita and school attainment in 1960.

The first two comparisons in table 3.2 (columns 2–3 and columns 4–5) present evidence on whether cognitive skills are more or less important in developed countries. The first comparison divides the estimation into the twenty-four OECD and twenty-six non-OECD countries in the sample, while the second divides the countries into those above and those below the median level of per-capita GDP in 1960.[14] The (statistically significant) difference between high- and low-income countries indicates developing countries are somewhat more affected by cognitive skills than developed countries.[15] This finding is consistent with the arguments by Glaeser and others (2004) that nearly all poor countries in 1960 were dictatorships, some of which developed better societal institutions as an outcome of growth rather than a cause. The countries that did better in terms of growth were those with higher human capital, supporting the larger coefficient on human capital in the poor countries. Nonetheless, variations in math and science skills remain very important in distinguishing among growth rates of the developed countries.[16] We investigate these issues in greater detail in chapters 5 and 6.

The influence of cognitive skills comes in part from the high growth of East Asian countries. As shown in column 6, excluding the ten East Asian countries lowers the estimated impact of math and science skills to 1.3, but it remains highly significant in the remaining countries. In other words, the overall estimates, while influenced by the East Asian growth experience, are not simply identifying the high growth–high test score position of East Asia, which would raise the possibility that the growth relationships are driven by other factors that are simply correlated with East Asian test performance. The high growth in East Asia is, of course, an important topic in itself that has received considerable and broad attention.[17] We return to a more detailed discussion of it—and of the proper functional form of the skills–growth relationship—in chapter 5.

Table 3.2
Estimated effects of cognitive skills in different country samples and test-score specifications

Country sample ▶ ▼ Test-score specification	(1) Full	(2) OECD	(3) Non-OECD	(4) High income[a]	(5) Low income[a]	(6) W/o East Asia
All math and science	1.980***	1.838***	2.064***	1.287***	2.286***	1.301***
	(9.12)	(4.56)	(6.00)	(5.37)	(6.98)	(4.90)
Only lower secondary	1.759***	1.746***	1.801***	1.040***	2.083***	1.137***
	(9.22)	(4.35)	(6.09)	(4.70)	(7.44)	(4.82)
Number of countries	50	24	26	25	25	40

Notes: Reported numbers are the coefficient on cognitive skills in each model specification. Dependent variable: average annual growth rate in GDP per capita, 1960 to 2000. Control variables: Initial GDP per capita, initial years of schooling, and a constant. Unless noted otherwise, cognitive skill measure refers to average score on all international tests 1964 to 2003 in math and science, primary through end of secondary school. t-Statistics in parentheses: statistical significance at * 10 percent, ** 5 percent, *** 1 percent.
a. Countries above/below sample median of GDP per capita 1960.

Table 3.3
Estimated effects of cognitive skills in different time periods and for score-schooling outliers

Year/country sample ▶	(1) 1960–1980	(2) 1980–2000	(3) 1980–2000	(4) Score-schooling outliers[a]	(5) Score-schooling core[a]
▼ Test-score specification			Only tests until 1984		
All math and science	1.522***	2.996***	3.782***	1.888***	2.175***
	(4.29)	(9.42)	(3.11)	(7.81)	(3.47)
Only lower secondary	1.407***	2.580***	4.386***	1.673***	1.887***
	(4.56)	(8.88)	(4.49)	(7.83)	(3.45)
Number of countries	50	50	25	25	25

Notes: Reported numbers are the coefficient on cognitive skills in each model specification. Dependent variable: Unless noted otherwise, average annual growth rate in GDP per capita, 1960 to 2000. Control variables: Initial GDP per capita, initial years of schooling, and a constant. Unless noted otherwise, cognitive skill measure refers to average score on all international tests 1964 to 2003 in math and science, primary through end of secondary school. t-Statistics in parentheses: statistical significance at * 10 percent, ** 5 percent, *** 1 percent.

a. Countries with largest (outliers)/smallest (core) residuals when regressing years of schooling on test scores.

The growth estimates are meant to identify long-run factors, but the sample period of 1960 to 2000 includes subperiods of world stagnation, fast growth, and financial crises. Some have suggested, for example, that the observed growth rates are dominated by the growth explosion of East Asia early in the period, and that this changed considerably with the financial crises of the late 1990s (Ramirez et al. 2006). Our results in the first two columns of table 3.3 indicate, however, a consistent impact of cognitive skills across the periods 1960 to 1980 and 1980 to 2000, which, if anything, grows stronger in the second half of the observations. Indeed the estimated impact doubles in the more recent period, consistent with various arguments that, at least for the United States and OECD countries, the importance of skills has increased.[18]

Our analysis relies on educational assessments made throughout the period of economic observation. We made this choice to maximize the number of countries and include the more precise testing of recent periods, but it raises questions of reverse causality. If greater growth adds resources that can be used to improve schools and test scores, our estimates could suffer from simultaneity bias. One set of estimates addresses this issue directly: we find the same impact on 1980 to 2000 growth when we restrict the test scores to measures obtained before 1985 (available for only twenty-five countries)—that is, when we use test scores nearly fully predating the growth period (column 3). In fact the point estimate for cognitive skills becomes substantially larger in this specification, which, by using predetermined test scores, excludes the possibility of simple reverse causation. The conclusion that simple reverse causation is not driving the results is reinforced in analyses using data updates that extend the economic series to 2009, where we can relate test scores measured in 1964 to 1984 to long-run growth in 1985 to 2009 (see appendix 3A).[19] Reverse causation from economic growth to test scores is also unlikely because additional spending on education (which might become affordable with higher growth) does not systematically relate to better test scores.[20] We return to analyses of the resource question, as well as broader policy discussions, in chapter 8, showing that the differences in international tests are not driven by differences in resources across countries, and we return to a more detailed investigation of causality in chapter 4.

Levels of schooling and cognitive scores are correlated in our sample of countries ($r = 0.62$), in part because of the differences between developed and developing countries. The separation of the impact of cognitive skills from that of school attainment in our estimation relies upon information where these two diverge, and the countries where the pattern of school attainment and skills varies most might be peculiar in terms of growth. The final two columns of table 3.3 divide countries based on deviations of cognitive scores from school attainment. Specifically, the "score-schooling outliers" are the twenty-five countries with the largest residuals when test scores are regressed on attainment, and the "score-schooling core" are the twenty-five with the smallest residuals. Interestingly, the relationship between cognitive skills and growth is virtually the same in these two samples, which reveals the results are not indeed driven by countries whose production of cognitive skills is "peculiar."

Estimation with Different Cognitive Skill Measures

The preceding results hold when we look across columns, but the pattern also obtains for the alternative measures of test scores presented in the second row of tables 3.2 and 3.3. The estimated coefficients using only lower-secondary school math and science scores are systematically a little smaller than those from all scores, which may reflect attenuation bias when using fewer test observations in the construction of the cognitive skill measure, but no changes occur in patterns across any of the columnar comparisons. This test score measure excludes any test in primary school or the final year of secondary education. Although test scores at the end of the secondary level, which combine the knowledge accumulated over primary and secondary schooling, may be most relevant with respect to the skills of the labor force, the duration of secondary education differs across countries, so they may not be as readily comparable across countries. Furthermore, given differing school completion rates, tests in the final year of secondary schooling may produce samples with differential selectivity of test takers. Yet neither the primary school tests nor the tests in the final secondary year are crucial for the results. (Note that our cognitive skills measures may be affected by potential biases not just from enrollment rate differences but also from test exclusions. Appendix 3B directly addresses both possibilities and finds they are not important in the analysis of economic growth.)

Table 3.4 provides more detail on sensitivity to the measure of cognitive skills, comparing several additional plausible alternatives for the aggregation of scores, which include using math, science, and reading scores separately. We also provide breakdowns by OECD and non-OECD countries, although this makes little qualitative difference, and we concentrate on the variations in aggregate test information found in the table rows.

Recent tests are generally viewed as having the highest standard of sampling and quality control. Results are qualitatively the same when using

Table 3.4
Estimated effects of cognitive skills for different measurement of skills

Country sample ▶	(1) Full	(2) OECD	(3) Non-OECD	
▼ Test-score specification				Number of countries
(A) Only since 1995	1.814*** *(9.91)*	1.568*** *(4.15)*	1.864*** *(6.66)*	47
(B) Only lower secondary since 1995	1.644*** *(9.57)*	1.475*** *(3.79)*	1.669*** *(6.39)*	47
(C) Only until 1995	3.156*** *(6.57)*	1.377* *(1.93)*	3.668*** *(4.44)*	37
(D) Early as instrument for average[a]	2.341*** *(7.71)*	1.212* *(1.98)*	2.915*** *(5.80)*	37
(E) Only math	2.009*** *(8.98)*	1.559*** *(4.41)*	2.082*** *(5.73)*	47
(F) Only science	1.576*** *(7.00)*	1.806*** *(3.88)*	1.559*** *(4.39)*	50
(G) Only reading	2.351*** *(6.21)*	1.727*** *(3.57)*	2.678*** *(3.70)*	46
(H) All subjects entered jointly				41
Math	1.662*** *(3.69)*	2.270*** *(2.97)*	1.882* *(1.97)*	
Science	1.007** *(2.34)*	-2.414 *(1.62)*	1.270* *(1.92)*	
Reading	-0.793 *(1.15)*	1.333 *(1.44)*	-1.457 *(0.94)*	

Notes: Reported numbers are the coefficient on cognitive skills in each model specification. Dependent variable: Average annual growth rate in GDP per capita, 1960 to 2000. Control variables: Initial GDP per capita, initial years of schooling, and a constant. Unless noted otherwise, cognitive skill measure refers to average score on all international tests 1964 to 2003 in math and science, primary through end of secondary school. t-Statistics in parentheses: statistical significance at * 10 percent, ** 5 percent, *** 1 percent.
a. 2SLS with average of test scores until 1995 as instrument for average of all test scores.

only scores on those performed since 1995 (row A). Likewise, they are robust to using scores since 1995 for just lower secondary grades (row B).

A drawback of using only the more recent tests is that doing so requires a strong version of the assumption that test performance is reasonably constant over time, because it relates test performance measured since 1995 to the economic data for 1960 to 2000. To make sure that higher previous economic growth is not driving the measured test performance, the test score measure used in row C disregards all tests since the late 1990s. Our results turn out to be robust, with a significantly higher point estimate on the test score variable (although the sample is reduced to thirty-seven countries). Our results are also robust to using the average early test scores as an instrument for the average of all test scores in a two-stage least-squares regression, which effectively utilizes only that part of the total test score measure that can be traced back to the early scores (row D). Again, this has little impact on the achievement-growth parameter. In sum, the results do not appear to be driven by either early or late test scores alone.

The remainder of the table shows results of investigating different combinations of the math, science, and reading tests. While concerns about the reliability of the reading tests have led us to focus on math and science, the use of them does provide similar results in the growth models (rows E–G). In a specification that enters the different subjects together (panel H), the three are always jointly significant at the 1 percent level and higher, even though the science effect gets smaller and the reading effect loses significance.

The overall picture from this sensitivity analysis is that the estimated effect of cognitive skills on growth is quite robust to a range of samples, specifications, and measurements.[21] This finding contrasts sharply with the results of many previous analyses that use years of schooling as the human capital measure, beginning with Levine and Renelt (1992) and continuing through Pritchett (2006). But, of course, the similarity of our results, while ruling out some specification and measurement issues, cannot guard against all plausible threats to the identification of causal growth relationships.

A central theme of this book is that cross-sectional growth regressions using existing variation across countries provide stylized facts about long-term development, but their interpretation may be hampered by endogeneity biases. Endogeneity of cognitive skills could, for example, arise because nations with conditions favorable to economic growth also produce high test performance. This correlation in turn could arise because cultural factors, historically good economic institutions, variations in health status, or any other set of factors that lead to strong economic performance might also be systematically related to high cognitive skills. Indeed, whether such relationships are causal or purely associational does not matter. If these factors are omitted from the growth estimation, they will tend to bias the coefficient on cognitive skills. Likewise, as suggested previously, reverse causality may occur if economic growth facilitates investments in the school system or increases family resources that improve cognitive skills. These potential critiques of our basic focus on knowledge capital lead naturally into a broader investigation of how institutions fit into the picture of world growth. Larger questions of causality are at the heart of the next chapter.

3.2   Institutions, Knowledge Capital, and Growth

Although emphasis on the role of economic institutions as the fundamental cause of differences in economic development has been increasing, for the past decade fierce debate has also surrounded questions about the roles of societal institutions and human capital in economic growth and development. Here we consider how allowance for various economic institutions affects our picture of the pattern of growth across nations.

On the one hand, an innovative and influential line of research by Acemoglu, Johnson, and Robinson (2001, 2002, 2005) argues that major societal institutions created the fundamental building blocks for modern development. In their testing of this idea, they cleverly used information about the colonial origins of countries to circumvent obvious endogeneity concerns about the development of institutions.[22] They particularly fixed on the central notion of strong property rights, arguing that the causal role of these institutions can be seen analytically by tracing it back to the different colonial paths of countries.

On the other hand, Glaeser and others (2004) argue (and marshal a broad body of evidence to support their view) that the colonists brought to their new lands human capital in addition to knowledge of good societal institutions, and that better human capital more likely led both to the development of good institutions and higher economic growth. Acemoglu, Gallego, and Robinson (2014) responded to this argument with new tests and evidence—partially involving another set of early institutions closely related to establishing the rule of law in different countries—that indicated human capital is endogenous, reestablishing their conclusions that institutions are more fundamental to growth.

Our analysis is not designed to resolve either this debate about the predominance of institutions or other debates about the measurement of precise institutions. Our view is simply that societal institutions are almost certainly a component of differences in economic growth, and understanding how they interact with the knowledge capital of nations is important. This investigation is not, however, just replaying the previous debates. Our concerns at this point again relate to the measurement of human capital in the earlier analyses. All of them are based on school attainment, which we have demonstrated is a very inaccurate measure of the relevant skills of nations.

Table 3.5 considers alternative measures of economic institutions within the context of our basic growth models. The first column simply adds to our baseline models two common (and powerful) institutional measures related to the quality of the underlying economic environment: openness of the economy and security of property rights.[23] These measures are jointly significant in explaining growth, and the property rights measure is individually significant. (Note that protection against expropriation and openness are strongly correlated, with a simple correlation of 0.71.) At the same time, however, the results show cognitive skills exert a positive and highly significant effect on economic growth independent of these measures of the quality of institutions, although their estimated impact is reduced to around 1.3. This reduced estimate can be viewed as a lower bound of the total effect of cognitive skills to the extent that any effects they have on the development of good institutions are captured by the institutional measures.

While this evidence confirms the presence of an independent effect of cognitive skills on economic growth, there are reasons to believe their effect may differ depending on the economic institutions of a country. North (1990), for example, emphasized the important role played by the institutional framework in shaping the relative profitability of piracy versus productive activity. If the available knowledge and skills are used in the former rather than the latter activity, one may certainly expect the effect on economic growth to be substantially different and maybe even to turn negative.

Similarly Murphy, Shleifer, and Vishny (1991) showed the allocation of talent between rent seeking and entrepreneurship matters for economic growth: countries with relatively more college engineering majors grow faster, and those with relatively more law concentrators grow more slowly. Easterly (2001) argued that education might have little impact in less developed countries that lack other facilitating factors, such as

Table 3.5
Cognitive skills, institutions, and economic growth

	(1)	(2)	(3)	(4)	(5)
Cognitive skills	1.265***	1.995***	1.494***	1.239***	1.257***
	(4.06)	(7.60)	(4.46)	(4.12)	(4.00)
Initial years of schooling (1960)	0.004	-.031	-0.017	-0.049	-0.003
	(0.05)	(0.41)	(0.22)	(0.66)	(0.03)
Initial GDP per capita (1960)	-0.351***	-0.297***	-0.355***	-0.310***	-0.381***
	(6.01)	(5.64)	(6.03)	(5.73)	(4.72)
Openness	0.508	0.732**		0.859**	0.503
	(1.39)	(2.13)		(2.18)	(1.36)
Protection against expropriation	0.388**		0.485***	0.183	0.396**
	(2.29)		(3.00)	(1.08)	(2.31)
Cognitive skills × openness		1.609**			
		(2.34)			

	(1)	(2)	(3)	(4)	(5)
Cognitive skills × protection against expropriation			0.210		
			(1.19)		
Tropical location				0.043	
				(0.14)	
Fertility				-0.135	
				(0.83)	
Initial physical capital per capita					0.014
					(0.55)
Constant	-6.447***	2.813***	2.845***	-4.114**	-4.695***
	(6.65)	(6.48)	(6.51)	(2.63)	(5.04)
Number of countries	47	47	47	45	47
R^2 (adj.)	0.784	0.785	0.781	0.797	0.780

Notes: Dependent variable: average annual growth rate in GDP per capita, 1960 to 2000. Cognitive skill measure refers to average score on all international tests 1964 to 2003 in math and science, primary through end of secondary school. All interacted variables are centered on zero. t-Statistics in parentheses: statistical significance at * 10 percent, ** 5 percent, *** 1 percent.

functioning institutions for markets and legal systems. Pritchett (2001, 2006) likewise suggested that deficiencies in the institutional environment in many developing countries might lead to cognitive skills being applied to socially unproductive activities, rendering the average effect of education on growth negligible.

While the empirical support for these latter arguments may be affected by the measurement of education and human capital, the basic point that the social returns to education and skills may be low in countries with perverse institutional environments is certainly worth pursuing. Thus in columns 2 and 3 of table 3.5 we add an interaction term between cognitive skills and each of our institutional measures.[24] The results suggest openness and cognitive skills not only have significant individual effects on economic growth but also a significant positive interaction (column 2), which is depicted in figure 3.3. The effect of cognitive skills on economic growth is indeed significantly higher in countries that have been fully open to international trade than in those that have been fully closed.[25] In closed economies, skills have a relatively low impact of 0.9 on growth rates, but this increases to 2.6 in open economies.[26]

When we use protection against expropriation rather than openness to trade as the measure of quality of institutions in column 3, we similarly find a positive interaction term with cognitive skills, although it lacks statistical significance (see also figure 3.3), and cognitive skills remain as a significant determinant of growth differences.

In a similar vein, others have argued for an expansion of our basic models. For example, McArthur and Sachs (2001) held that geographical features exert an effect on economic growth independent of institutions. To address this possibility, column 4 adds tropical location (along with fertility, another potential factor). Neither is significant nor changes the impact of cognitive skills. The final column adds the initial physical capital stock of each nation, but this also leaves the basic model unchanged.

We interpret the estimates of test scores in the presence of institutional factors as a lower bound on the overall true effect, since the institutional measures include any direct effects of cognitive skills on the development of good institutions. Yet the interpretation must also be more nuanced, since the developed nations almost uniformly show no variation in either property rights or openness to international trade. This suggests that developing countries (with restrictive institutions) have room to improve their economic performance by moving toward better institutions. But once they have in fact corrected the imperfect economic institutions, they, too, must return to relying on knowledge capital for any further improvements in growth.

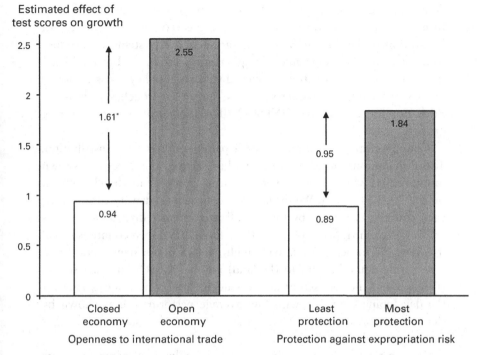

Figure 3.3
How the impact of knowledge capital on growth varies with societal institutions

Notes: Estimated effect of average achievement test scores on the average annual rate of growth of real GDP per capita in 1960 to 2000, depending on the degree of openness to international trade and on the protection against expropriation risk of a country. Authors' calculations; see table 3.5, columns 2 and 3. *Statistical significance at 5 percent.

The developed countries, of course, do not have perfect institutions from an economic perspective, and much discussion still goes on in Europe, for example, about restrictions in labor and product markets and various governmental intrusions into markets. We analyze those separately in chapter 6.

3.3 Rocket Scientists or Basic Education for All?

We address a range of schooling policy options in chapter 8, but one potentially important issue of policy overall is useful to consider at this point: whether to concentrate on the lowest or the highest achievers.

Some argue in favor of elitist school systems that focus on the top performers as potential future managers of the economy and drivers of innovation. Others favor more egalitarian school systems, to produce well-educated masses capable of implementing established technologies. In other words, the question is, Should education policy focus on forming a small group of "rocket scientists," or are approaches such as the Education for All initiative (UNESCO 2014) more promising for spurring growth?

Countries vary significantly in their patterns of test score distribution. The distributions of achievement within selected countries are shown in figure 3.4, which presents kernel density plots for math achievement on the 2003 PISA test. We display the achievement density function for each country as framed by the overall performance distribution across all OECD countries. The plots for the selected developed countries reveal it is possible to achieve relatively high median performance, both with a relatively equitable spread (Finland) and a relatively unequal spread (Belgium), in the test scores at the student level. The same is true for the developing countries with low average performance, as shown by the contrast between Brazil's long right tail and Indonesia's much greater density around its median.

To investigate these issues in our growth analysis, we again aggregate country performance, now in distributional terms, across the international assessments in which each country participated. We use the microdata from each assessment to calculate measures of the share of students in each country who reach at least basic skills, as well as those who reach superior performance levels.[27] As figure 3.4 shows, these differences represent more than simple mean displacement, and they are not readily captured by such simple measures as the standard deviation in national test scores.[28]

We use performance of at least 400 test score points on our transformed international scale—one standard deviation below the OECD mean—as our threshold of basic literacy and numeracy. The PISA 2003 science test uses 400 points as the lowest bound for a basic level of science literacy (Organisation for Economic Co-operation and Development 2004: 292); on the math test, this corresponds to the middle of the test's level 1 range of performance (358–420 test score points), which denotes that fifteen-year-old students can answer questions involving familiar contexts where all relevant information is present and the questions are clearly defined. For example, given the exchange rate between dollars and euros, a student at level 1 can calculate the euro equivalent of a given

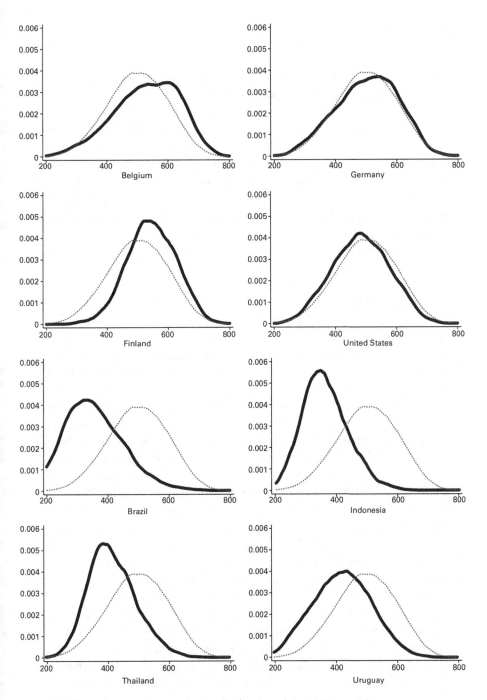

Figure 3.4

Selected country examples of the distribution of student achievement

Notes: Kernel densities of student achievement on the PISA 2003 math test. Bold solid line: specified country; thin dotted line: OECD countries.

number of dollars. The international median of this share of students is 86 percent in our sample, ranging from 18 percent in Peru to 97 percent in the Netherlands and Japan (see table 2A.1).

As our threshold for superior performance, we use 600 points, or one standard deviation above the OECD mean. A score of 600 points is near the threshold of the level 5 range of performance on the PISA 2003 math test, which denotes that fifteen-year-old students can develop and work with models for complex situations, identifying constraints and specifying assumptions, and they can reflect on their answers and formulate and communicate their interpretations and reasoning. This level is reached by an international median of only 5 percent, although it ranges from below 0.1 percent in Colombia and Morocco to 18 percent in Singapore and Korea and 22 percent in Taiwan.

It turns out that both distributional measures of a nation's cognitive skills are significantly related to economic growth, either when entered individually or jointly (table 3.6).[29] Both the basic skill and the top-performing dimensions of educational performance appear separately important for growth (columns 1 and 2). From the estimates in column 3, an increase of 10 percentage points in the share of students reaching basic literacy is associated with annual growth 0.3 percentage points higher, and an increase of 10 percentage points in the share of top-performing students is associated with annual growth 1.3 percentage points higher.

It is difficult to compare directly the impacts of the two performance measures. For example, increasing the basic literacy share may be much more feasible than increasing the top-performing share by the same amount, as suggested by the international standard deviations of 0.215 and 0.054, respectively, of these two shares. Thus increasing each share by roughly half a standard deviation (10 percentage points for the basic literacy share and 2.5 percentage points for the top-performing share) yields a similar growth effect of roughly 0.3 percentage points.

On the one hand, the impact of having more top performers is only slightly reduced by introducing the measures of economic institutions, fertility, and tropical geography (column 4). On the other hand, the separate influence of basic literacy levels falls quantitatively and becomes statistically insignificant in the expanded model (for the forty-five countries with complete data). This is in line with an interpretation where part of the effect of basic literacy comes through improved institutions (Glaeser et al. 2004).

The effect of the basic literacy share does not vary significantly with the initial level of development, but the effect of the top-performing share

Table 3.6
Rocket scientists or basic education for all?

	(1)	(2)	(3)	(4)[a]	(5)	(6)	(7)
Share of students reaching basic literacy	4.717***		2.732***	1.002	3.460***	5.150***	5.869***
	(6.64)		(3.61)	(1.33)	(3.81)	(2.87)	(3.33)
Share of top-performing students		19.347***	12.880***	11.735***	8.460**	4.226	-1.530
		(7.29)	(4.35)	(4.18)	(2.37)	(0.65)	(0.22)
Share of students reaching basic literacy × Initial GDP per capita					0.376		
					(1.25)		
Share of top-performing students × Initial GDP per capita					-2.148**		-1.649**
					(2.11)		(2.07)
Share of students reaching basic literacy × Share of top-performing students						42.357	53.538*
						(1.48)	(1.91)
Number of countries	50	50	50	45	50	50	50
R^2 (adj.)	0.610	0.646	0.719	0.823	0.734	0.727	0.746

Notes: Dependent variable: Average annual growth rate in GDP per capita, 1960 to 2000. Control variables: Initial GDP per capita, initial years of schooling, and a constant. The aggregate shares are averages constructed from all international tests 1964 to 2003 in math and science, primary through end of secondary school. All interacted variables are centered on zero. t-Statistics in parentheses: statistical significance at * 10 percent, ** 5 percent, *** 1 percent.
a. Specification includes additional controls for openness, protection against expropriation, tropical location, and fertility.

is significantly larger in countries with more scope to catch up to the initially most productive countries (column 5). These results appear consistent with a mixture of the basic models of human capital and growth mentioned earlier. The accumulation of skills as a standard production factor, emphasized by augmented neoclassical growth models (e.g., see Mankiw, Romer, and Weil 1992), is probably best captured by the basic literacy term, which has positive effects similar in size across all countries. The larger growth effect of high-level skills in countries farther from the technological frontier, though, is most consistent with technological diffusion models (e.g., Nelson and Phelps 1966). From this perspective, countries need high-skilled human capital for an imitation strategy, and the process of economic convergence is accelerated in those with larger shares of high-performing students.[30] Obvious cases are East Asian countries, such as Korea, Singapore, and Taiwan, that all have particularly large shares of high performers and that started from relatively low levels and have shown outstanding growth performances (see chapter 5); but the results of column 5 are nonetheless robust to the inclusion of an East Asian dummy, or a full set of regional dummies.

Another informative extension considers the interaction of the top-performing and basic literacy shares (columns 6 and 7). The complementarity between basic and top-level skills depicted by the results suggests that to be able to implement the imitation and innovation strategies developed by scientists, a country needs a workforce with at least basic skills.[31]

Many countries have focused on either developing basic skills or producing engineers and scientists. In terms of growth, our estimates suggest that developing basic skills and producing highly talented people reinforce each other. Moreover achieving basic literacy for all may well be a precondition for identifying those who can reach "rocket scientist" status. In other words, tournaments among students in a large pool of those with basic skills may be an efficient way to obtain a large share of high performers.

3.4   Conclusions on the Empirical Relevance of Knowledge Capital

The simplest conclusion from our baseline modeling is that the knowledge capital of nations is powerfully related to long-run growth rates. The relationship is robust to a variety of specification issues, which implicitly rules out a number of possible concerns about the interpretation of the models.

The now extensive literature cataloging the sensitivity of cross-country growth models to samples, model specifications, and the like immediately triggers concerns about the ability to interpret cross-country analyses in a sensible way, as it suggests that a variety of omitted variables are driving the observed growth regressions. With their insensitivity to significant specification and sample issues, however, our fundamental results pass the first test of whether they can be interpreted in a causal manner. In other words, our models can be interpreted as saying that if a country finds a way to increase its knowledge capital—say, through improved schools—it can realistically expect its long-run economic fortunes to improve.

The basic specification investigations obviously do not rule out all threats to such a causal interpretation. The next chapter provides more information on this.

Appendix 3A: Alternative Data and Expansion of Growth Period

The analysis in chapter 3 concentrates on measurement issues surrounding cognitive skills, but these are not the only measurement issues that have been raised in the context of empirical growth analysis. In this appendix, we analyze the impact of other such issues with respect to data on school attainment and on economic growth. We also consider the most recent wave of cognitive skills data. These updates and revisions do not substantially change the results presented in our main analyses.

The measurement of school attainment has been discussed at various times. Barro and Lee (1993) developed the initial international database for school attainment. This was criticized by Cohen and Soto (2007), who produced the data set that is the basis of our estimation. Most recently, Barro and Lee (2013) have produced a new data set. Using this latest cross country data on school attainment (data version 1.0, 03/10, accessed on May 17, 2010) has no effect on the estimates of the impact of cognitive skills and only slightly increases the attainment coefficient. As shown in table 3A.1, column 2, the estimated cognitive skills coefficient is 1.92, as opposed to 1.98 in our base estimates (column 1).

The economic data underlying growth analyses are the second area of concern. Some have argued that changes in the Penn World Tables (PWT), particularly the 6.2 revision, lead to significant alterations in standard estimates of growth models (Ciccone and Jarocinski 2010; Appleton, Atherton, and Bleaney 2011; Johnson et al. 2013).[32] To assess the impact of these data, we compare estimates using the more recent version of the PWT (version 7.0, released on June 3, 2011; Heston, Summers, and Aten 2011) to our estimates based on version 6.1. As is apparent from column 3, the estimate for cognitive skills is hardly affected when estimating the same model with the same growth period (1960 to 2000) using the new economic data; in fact, the point estimate is slightly higher.

The new version of the PWT allows us to expand the growth period to 2007. Again, results are strongly confirmed in this forty-seven-year period (column 4), with the point estimate closer to the original estimate again. We use 2007 as the endpoint of the considered growth period here rather than 2009 (which is the latest year available in PWT 7.0) because we do not want the long-run growth analysis to be affected by the global recession that started at the end of 2008 (as is clearly visible in the PWT data, where average growth rates in our sample drop from around 4 percent in the preceding years to 1.6 in 2007–2008 and to –2.5 in 2008–2009). Still our result on cognitive skills is confirmed in the 1960

Table 3A.1
Growth regressions with updated data series on school attainment and economic growth

	6.1	6.1	7.0	7.0	7.0
PWT version					
Years of schooling data	Cohen and Soto (2007)	Barro and Lee (2013)	Barro and Lee (2013)	Barro and Lee (2013)	Barro and Lee (2013)
Growth period	1960–2000	1960–2000	1960–2000	1960–2007	1985–2007
Test scores	all years	all years	all years	all years	until 1984
	(1)	(2)	(3)	(4)	(5)
Cognitive skills	1.980***	1.921***	2.133***	1.881***	3.593**
	(9.12)	(9.25)	(9.01)	(7.78)	(2.56)
Initial years of schooling (1960)	0.026	0.079	0.018	0.018	-0.079
	(0.34)	(1.09)	(0.23)	(0.22)	(0.41)
Initial GDP per capita (1960)	-0.302***	-0.324***	-0.219***	-0.212***	-0.123**
	(5.54)	(7.01)	(5.59)	(5.29)	(2.20)
Constant	-4.737***	-4.585***	-5.563***	-4.465***	-11.850*
	(5.54)	(5.50)	(5.82)	(4.57)	(1.93)
Number of countries	50	50	50	50	25
R^2 (adj.)	0.728	0.734	0.667	0.610	0.318

Notes: Dependent variable: average annual growth rate in GDP per capita (growth period depicted on top of each column). Unless noted otherwise, cognitive skill measure refers to average score on all international tests 1964 to 2003 in math and science, primary through end of secondary school. t-Statistics in parentheses: statistical significance at * 10 percent, ** 5 percent, *** 1 percent.

to 2009 growth period (not shown), as well, with a point estimate of 1.76 ($t = 7.32$).

The expanded PWT data also allow us to perform an analysis in which the observation period of test scores strictly predates the observation period of economic growth. For a sample of twenty-five countries, we have test score data observed between 1964 and 1984, which we use to predict economic growth in 1985 to 2007 (column 5). Again, the significant effect of cognitive skills on growth is confirmed, with a point estimate substantially larger than in the base model. (And, again, results are very similar for the growth period expanded to 2009.)

While we are reluctant to perform analyses on shorter growth periods because they are prone to country-specific shocks and business cycle fluctuations, we can expand to thirty-seven our sample of countries with test scores predating the observed growth period when we use the tests conducted until 1995 to predict growth in 1995 to 2009 or 2000 to 2009. Yet again, results confirm a strong estimate on cognitive skills with a point estimate larger than in the base model (not shown), although the precise point estimate is sensitive to excluding individual countries when considering this shorter growth period.

We have also experimented with newer waves of test score data, specifically the 2009 wave of the PISA study. Our test score measure derived from the tests conducted in 1964 to 2003 is strongly correlated with the PISA 2009 data (with a correlation coefficient of 0.94 for the thirty-seven countries available in both datasets). This corroborates the assumption of relative stability underlying our main analysis. Using the PISA 2009 as an alternative measure of cognitive skills in the growth regressions fully confirms our results, with a highly significant point estimate extremely close to that of our main analysis (1.96).

Appendix 3B: Relevance of Sample Selectivity

Critics of international assessments suggest underlying sampling issues may compromise comparability across countries. Nonrandom differences in patterns of school enrollment, sample exclusions, and nonresponse can clearly influence rankings of countries on international league tables of average student achievement. In fact, we show below that larger rates of exclusion, nonresponse, and age-specific enrollment are indeed related to better country average scores on international student achievement tests. But, as this appendix shows, accounting for these patterns of sample selectivity does not alter the evidence about the importance of cognitive skills in economic growth regressions.[33]

To critics of international comparisons, "the basic problem is student selectivity: ... the average score ... simply reflects the fact that the students represented in the test comparisons have been much more highly selected in some countries than in others" (Rotberg 1995: 1446). Simple calculations indicate that sample bias certainly has the potential to move country mean scores substantially. For example, if exclusion propensity and student achievement are bivariate normally distributed and correlated at 0.5, a 10 percent exclusion rate—not uncommon in some countries—leads to an upward bias in the resulting country mean score of 10 percent of a standard deviation.[34]

The basic notion of measurement error in econometric analyses tells us that whether and how such mismeasurement of country mean performance biases results of econometric analyses of relationships is another matter. First, any bias depends on whether sample selectivity is idiosyncratic or persistent over time—that is, whether some countries have systematically more selective samples. If idiosyncratic, sample selectivity introduces classical measurement error that works against finding statistically significant associations. In our economic growth modeling, however, the use of averages of scores across several tests lessens the importance of any idiosyncratic measurement error, since the error variance is reduced by averaging. When sample selectivity is persistent over time, the second issue is whether it is correlated with the error term of the estimation equation. If it is orthogonal to the (conditional) growth rates—that is, to the errors in the growth equation—even systematic sample selectivity simply works against finding statistically significant results. Only if it is correlated with the error term of the growth equation does it introduce bias to our econometric analyses.

Sample Selection and Average Test Scores

This analysis focuses on sample selectivity for the five international tests in math and science conducted at the lower secondary level between 1995 and 2003. The relevant tests are the Trends in International Mathematics and Science Study (TIMSS), conducted in 1995, 1999, and 2003, and the Programme for International Student Assessment (PISA) tests, conducted in 2000 and 2003 (see chapter 2).

There are three main sources of sample selectivity, each of which may have very different impacts on the validity of testing and the importance of statistical bias. First, both tests allow exclusions for small, geographically remote schools, for schools focused on students with intellectual or functional disabilities, and, within schools, for individual students in the latter group or with limited proficiency in the test language. Exclusion from the target sample is generally permissible for students who are unable to follow the general instruction of the test but not simply for those who have poor academic performance or normal disciplinary problems. To limit such exclusions, the tests generally require participating countries to keep exclusion rates below 5 percent.

Second, sampled schools in many nations are not required to participate. Moreover individual students may be absent on the day of the assessment. Again, to limit the extent of such nonparticipation, response rates are generally deemed acceptable only if they reach 85 percent both at the school and student levels (80 percent at the student level in PISA).

Given the nature of the permissible exclusions—small, remote schools and students with special needs or language deficiencies—higher exclusion rates are likely to introduce positive selection bias into estimates of national mean performance. The direction of selection bias is not as obvious for nonresponse rates, but if weaker performing schools and students are less likely to participate in the test, it would be the same as for exclusion rates.

Third, testing is always focused on students in school. Some children in the tested age range may no longer be in school. This problem is not associated with the testing so much as with the character of schooling in each country. Here, however, the direction of bias is unclear. In lower secondary school to which the tests refer, virtually all developed countries have close to universal enrollment. Consequently sampling differences come into play mostly when comparing developed to less developed countries. Generally, students with higher ability or other background features supportive of higher achievement are more likely to be enrolled in school, introducing bias similar to that introduced by exclusion rates. But at the country level, this bias is likely to be overwhelmed by the fact that low enrollment rates in lower secondary education are a sign of a generally underdeveloped or dysfunctional education system, leading potentially to a positive association between enrollment rates and test performance.

The first two columns of table 3B.1 report descriptive statistics of the data on sample coverage for the 196 country observations on the five international tests. Column 3 reports the correlations of the three components of sample selection with reported mean test performance, which reveal that exclusion and nonresponse rates are, as expected, significantly positively associated with reported test scores—that is, the larger the share of schools and students excluded by the national testing authority and the larger the share of schools and students sampled but not participating, the higher the reported country mean test score. At the same time, enrollment rates are also positively correlated with test scores, suggesting no simple upward bias where a substantial share of the age group is not enrolled in school.

These overall results for average test scores are quite robust. The significant correlation of the three measures of sample coverage with test scores is robust to controlling for fixed effects for the five underlying tests. The reported correlations are similar when test scores in math and science are used separately. Within each of the five international tests, enrollment rates are always significantly positively correlated with test scores. Correlations with exclusion rates are significant in PISA 2003, marginally significant in PISA 2000 and TIMSS 2003, and not significant otherwise. Correlations with nonresponse rates are significant in the PISA tests but not in the TIMSS tests. As the last two columns of table 3B.1 show, exclusion rates and nonresponse rates are significantly correlated with enrollment rates but not with each other. When all three are entered in a regression to predict test scores, only enrollment rates remain significant.

Table 3B.1

Sample coverage: descriptive statistics and correlation with test scores

| | Mean | Min | Correlation with | | |
| Source of sample selection problems | (standard deviation) | Max | Test score | Enrollment rate | Exclusion rate |
	(1)	(2)	(3)	(4)	(5)
Enrollment rate	91.8	42.7	0.571***	1.000	
	(11.3)	103.0	(0.000)		
Exclusion rate	3.1	0.0	0.133*	0.127*	1.000
	(2.8)	22.5	(0.063)	(0.076)	
Nonresponse rate	11.6	0.0	0.198***	0.207***	0.097
	(9.4)	54.9	(0.005)	(0.004)	(0.177)

Notes: 196 country-level observations: all participants in five international tests (TIMSS 1995, 1999, 2003; PISA 2000, 2003). Test score is average of math and science on the comparable scale used throughout this book. Correlations: p-values in parentheses. Significance level: * 10 percent, ** 5 percent, *** 1 percent.

To elucidate persistence of sampling issues, we report in table 3B.2 the correlations of exclusion and nonresponse rates across tests. (Of course, enrollment rates are relatively constant over the short time period and are not reported in the table.)[35] Nonresponse rates are positively correlated across the five tests. By contrast, exclusion rates are significantly correlated in only three of the ten pairs of tests. Thus sample selectivity is only to a limited degree systematic over time and has a substantial idiosyncratic component.

Sample Selection and the Results of Growth Regressions

Our main interest, however, is whether these test selection issues affect our estimation of growth models. The first column of table 3B.3 is simply our baseline model from table 3.1, where the average annual growth rate in real GDP per capita over 1960 to 2000 is regressed on initial GDP per capita, initial years of schooling, and our measure of knowledge capital that combines performance on all international student achievement tests between 1964 and 2003. Column 2 gives the same model for the sample of forty-five (of our fifty) countries for which we have information on sampling quality, where the estimate on test scores is slightly lower at 1.74.

Column 3 adds our three measures of sample coverage—enrollment, exclusion, and nonresponse rates—to the growth model. They enter statistically insignificantly, individually or jointly, and do not significantly affect the coefficient on test scores—that is, the variation in the extent to which sampling is selective across countries is orthogonal to the variation in conditional economic growth. Thus the positive association between test scores and economic growth cannot be explained by international differences in sample selectivity.

To this point, the test score measure refers to all international achievement tests, whereas our sampling information refers only to the five tests conducted at the lower secondary level since 1995. In column 4 we therefore use as a test score measure the average of just these five tests. While the point estimate on the measure is slightly (but not significantly) smaller—presumably because of attenuation when using a measure based on less test information—qualitative results on the effect of including sampling information are the same.

To ensure the latter specification does not just capture variation that emerged toward the end (1995 to 2003) of the growth period of our analysis (1960 to 2000), we use in column 5 the average score of all international tests (from 1964 to 2003) as an instrument for the recent tests. Qualitative results are unchanged in this two-stage least-squares

Table 3B.2
Sample coverage: correlation across tests

	Exclusion rate				Non-response rate			
	TIMSS			PISA	TIMSS			PISA
	1995 (1)	1999 (2)	2003 (3)	2000 (4)	1995 (5)	1999 (6)	2003 (7)	2000 (8)
TIMSS 1999	0.132				0.514***			
	(0.519)				(0.007)			
TIMSS 2003	-0.036	0.670***			0.336	0.790***		
	(0.866)	(0.000)			(0.100)	(0.000)		
PISA 2000	-0.266	0.250	-0.041		0.531***	0.738***	0.740***	
	(0.163)	(0.263)	(0.862)		(0.003)	(0.000)	(0.000)	
PISA 2003	0.036	0.500**	0.274	0.384**	0.577***	0.708***	0.893***	0.756***
	(0.856)	(0.021)	(0.257)	(0.023)	(0.001)	(0.000)	(0.000)	(0.000)

Notes: Columns 1–4: correlations among exclusion rates across tests. Columns 5–8: correlations among nonresponse rates across tests. p-values in parentheses. Significance level: * 10 percent, ** 5 percent, *** 1 percent.

Table 3B.3

Sample coverage and the role of cognitive skills in growth regressions

Test-score measure:	All grades and years (AA)			Lower secondary, 1995–2003 (LR)	LR instr. by AA	LR instr. by tests before 1985
	(1)	(2)[a]	(3)	(4)	(5)[b]	(6)[b]
Cognitive skills	1.980***	1.741***	1.690***	1.338***	1.396***	1.651***
	(9.12)	(7.64)	(6.07)	(6.25)	(6.16)	(3.85)
Initial years of schooling (1960)	0.026	0.041	0.028	0.068	0.060	0.114
	(0.34)	(0.56)	(0.35)	(0.92)	(0.80)	(1.03)
Initial GDP per capita (1960)	-0.302***	-0.294***	-0.310***	-0.320***	-0.320***	-0.362***
	(5.54)	(5.79)	(5.91)	(6.21)	(6.19)	(4.26)
Enrollment rate			0.009	0.011	0.010	-0.007
			(0.89)	(1.12)	(0.98)	(0.18)
Exclusion rate			-0.055	-0.050	-0.049	-0.019
			(0.95)	(0.89)	(0.87)	(0.25)

Nonresponse rate		0.016	0.012	0.013	0.003
		(1.06)	(0.81)	(0.86)	(0.15)
Constant	-4.737***	-4.255***	-2.954***	-3.071***	-2.741
	(5.54)	(4.42)	(3.61)	(3.69)	(0.91)
Number of countries	50	45	45	45	20
R^2 (adj.)	0.728	0.680	0.689	0.688	0.777
F-test (3 coverage rates)		0.79	0.74	0.68	0.03
p-value		(0.505)	(0.533)	(0.571)	(0.993)
F-test (instr. in 1st stage)				311.92	32.14

Notes: Dependent variable: average annual growth rate in GDP per capita, 1960 to 2000. Unless noted otherwise, cognitive skill measure refers to average score on all international tests 1964 to 2003 in math and science, primary through end of secondary school. AA = all grades, all years. LR = lower secondary, recent years (1995 to 2003). t-Statistics in parentheses: statistical significance at * 10 percent, ** 5 percent, *** 1 percent.
a. Sample of countries with available information on measures of sample coverage.
b. Two-stage least-squares regression.

regression. In column 6 we restrict the analysis to only that part of the variation in recent scores that is related to variation on the early tests (1964 to 1985), ensuring that only variation traceable to the early tests is used in the estimation of growth effects. While this reduces the sample to the twenty countries participating in the early tests, the qualitative result on the effect of test scores on economic growth is unaffected. Similar to our specification tests above, the same is true if (not shown) we use only growth rates from 1980 to 2000 in this final specification (coefficient on test score equals 1.707). This last specification relies for identification on only test score variation that mostly predates growth rates while it still permits focusing on tests for which we have the relevant sampling information as control variables.

This analysis indicates the most serious issues in terms of the reliability and validity of the international tests are not significantly affecting our analysis. Although enrollment, exclusion, and nonresponse rates are positively correlated with reported country mean scores on international student achievement tests, the sample selectivity indicated by these measures does not affect the results of our analysis of economic growth.

Appendix 3C: IQ Models

The international assessments of student achievement used in our analysis are not the only sources of information about cognitive skills or the knowledge capital of nations. An extensive set of estimates of intelligence quotient (IQ) differences across nations exists that could potentially supplement, or even replace, the international achievement data. These estimates should be considered for two basic reasons. First, they may provide additional insights into the sources of the differences we measure in skills, with possible implications for the nations' policy choices. Second, they may simply broaden the set of countries that can be included in the analysis.[36]

Perhaps the largest potential difference in interpretation between our general analysis of cognitive skills and one using IQ as a measure is the common view that IQs are fixed and not subject to schooling or environmental influences. If true, this would suggest both that IQ measures might more accurately represent the relevant cognitive skills, and that the analytics of them might be less prone to the types of identification issues discussed in the next chapter.[37] Nonetheless, this fixed-factor view, often related to ideas of IQ being highly heritable, is not uniformly held by researchers in the area. Indeed, in the economics literature, analyses by Goldberger and Manski (1995) and Heckman (1995) clearly show that families and schools have strong effects on measured IQ.[38] This and related work in psychology suggest the most reasonable interpretation of IQ studies is that they provide an alternative measure of cognitive skills to the international assessments described here.

All studies of the economic impacts of IQ are based on the international IQ scores compiled by Lynn and Vanhanen (2002, 2006),[39] who assembled data from specific national samples using a variety of measurement instruments. The earliest work by Weede and Kämpf (2002) mimicked our basic models but included ninety-seven countries. As in our analyses using achievement data as a measure of cognitive skills, differences in measured IQ have a strong and significant effect on growth rates, even allowing for differences in school attainment. Jones and Schneider (2006) provided a series of robustness analyses similar to those of Sala-i-Martin, Doppelhofer, and Miller (2004), with the addition of the Lynn and Vanhanen (2002) IQ measures. They demonstrated that IQ has strong predictive power for economic growth. They also showed the measures are very strongly correlated with the cognitive skill measures of Hanushek and Kimko (2000). Ram (2007) estimated models similar to the augmented neoclassical production functions of Mankiw, Romer, and Weil (1992).

The general conclusion is that school attainment appears less relevant when IQ measures are included in the analysis. Jones and Schneider (2010) used IQ measures of skills to account for variations in immigrant wages, similar to analyses discussed in chapter 4. They concluded IQ is a powerful predictor of wages and, relatedly, that it explains a significant portion of earnings differences across countries.

The real question about these analyses is what, exactly, is being measured. The underlying IQ scores by country come from an idiosyncratic collection of national data that relies on specialized samples for specific cohorts and subsets of the population.[40] Thus we need to ask, how much measurement error is in the underlying skill dimension? In a direct analysis (albeit in terms of the level of GDP per capita) of the empirical value of IQ scores versus PISA scores, Hunt and Wittmann (2008) concluded that PISA scores are better predictors of GDP per capita than the Lynn and Vanhanen (2002) measures of IQ. Lynn and Mikk (2007, 2009) confirmed the very high correlations between IQ scores and either TIMSS or PISA scores. More important, Lynn and Mikk question whether the simple relationships estimated in Lynn and Vanhanen (2002) are causal, as originally asserted.

The conclusion from the various models of the impact of national IQ scores on rates of economic growth is that IQ provides another potential measure of cognitive skills. If accurate, the Lynn and Vanhanen IQ data provide for a considerable expansion of the sample sizes, reaching 113 nations (Lynn and Vanhanen 2006: app. 1). Nonetheless, most analyses would suggest this measure is noticeably more error prone than the international test data stressed here. Additionally, rather than capturing innate differences, they are amenable to family and school influences, which opens a similar set of identification issues to those discussed below (but not addressed in the IQ analyses).

Appendix 3D: Basic Descriptive Statistics

Table 3D.1

Descriptive statistics for the basic growth models

	Mean	Standard deviation	Min	Max
Average annual growth rate in GDP per capita (1960–2000)	2.903	1.387	0.967	6.871
Cognitive skills (all math and science)	4.546	0.611	3.089	5.452
Cognitive skills (only lower secondary)	4.535	0.671	2.683	5.599
Share of students reaching basic literacy	0.761	0.215	0.182	0.967
Share of top-performing students	0.062	0.054	0.000	0.219
Initial GDP per capita (1960)	4,991	3,676	685	14,877
Initial years of schooling (1960)	5.447	2.877	0.611	10.963
Average years of schooling (1960, 2000)	7.425	2.654	2.098	11.845

Notes: Descriptive statistics for variables used in the basic growth models, 50 country observations. See main text for data sources.

4

Causation

Fundamental to all of the prior analysis is a deceptively simple question: should we interpret the tight relationship between cognitive skills and growth as reflecting a causal relationship that can support direct policy actions? Questions about identifying underlying causal effects in cross-country growth models have been asked for a long time and go beyond just the impact of human capital. Beginning with Levine and Renelt (1992), plentiful evidence of their general sensitivity to alternative samples and specifications has convinced many that cross-country empirical models are not fruitful as policy investigations. Bils and Klenow (2000), for instance, provided convincing evidence of the endogeneity of school attainment in growth models. Moreover it is unclear to what extent prior attempts to deal with endogeneity—such as the panel data approaches of Barro (1997) and Vandenbussche, Aghion, and Meghir (2006)—have been successful in a setting where the dominant information is found in the cross-country variation.[1] Perhaps the strongest evidence on causality comes from analyses of the importance of fundamental economic institutions with identification through historical factors (Acemoglu, Johnson, and Robinson 2001, 2005), but as noted in the previous chapter, this evidence has also been subject to question. Furthermore from a policy perspective, it has not yielded clear advice on what kinds of feasible actions will lead to national payoffs, particularly for more developed countries.

The main causality concerns relate to reverse causality and to omitted country variables, such as inherent but unmeasured differences in nations' cultures and economic institutions, that are correlated both with economic growth and cognitive skills or their determinants. The previous chapter presented evidence based on test scores fully predating the observed growth period that already guards against simple reverse causality concerns. Here we assess the endogeneity issues from a number of additional angles with the objective of narrowing the range of threats to a causal interpretation.

Of course, identifying causality in a thoroughly convincing manner is virtually impossible, given the limited observations underlying our cross-country growth models. Each approach we use deals with one or more common concerns, such as the influence of cultural differences, faulty measurement of cognitive skills, or simple reverse causality. But each relies upon certain maintained assumptions that may or may not be completely persuasive.

We essentially apply to the macroeconomic examination of growth a series of three approaches to identifying causal parameters that are now common in microeconometric studies. These important new analyses include estimation with instrumental variables (section 4.1) and consideration of intertemporal changes in growth rates within countries (section 4.2). More recent US data also permit important refinements to the analysis of the effect of cognitive skills on the labor market earnings of immigrants (section 4.3) previously introduced in Hanushek and Kimko (2000), including the specification of full difference-in-differences models.[2]

Each of our three approaches deals with a particular class of reverse causation or omitted variables. By identifying variation in skills stemming from institutional school policies in the different countries, the instrumental variable models highlight the role of schools while addressing issues of simple reverse causality and of inherent cultural differences across nations that might be related to attitudes and performance in learning. By using the intertemporal dimension of our new database for knowledge capital, our longitudinal analysis of changes in growth rates eliminates stable country-specific factors in a general way in the spirit of country fixed effects. By focusing on US labor market outcomes for immigrants, the difference-in-differences approach deals not only with reverse causality but also the possibility that cultural differences or economic institutions and structures of national economies may be correlated with favorable educational outcomes. In each of the three investigations, we explicitly describe the assumptions that are key to interpreting the results. This is important because the different approaches rely on different assumptions, guard against different threats to identification, and would fail for quite different reasons. But empirically, each approach fully supports giving a causal interpretation to the stylized fact of the crucial role of knowledge capital in economic growth found in the previous chapter.

A related aspect of these separate causal investigations is the pinpointing of a specific policy role for improved school quality. While variations in cognitive skills can arise from various influences—including families, culture, health, and ability—the instrumental variable results indicate that schools, and in particular the institutional structures of school systems, are one means of improvement available to policymakers. This conclusion is reinforced in the immigrant analysis by the importance of country of schooling—United States versus home country—for identifying individual skills.

Finally, we complement our regression analysis with a development accounting analysis that extends human capital measurement to include our cognitive skills measure (section 4.4). Here we focus directly on differences in income levels across nations and consider whether knowledge capital can explain the observed variations in GDP per capita. Beginning with a standard functional form of the macroeconomic production function that includes cognitive skills, our development accounting introduces production parameters from the microeconometric literature. This avoids relying on parameters from a macro regression that would be particularly susceptible to endogeneity concerns when viewed in levels instead of growth. In particular, we map years of schooling and cognitive skills onto aggregate human capital using consistent estimates of their micro returns on the US labor market, thereby avoiding potential bias from estimating parameters in cross-country regressions. While we look across all countries, we are particularly interested in performance for the outlying growth regions of Latin America (at the bottom) and East Asia (at the top; see figure 1.1).[3]

Results show that when we consider both school attainment and cognitive skills, human capital can account for about 40 percent of the total variation in current levels of per-capita income across the countries in our global sample. In contrast, it accounts for only about a quarter of the variation when we rely just on school attainment without considering differences in cognitive skills. What is more, knowledge capital accounts for about 60 percent of the income differences between Latin American countries and the rest of the world and about three-quarters between Latin American countries and East Asian countries. These results corroborate the major relevance of knowledge capital to understanding differences in economic prosperity around the world, and especially differences between the outlying growth regions of Latin America and East Asia.[4]

4.1 Variations in Cognitive Skills Driven by School Institutions

One general concern in cross-country investigations is that the omission of cultural features simultaneously influences both economic behavior and school outcomes—that is, some (or all) of the previously estimated impacts of cognitive skills may reflect other forces, and not a causal impact of measured human capital. Additionally, as noted, cognitive skills are likely to depend not only on formal schooling but also on nonschool factors, such as families, peers, and ability. Thus, even if the previous cognitive skills–growth results are causal, they would only be relevant for school policy if the variations in cognitive skills emanating from school policies were related to economic growth, making it important to establish links with school policy per se.

One means of addressing both issues is to focus on only the part of the international variation in cognitive skills that can be traced back to international differences in school systems. For this, we use measures of the institutional structure of the school systems as instruments for the cognitive skill measure. The key for this analysis is that any specific schooling institution must be related to student outcomes but not directly related to economic growth (except through the impact on achievement). Many school policies, such as those surrounding educational spending levels, would be inappropriate because they are likely to be endogenous to the growth process.

Nonetheless, we have consistent international data for institutional features we can plausibly assume are uncorrelated with the regression disturbances of our growth models. Based on the literature on international education production pertaining to factors associated with student achievement, several such features are appropriate: notably, the existence of external exit exam systems, the share of privately operated schools, the impact of varying Catholic church history, the centralization of decision making, and relative teacher pay.[5] We discuss the suitability of each below within the context of our estimation.

External Exit Exams

We begin with external exit exam systems, a device to increase accountability in the school system that has been repeatedly shown to be related to better student achievement.[6] For the estimates shown in the first column in table 4.1, we use the share of students in a country who are subject to external exit exams as an instrument for our measure of cognitive skills in the growth regression.[7] The first-stage results (in the bottom panel of the table) confirm a statistically significant association between external exit exams and cognitive skills.

The effect of cognitive skills on economic growth in the second stage of the instrumental variable (IV) estimation indicates that the variation in skills emanating from the exam systems is statistically significantly related to growth, and the resulting impact is close to the OLS estimate.[8] The relatively low F-statistic of the instrument in the first stage, however, indicates the possibility of a weak-instrument problem—that is, instruments that are only weakly correlated with the endogenous explanatory variable may actually increase estimation bias and compromise the reliability of the conventional asymptotic approximations used for hypothesis testing. To address this, we also report estimates based on the modification of the limited information maximum likelihood (LIML) estimator by Fuller (1977), but the results are hardly affected.[9] While the confidence band of the conditional likelihood ratio test proposed by Moreira (2003) and Andrews, Moreira, and Stock (2007) gets large at the upper end in this specification, difference from zero is still significant at the 10 percent level.[10]

Because initial years of schooling is insignificant in the growth model once test scores are controlled for (both in the OLS and in the IV specification), another possibility is to include years of schooling as a second instrument for test scores.[11] This approach is also suggested by the prior model, as long as cognitive skills are a measure of human capital in equation 2.1. Given that years of schooling are measured in 1960, this instrument also rules out simple reverse causality. Column 2 of table 4.1 reveals that years of schooling is significantly associated with test scores in the first stage, and the first-stage F-statistic increases substantially.[12] The Sargan test does not reject the over-identifying restrictions of the model, suggesting that, if presence of external exit exams is a valid instrument, years of schooling is also valid. Both the 2SLS and the Fuller estimates, as well as inference based on Moreira confidence bands, confirm the schooling-induced differences in cognitive skills are significantly related to economic growth.

Private School Competition

Greater school choice, as measured by the share of privately operated schools in a system, consistently shows a positive association with student achievement in OECD countries and provides an additional instrument.[13] In our sample, the share of private enrollment in a country is significantly positively associated with cognitive skills in the first stage of our IV model (column 3 of table 4.1).[14] The second-stage estimate of the growth model confirms our previous results: schooling-induced differences in cognitive skills are significantly related to economic growth. Again, the Sargan test does not reject the validity of the over-identifying restrictions, and the

Table 4.1
From schooling institutions to cognitive skills to economic growth: Instrumental variable estimates

Second stage:	(1)	(2)	(3)a	(4)	(5)a	(6)
2SLS:						
Cognitive skills	2.151***	2.023***	2.978***	2.207***	3.914***	1.749***
	(2.73)	(5.81)	(5.84)	(6.54)	(4.17)	(5.77)
Initial years of schooling	-0.028					
	(0.18)					
Catholic share in 1970				0.003		
				(0.01)		
Fuller (1) modification of LIML:						
Cognitive skills	2.121***	2.022***	2.969***	2.197***	3.797***	1.753***
	(3.01)	(5.94)	(5.93)	(6.64)	(4.17)	(5.92)
Moreira 95% confidence band:						
Cognitive skills	[-3.888, 19.871]	[1.190, 2.868]	[1.734, 4.343]	[1.465, 3.093]	[2.063, 7.006]	[0.865, 2.525]
p-value	(0.100)	(0.001)	(0.0004)	(0.0001)	(0.0000)	(0.007)
First stage (dependent variable: cognitive skills):						
External exit exam system	0.286**	0.286**				
	(2.01)	(2.01)				

Initial years of schooling	0.176*** (4.11)	0.176*** (4.11)	0.137*** (4.19)	0.186*** (4.32)	0.065* (2.06)	0.161*** (3.05)
Private enrollment share			0.520** (2.36)			
Catholic share in 1900				2.301** (2.15)		
Catholic share in 1970				-2.801** (2.46)		
Centralization (share) of decisions on organization of instruction					-0.941*** (3.24)	
Relative teacher salary						0.188** (2.19)
Number of countries	43	43	20	50	18	34
Centered R^2	0.752	0.753	0.791	0.743	0.590	0.819
First-stage F-statistic	4.04	10.28	12.15	10.60	13.35	6.94
Sargan statistic p-value	0.034 (0.855)	0.033 (0.856)	0.158 (0.691)	0.193 (0.661)	0.011 (0.917)	0.377 (0.540)
Durbin–Wu–Hausman χ^2 test p-value		0.003 (0.957)	0.113 (0.737)	0.479 (0.489)	4.744 (0.029)	0.081 (0.776)

Notes: Dependent variable (of the second stage): average annual growth rate in GDP per capita, 1960 to 2000. Control variables: Initial GDP per capita and a constant. Cognitive-skill measure refers to average score on all international tests, 1964 to 2003, in math and science. t-Statistics in parentheses unless otherwise noted: statistical significance at * 10 percent, ** 5 percent, *** 1 percent. a. Dependent variable: average annual growth rate in GDP per capita, 1980 to 2000; sample of OECD countries.

Durbin–Wu–Hausman test presents no evidence of endogeneity of the cognitive skill measure. Results are also very similar without years of schooling as a second instrument.

Varying Catholic Church History

An additional way to exploit the effect of private competition focuses on religious schools and the influence of the historical origins of international variation in the size of the Catholic school sector. Specifically, we investigate whether competitive forces set in the historical development of different countries' schooling systems provide variations in educational achievement related to current growth. West and Woessmann (2010) showed that the resistance of the Catholic church in the nineteenth century to emerging state-run schooling systems created private school sectors in many countries that have remained over time, with a higher share of Catholics in a country's population in 1900 significantly increasing the share of privately operated schools today. This increased competition in a country's school system in turn raises educational achievement. Without having to rely on the limited number of internationally consistent observations on private school shares, we can use the "reduced form" of West and Woessmann's (2010) model to obtain arguably exogenous variation in test scores—that is, we use the share of Catholics in a country in 1900, available for our whole fifty-country sample, as an instrument for our test score measure.[15]

Of course, religious affiliation may itself be related to educational achievement and to economic growth. Consequently this IV specification conditions on Catholic shares in the modern population. Thus the identifying assumption of this IV model is that, holding constant the effects of modern religious affiliation, historical religious affiliation is not otherwise related to modern growth, apart from the indirect effect through its bearing on competition and thus productivity in the modern school system.

The IV estimation reported in column 4 of table 4.1 provides additional support for our underlying model of cognitive skills and growth. The share of Catholic population in 1900 is indeed positively related to our measure of cognitive skills in the first stage, while in 1970 it is negatively related, which is in line with the previous literature.[16] At the same time, the 1970 Catholic share does not enter the second-stage growth model significantly. But importantly, the variation in cognitive skills that is related to historical Catholic shares has a significant positive effect on economic growth that is close to the OLS estimate. The F-statistic of the instruments in the first stage is just above 10, and LIML estimates and Moreira bands confirm the result is not driven by weak-instrument problems.

Centralization of Decision Making

Another institutional feature regularly shown to be positively associated with student achievement—at least in developed countries—is the extent to which schools or local decision makers are empowered to make their own decisions about the organization of instruction.[17] As column 5 of table 4.1 shows, the share of such decisions that are made at the central government level is significantly negatively associated with our cognitive skill measure, even within our limited sample of developed countries. The second-stage estimators confirm the significantly positive effect of cognitive skills on economic growth.[18]

Relative Teacher Pay

Finally, a key finding in the economics of education literature in recent years is that the quality of the teaching force is a leading observable determinant of student test scores.[19] In a cross-country perspective, Dolton and Marcenaro-Gutierrez (2011) suggested relative teacher salaries as a useful proxy for the overall quality of the teaching force.[20] We therefore use their measure of teacher salary, expressed relative to the per-capita income of each country, as an instrument for our achievement measure.[21] By expressing teacher salary *relative* to the earnings distribution in a country, we focus on the point in the overall "ability" distribution from which a country is likely to draw its population of teachers and avoid capturing just the overall income levels that would be correlated with growth.[22]

In the first-stage model, teacher salaries relative to per-capita income are indeed significantly related to our cognitive skill measure (column 6 of table 4.1). And, again, the second-stage results confirm the significant growth effect of cognitive skills, in the same order of magnitude as the OLS estimates, as well as the robustness to LIML estimation and Moreira bands.

One potential concern about the exogeneity of our instruments is that the institutional features of school systems may be correlated with economic institutions, which are themselves correlated with economic growth. To test whether this affects our identification, we add to our IV models the two measures of differences in economic institutions that tend to enter most robustly in growth regressions: openness and security of property rights (remembering, however, our prior reservations about the distinct possibility that these economic institutions capture part of the human capital effect). Our basic result is unaffected. The measures of economic institutions in fact do not enter significantly (individually or jointly) into any of the IV models except in column 2, and the effect of cognitive skills remains significant in all models except in column 1. The point estimates for cognitive skills are hardly affected except in columns 2 and 4, where they are reduced to 1.1 and 1.3, respectively, similar to our OLS estimate in table 3.5 of the lower bound for the effect.[23]

The results suggest that improvements in cognitive skills generated in the school system—through institutional features affecting school quality—lead to higher long-run growth of economies. Cross-country regressions with small data samples have obvious limits, and this is particularly salient in our IV specifications. Caution is appropriate in interpreting IV results for our relatively small samples of countries and employing the aggregate nature of the institutional measures, but the results are nonetheless statistically significant, reasonably precise, and quantitatively robust, which is striking.

A significant concern remains, however. The institutional characteristics of the school system might still be related (either causally or correlationally) to important unmeasured aspects of economic institutions. Nevertheless, any such problems must go beyond the traditional measures of differences in economic institutions that are commonly employed and that are tested here.

4.2   Skill Improvement and Improved Growth

Our analysis so far has relied upon the average test score for each nation to characterize differences in skills among all their labor forces, but we now turn to the intertemporal variations in skills. As noted, most of the variation in test scores occurs among countries, but the existence of some systematic change suggests the possibility of using the time series evidence on performance within each to identify the impact of skills on growth. Specifically, according to the underlying model, countries that improve the skills of their populations—no matter how they do it—should see commensurate improvements in their rates of growth. For a subset of countries, we can look at the time series patterns within our data. This estimation, in the spirit of a difference-in-differences approach, removes any country-specific fixed effects on growth rates, including effects from basic economic institutions, cultural factors, political environments, and the like, that are constant over the period. This permits focusing on whether a country that improves the cognitive skills of its population is observed to receive an economic return.

While others have investigated turning points in growth, we focus on low-frequency changes such as those that might result from evolutionary schooling policies that alter the path of economic growth.[24] Policies affecting the skill composition of the labor force necessarily unfold over lengthy periods and are not seen as sharp changes in outcomes.

To characterize the longitudinal patterns of test scores for each country, we regress performance on the different international student achievement tests, expressed on our standardized test metric described in appendix 2A, on the year the test was conducted, as well as age group and subject indicators. The unit of observation in these country-specific regressions is each subject, by age and by year, on the occasion of an international student achievement test, using all available tests, subjects, and age groups until 2003 (see table 2.1).[25] The coefficient on the year variable provides us with the measure of change in cognitive skills for each nation we are interested in. The amount of noise in each test observation, particularly with our common scaling, implies such trends are also estimated with considerable noise. We therefore trust the rough cross-country pattern more than the specific point estimates of changes in each country. To limit the amount of noise affecting our analyses, we rely on the sample of OECD countries that have test observations both before 1985 and up to 2003.[26]

The estimated time trends for each country are shown in figure 4.1, which simply extrapolates scores for the range of 1975 to 2000, anchored by the PISA 2000 score. As is evident, substantial changes—both positive and negative—have occurred in test performance for the sample of OECD countries.[27] The rapid rise in performance of such countries as Canada, Finland, and the Netherlands contrasts sharply with the declining scores in Germany, Italy, and Norway over this period. For our purposes, however, we are not interested in test scores for the school-aged population, but rather in the skills of the relevant portions of the labor force. Thus we need to assume that the observed trends in performance reflect long-run patterns of skill change and, specifically, the patterns during the earlier time periods.

In a parallel manner, we estimate a time trend for annual growth rates in each country using the Penn World Tables data. These series contain considerable noise, largely reflecting short-run business cycle phenomena or financial crises, and the trend estimation is designed to extract long-run changes in growth.[28]

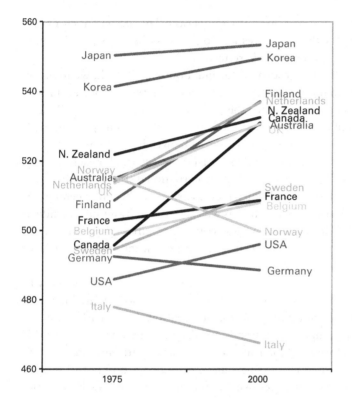

Figure 4.1

Trends in test scores

Notes: Depiction based on PISA 2000 performance and a backward extrapolation based on the coefficient on a time variable from a regression of all available international test scores (by year, age group, and subject) on the time variable and dummies for age group and subject. See text for details.

The consistency of changes in both test performance and growth rates is evident in figure 4.2. When we split countries into those above and those below the median change in growth rates and those above and those below the median change in cognitive skills, all countries fall into either the positive or negative quadrants on both measures. The largest outliers from the trend line are precisely those countries that have less historical test score data (Canada, Korea, and Norway) and thus poorer trend data.

We provide estimates of simple models of the change in growth rates over the 1975–2000 period in table 4.2. By focusing on changes in test scores and growth rates, these specifications are essentially equivalent to

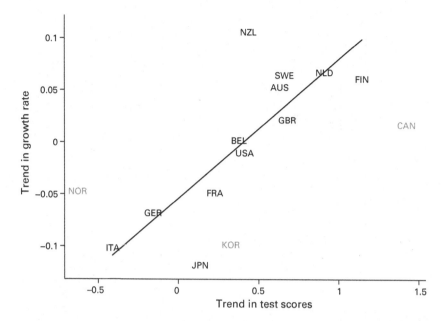

Figure 4.2

Trends in test scores and trends in growth rates

Notes: Scatter plot of trend in the growth rate of GDP per capita from 1975 to 2000 and trend in test scores, which is equivalent to the first column of table 4.2. Three countries without test scores before 1972 in light gray; regression line refers to the remaining twelve countries. See text for details.

panel estimates with country fixed effects that eliminate time-invariant factors of cultural, institutional, or other potential influences. For the fifteen OECD countries, 38 percent of the variance in growth rate changes is accounted for by test score changes. If we add measures for the average growth rate in each country and the initial GDP per capita (columns 2–3), the change in achievement scores remains statistically significant at nearly the same level found in the simple regression of column 1. The same is true when we add the change in quantitative educational attainment to the model (column 4). Importantly, the change in educational attainment is orthogonal to the change in growth rates (either with or without controls for the test score trend), reinforcing the general theme of this analysis regarding the limited information about human capital in international measures of school attainment. Likewise results are hardly affected if we weight each observation by the inverse of the standard error

Table 4.2.
Changes in cognitive skills and changes in growth paths

	(1)	(2)	(3)	(4)	(5)[a]	(6)[b]	(7)
Trend in cognitive skills	0.084***	0.073***	0.074***	0.074***	0.080***	0.117***	0.073***
	(3.10)	(3.21)	(3.07)	(3.04)	(3.34)	(6.90)	(2.97)
Average annual growth rate in GDP per capita 1975–2000		−0.030**	−0.035	−0.028	−0.039**	−0.085***	−0.031**
		(2.73)	(1.61)	(1.69)	(2.32)	(5.26)	(2.55)
Initial GDP per capita			−0.002				
			(0.27)				
Change in years of schooling 1975–2000				−0.004			
				(0.21)			
Trend in cognitive skills in 1999–2009							0.0004
							(0.03)
Number of countries	15	15	15	15	15	12	15
R^2 (adj.)	0.380	0.586	0.551	0.550	0.582	0.891	0.548

Notes: Dependent variable: trend in the annual growth rate of GDP per capita from 1975 to 2000. Regressions include a constant. Sample: OECD countries with test-score data both before 1985 and up to 2003. Cognitive-skill measure refers to average of math and science. t-Statistics in parentheses: statistical significance at * 10 percent, ** 5 percent, *** 1 percent.
a. WLS with inverse of standard error with which the trend in test scores was estimated as weights.
b. Excluding countries without test scores before 1972 (Canada, Korea, and Norway).

with which the trend in test scores was estimated, to down-weight those that are more noisily estimated (column 5).

If, however, we restrict the analysis to those countries with test scores spanning a range of more than three decades (from at least 1971 to 2003), both the coefficient estimate and the explained variance become larger (column 6), as suggested in figure 4.2. In the sample without the three countries with limited time series information (Canada, Korea, and Norway), the test score trend alone accounts for 64 percent of the variation in growth trends.[29]

The underlying identifying assumption of these analyses is that the observed test score trend captures a prior trend and is not affected by the partly overlapping growth trend. One way to test the validity of this assumption is to use the most recently available test score data to estimate the trend in test scores after the period over which the growth trend is estimated. To do so, we estimate the test score trend from the twenty-four available test observations in 1999 to 2009 (details available on request). Entered to our regression, this test score trend is totally unrelated to the prior growth trend and does not affect the result on the prior test score trend (column 7). The test score trend in 1999 to 2009 is in fact not correlated with the prior long-term test score trend (correlation coefficient −0.302, p-value 0.274) nor with the growth trend in 1975 to 2000 (correlation coefficient −0.293, p-value 0.289).[30] This result corroborates the assumption that the identifying test score variation is not itself caused by variation in growth. Furthermore analysis using the updated Penn World Table data (version 7.0), appearing in appendix table 4A.2, shows results are strengthened when the initial test score trend is related to the growth trend in 1985 to 2007 (rather than 1975 to 2000).[31]

Still this analysis requires backward extrapolation of the test score data to capture changes for people in the labor force. Thus it cannot be considered definitive. We can, however, relate these estimates to the prior growth models. If we assume the observed trend in test scores has been going on since the oldest person in the current labor force went to school, an annual increase in test scores by 1 percent of a standard deviation will translate into an annual increase in the growth rate by 0.07 to 0.12 percentage points. If, however, we more realistically assume any change in test scores began at the beginning of our observation period, then the impact of student improvements on the average labor force is much less, and the projected change in growth rates is commensurately reduced. Back-of-the-envelope calculations suggest that, in such a setting, the estimates based on the trend analysis in table 4.2 are close to the steady-state estimates in table 3.1.

In conclusion, the positive relationship between improving cognitive skills and improving growth rates represents another set of surprisingly consistent results based on a different approach to identifying the causal impact of cognitive skills: a focus on changes within each country that removes country-specific fixed effects. While the analysis requires large extrapolations of changes to cover existing workers, the results are remarkably compatible with the underlying growth model showing growth rates changing in a manner consistent with changes in cognitive skills.

4.3   Micro Evidence from US Immigrants

Yet another approach to assessing the causal importance for economic outcomes of schools and our measured skill differences relies on microdata on earnings differences within a single labor market. This strategy, first proposed by Hanushek and Kimko (2000), looks within the US labor market, thereby explicitly holding constant the quality of economic and cultural factors affecting the operations of the overall economy and focusing on whether measured cognitive skills directly relate to productivity.[32] Following a difference-in-differences strategy, we can compare the returns to skills of immigrants schooled in their country of origin to those of immigrants from the same country schooled within the United States. If it is the measured differences in cognitive skills and not other economically relevant attributes of the families and home economies that are important, the impact of skills can be derived from the different earnings of the two groups.

Micro Returns to Knowledge on the Labor Market
The structure of the estimation is derived from a standard Mincer (1974) wage equation (as shown in appendix 2B), augmented by measured cognitive skills such as

$$\ln y_{ic} = \alpha_0 + \beta S_{ic} + \alpha_1 E_{ic} + \alpha_2 E_{ic}^2 + \gamma T_{ic} + v_{ic}, \qquad (4.1)$$

where y is annual earnings for immigrant i from country c, S is years of school attainment, E (= age $- S - 6$) is potential experience, T is cognitive skills, and v is a random error. Here β is the conventional Mincer return to schooling, and γ is the earnings return to cognitive skills.[33]

Before presenting our difference-in-differences strategy based on US immigrants, we briefly summarize what is known on the micro returns to cognitive skills on the labor market. So far, estimation of these returns has generally relied on US panel data that permit observing the earnings of youth as they go from school into their initial jobs. Estimates of models such as equation (4.1) for US workers indicate around 10 to 15 percent returns to a standard deviation of test scores for young workers.[34] For example, Murnane and others (2000) provided evidence from the High School and Beyond national longitudinal study and the National Longitudinal Survey of the High School Class of 1972. Their estimates suggest some variation, with males obtaining a 15 percent increase and females a 10 percent increase per standard deviation of test performance. Lazear (2003), relying on a somewhat younger sample from the National Education Longitudinal Survey of 1988 (NELS: 88), provided a single estimate of 12 percent. These estimates are also very close to those by Mulligan (1999), who found 11 percent for the normalized Armed Forces Qualification Test (AFQT) score in the National Longitudinal Survey of Youth (NLSY) data.[35] More recently Chetty and colleagues (2011) found a return of 18 percent to measured achievement in young workers using tax return data.

Looking across the full age range of US workers, Hanushek and Zhang (2009) estimated a return to skills of 19 percent from the International Adult Literacy Survey (IALS), which samples workers ages sixteen to sixty-five. More generally, Hanushek et al. (2015) showed that estimates based on early career earnings substantially underestimate the lifetime returns to skills. Their estimate for the United States from the more recent data of the Programme for the International Assessment of Adult Competencies (PIAAC) is 14 and 28 percent, respectively, with and without conditioning on years of schooling.

The international evidence in the studies by Hanushek and Zhang (2009) and Hanushek et al. (2015) also highlights the presence of considerable variation in the micro returns to skills across countries. In fact, estimated returns are higher in the United States than in any other country participating in the international testing programs. Across the twenty-two countries analyzed by Hanushek et al. (2015), the average return to skills (without conditioning on years of schooling) is 18 percent, with Sweden showing the lowest return at 12 percent. Hanushek et al. (2015) show that the cross-country pattern is related to differences in institutions and distortions in the labor markets across countries. In particular, returns to skills are systematically lower in countries with higher union density, stricter employment protection legislation, and larger public sectors. Thus the returns estimated on the relatively undistorted US labor market may best reflect payments of the marginal returns to individual productivity.

How these micro returns to knowledge map onto the macro returns that interest us in this book remains unclear, however. The microeconomic returns to cognitive skills on the labor market may not capture their full macroeconomic effect. On the one hand, the social return to skills may be higher than the private return if there are externalities—for instance, in the spirit of the innovation effects of endogenous growth models.[36] If highly skilled inventors produce innovations that raise the productivity of other workers and, ultimately, of whole economies without all these benefits accruing to the innovator, the macro returns to skills may be considerably larger than those estimated in the micro literature. At our current state of knowledge, the empirical bearing of the size of such externalities is open to debate.[37]

On the other hand, the social return to skills may, in principle, also be lower than the private return if part of the latter comes in the form of unproductive signaling or screening. Since the analysis of Spence (1973), questions have been raised about whether schools simply act as devices to select more able students as opposed to providing them with new knowledge and skills. According to this view, an individual may get more schooling simply to signal high ability to the labor market. The difficulty has been that the labor market implications for the returns to school attainment are the same in the alternative models: those individuals with more schooling have more skills and thus receive higher wages. This fact has generated a variety of alternative ways to identify production versus signaling.[38] One salient approach is to rely on what happens during schooling as opposed to the market returns to school attainment to identify the differences. In what follows, we provide one form of such evidence that points strongly toward an interpretation that the micro returns to knowledge are not limited to private payoffs, as would be implied in the screening model.

Comparing the Impacts of Home Country Education and US Education on the US Labor Market

Building on the framework of the within-country analyses, we apply a difference-in-differences model to compare the labor market experiences of immigrants to the United States who were either educated entirely in their countries of origin or entirely in the United States.[39] (We exclude any individuals partially educated in both countries to obtain a clear separation of treatment and control groups.) We assign the average cognitive-skill score of the home country $\left(\overline{T}_c\right)$ for each immigrant and estimate the Mincer earnings equation (4.1) as

$$\ln y_{ic} = \alpha_0 + \beta S_{ic} + \alpha_1 E_{ic} + \alpha_2 E_{ic}^2 + \left[\alpha_3 O_{ic} + \gamma_1 \overline{T}_c + \gamma_2 \left(O_{ic}\overline{T}_c\right)\right] + v_{ic}, \qquad (4.2)$$

where O is an indicator that is one if immigrant i was educated entirely in schools in the country of origin and zero otherwise, and the combined terms in brackets indicate the skills of individuals from country c. The parameter γ_2 is the relevant contrast in skills between home country schooling and US schooling.[40]

We interpret γ_2 as a difference-in-differences estimate of the effect of home country test scores on earnings, where the first difference is between immigrants educated in their home countries (the "treatment group") and US-educated immigrants (the "control group") from the same countries, and the second difference is in the average cognitive-skill scores of the home countries.[41] The parameter γ_1 captures the bias that would emerge in standard cross-sectional estimates from omitted variables, such as cultural traits that are correlated with home country test scores in the same way for all immigrants from the same country of origin (independent of where they were educated); in our more elaborate specifications with country-of-origin fixed effects, this parameter is not identified.

The first two columns of table 4.3 report the estimates of the impact of cognitive skills from stratified samples for the two groups of immigrants, effectively estimating equation (4.1) with average test scores of the home countries. Test scores are normalized to mean zero and a standard deviation of one, so the estimates indicate the proportionate increase in earnings from a one standard deviation increase in scores. Other things equal, there is essentially no relationship between US earnings and test scores of their countries of origin, either quantitatively or statistically, for the 50,597 immigrants educated entirely in the United States. However, one standard deviation greater performance in country-specific average test scores translates into a statistically significant earnings increase of approximately 16 percent for the 258,977 immigrants educated in their countries of origin.

This estimate is close to the recent estimates for cognitive skills of US workers discussed above—surprisingly close, given that just average country scores as opposed to individual specific scores are used in the estimation here, although the averaging of scores does eliminate the measurement error found in individual test data.

Column 3 combines the samples and fully estimates equation (4.2). These estimates indicate a significant impact of test scores emanating

Table 4.3

Difference-in-differences estimates of returns to country-of-origin cognitive skills for US immigrants

Sample:	US educated[a] (1)	Educated in country of origin[b] (2)	All immigrants (3)	W/o Mexico (4)	All immigrants (5)	W/o Mexico (6)	Growth sample[c] (7)	Only English speaking countries (8)
Cognitive skills × Educated in country of origin			0.087**	0.132***	0.138***	0.140***	0.167***	0.162***
			(2.02)	(3.31)	(3.16)	(4.13)	(3.77)	(3.57)
Cognitive skills	0.005	0.158**	0.063	-0.026	not identified	not identified	not identified	not identified
	(0.14)	(2.37)	(1.06)	(1.42)				
Educated in country of origin			-0.139***	-0.101***	-0.1298***	-0.063**	-0.131***	-0.021
			(3.95)	(3.03)	(2.98)	(2.07)	(2.58)	(0.83)
Fixed effects for country of origin	no	no	no	no	yes	yes	yes	yes
Observations	50,597	258,977	309,574	187,506	309,574	187,506	273,213	72,091
Number of countries	64	64	64	63	64	63	47	12
R^2	0.157	0.170	0.180	0.132	0.196	0.150	0.202	0.156

Notes: Dependent variable: log(annual earnings). Cognitive-skill measure refers to average score of country of origin (centered at zero) on all international tests 1964 to 2003 in math and science. All models control for years of schooling, potential experience, and potential experience squared. Sample: All immigrants identified by country of birth not in school whose age is greater than 25, who are employed, and who earned more than $1,000 in 1999. Immigrants who had obtained some but not all of their education in the United States were excluded from the sample. Immigrants from all countries of origin for which there are cognitive-skill scores, except for the following countries (areas), which could not be identified because of census restrictions on release of data for small cells: Swaziland, Slovenia, Macau-China, Luxembourg, Liechtenstein, Estonia, Botswana, Bahrain, Tunisia, and Iceland. Israel could not be identified separately from Palestine; both were assigned the Israeli score. Robust absolute values of t-Statistics in parentheses with clustering by country of origin: statistical significance at * 10 percent, ** 5 percent, *** 1 percent. Authors' calculations from 2000 Census IPUMS data.

a. US-educated immigrants are identified as immigrating to the United States before the beginning year of schooling.

b. Immigrants educated in their country of origin are identified as immigrants to the United States after the final year of schooling.

c. The economic growth sample relies on the data for immigrants from the 50 countries in the basic growth regressions of chapter 3.

from schooling in the immigrant's country of origin (γ_2). In contrast, the estimate of (home country) test score for US-educated immigrants (γ_1) is statistically insignificant, although the point estimate is noticeably greater than zero. Column 4 demonstrates this latter effect comes entirely from the influence of immigrants from Mexico (who constitute 37 percent of all immigrants to the United States). The estimation for immigrants from Mexico is prone to classification error because many Mexican families tend to move back and forth from their home country—thus making assignment to US or Mexican schooling prone to error.[42] Excluding Mexican immigrants, $\hat{\gamma}_2$ is highly significant with a point estimate of 0.13, while the coefficient for US-educated immigrants falls to –0.026 and remains statistically insignificant.

The prior estimates indicate the estimation strategy may be sensitive to variations in immigration patterns across the sixty-four sampled countries. In addition to the complications for Mexican immigrants, for example, the immigrants from other countries might vary by where they fall in the ability distribution of the home country and the like. For this reason, the remaining columns of table 4.3 contain country-of-origin fixed effects. Thus immigrants educated entirely abroad in their home countries are compared directly to immigrants *from the same countries* educated entirely in the United States. This eliminates any potential bias emanating from features specific to the country of origin, be they specific selectivity of the immigrant population or country-specific cultural traits. The only remaining assumption required for identification of our parameter of interest is that any potential difference between the early-immigrated, US-educated group of immigrants and the late-immigrated, home-educated group from each country (as captured by the indicator O) does not vary across countries in a way associated with country-of-origin test scores.

Column 5 displays the primary estimation across all sampled countries with country-specific fixed effects. The estimated impact of cognitive skills is a 14 percent increase in earnings from each standard deviation increase in origin country test scores (when educated there). This estimate is highly significant. Furthermore the point estimate is virtually unchanged by excluding the Mexican immigrants (column 6). The standard error is reduced by clearer assignment to the treatment category (when Mexicans are excluded), even though the sample is substantially reduced.

For the final two columns, we investigate the sensitivity of these estimates to sample definition. First, our estimation of growth models uses the fifty countries for which we could obtain the relevant economic data for GDP growth. Restricting this analysis to that smaller sample yields a slight increase in the magnitude of $\hat{\gamma}_2$ to 17 percent, while it remains statistically significant. Second, because immigrants from non–English-speaking countries may have lower earnings because of language difficulties, the final column shows estimates based entirely on immigrants from countries where English is the primary or official language.[43] Again, even for this sample of just twelve countries, variations in cognitive skills across countries have a strongly significant impact on earnings of 16 percent.

The estimates of equation (4.2) in table 4.3 indicate that being educated entirely in the country of origin (α_3) reduces average earnings by 6 to 13 percent except for English-speaking immigrants, who appear to suffer no significant average earnings loss compared to people educated entirely in the United States. The estimated "Mincer" parameters (β, α_1, and α_2) appear within the range of typical estimates for the general population (not shown).[44] Results remain qualitatively the same when indicators for decade of immigration and gender are added to the model.[45] These last specifications address in part concerns that unmeasured differences between late immigrants (those receiving schooling in their home countries) and early immigrants (those receiving schooling in the United States) might be driving the results.

These difference-in-differences estimates provide support for two conclusions about the potential causal impacts of cognitive skills. First, they contrast individuals receiving the treatment of home country schooling to immigrants from the same countries, all within the same labor market. Thus they cannot be driven by differences in underlying economic institutions around the globe that are correlated with differences in cognitive skills. Second, they pinpoint the impact of schooling differences across countries, as distinct from family or cultural differences in attitudes, motivation, child rearing, and the like. In sum, the estimates, which are highly stable across different estimation samples, provide evidence that the economic impact is a causal one, and not purely associational.

Comparing magnitudes of coefficients from the immigrant earnings models to the growth regressions is very difficult, however. As discussed above, these estimates are restricted to the private returns and leave out any of the externalities implicit in the estimated growth models. Thus, while the estimated earnings impacts of cognitive skills are remarkably close to existing micro estimates, they do not translate easily into aggregate growth estimates.

The estimates do, however, provide direct support for the production view of schooling as contrasted with the signaling or screening view. As indicated above, one approach to identifying production versus signaling is to rely on what happens during schooling as opposed to the market returns to school attainment. The results above provide just such evidence because they show that the quality of different schools and the cognitive skills related to different schooling have direct payoffs within the same labor market. These estimates yield even stronger evidence that policies to improve schools have social payoffs, as opposed to being limited to private payoffs, as implied in the screening model.

4.4   Accounting for Levels of Development across Countries

Finally, we also pursue a different, complementary approach to address the endogeneity concerns of cross-country macro regressions. As introduced above, a primary set of concerns arises from the fact that the estimated growth parameters may suffer from common problems of reverse causality and omitted variables. Development accounting, an alternative approach, does not depend on estimating the growth parameters but, rather, takes them from the microeconomic literature and derives its structure in the macroeconomic analysis by assuming a particular form of the macroeconomic production function.[46]

Development accounting permits us to see if the differences in economic outcomes around the world are consistent with the differences we observe in knowledge capital. By adding some basic economic structure to incomes, we can decompose differences in outcomes across any set of countries or regions.

We use development accounting to supplement our explanations for the wide disparities we see in growth and incomes. Returning to figure 1.1, which showed two outliers in terms of regional growth—Latin America and East Asia—we now consider whether knowledge capital can provide a consistent accounting for how the incomes of these regions differ from other regions of the world.[47] In particular, we leave consideration of how growth varies for a specific look at whether variations in GDP per capita today are consistent with variations in knowledge capital.

Consider a standard Cobb–Douglas macroeconomic production function

$$Y = (hL)^{1-\alpha} K^{\alpha} A^{\lambda}, \qquad (4.3)$$

where Y is output, h is per-capita human capital, L is labor, K is physical capital, and A is total factor productivity. With Harrod-neutral productivity ($\lambda = 1 - \alpha$), we can express the production function in per-capita terms in the following way:

$$y \equiv \frac{Y}{L} = h \left(\frac{k}{y}\right)^{\alpha/(1-\alpha)} A, \tag{4.4}$$

where $k \equiv K/L$ is the capital–labor ratio.

The decomposition of cross-country variation in per-capita output is then straightforward. Taking logarithms of equation (4.4), we see that the covariances of log GDP per capita with the inputs are additively separable:

$$\begin{aligned}
\mathrm{var}(\ln(y)) &= \mathrm{cov}(\ln(y), \ln(y)) \\
&= \mathrm{cov}(\ln(y), \ln(h)) + \mathrm{cov}\left(\ln(y), \ln\left(\left(\tfrac{k}{y}\right)^{\alpha/(1-\alpha)}\right)\right) \\
&\quad + \mathrm{cov}(\ln(y), \ln(A)).
\end{aligned} \tag{4.5}$$

Dividing equation (4.5) through the variance of GDP per capita puts each component in terms of its proportional contribution to the variance of income. The "covariance measure" proposed by Klenow and Rodriquez-Clare (1997) allows us to decompose the total variance in log per-capita output in the country sample into shares attributed to its covariance with the factor input components—in the case of human capital, $\mathrm{cov}(\ln(y), \ln(h))/\mathrm{var}(\ln(y))$. Here we are only interested in the share attributed to variation in human capital, for which no additional parameter assumptions are required (although we must still measure human capital).[48]

An alternative measure that is informative when we consider regional variations—say, Latin America versus other regions—follows in the spirit of the decomposition provided in Hall and Jones (1999). The share of income variation between countries in region i and countries in a comparison region j that can be accounted for by differences in human capital is given by $\ln(h_i / h_j)/\ln(y_i / y_j)$, based on geometric averages of the variables for the countries in each group.

To measure human capital, we employ the extended macro Mincer specification (following equation 4.1) to weight the components of education by micro labor market returns. This extends the usual Mincer model that considers only years of schooling to one that additionally considers test score performance and suggests the following measure of human capital:

$$h = e^{\beta S + \gamma T}, \tag{4.6}$$

where S is years of schooling, T is test scores, and β and γ come from the micro literature on Mincer log earnings functions.

In an international context, past research has suggested considerable variation in both β and γ.[49] As discussed in the previous section, the underlying reasons for the variation, while not fully understood, incorporate various labor market distortions around the world. This leads us to draw our parameter estimates from the United States because of the lesser distortions there, so the parameters best reflect marginal products. In terms of the school attainment parameter, we assume a standard US rate of return of $\beta = 0.10$ for each year of schooling. (Some variation of this assumed value moreover does not make any substantial difference for our pattern of results.)

Crucially for our interest in cognitive skills, we require a micro estimate of the return to them on the labor market. As discussed in the previous section, a range of estimates exists for γ. Our baseline parameterization is based on the estimate for the full age range of US workers in the mid-1990s by Hanushek and Zhang (2009), which indicates each individual-level standard deviation in test scores is associated with 0.193 higher earnings (conditional on years of schooling). For our calibration, we therefore use a return of $\gamma = 0.20$ per standard deviation in test scores, but also present versions for lower and higher values.

Sharp differences in regional levels of GDP per capita in 2000 put OECD countries far ahead of other regional groupings. Interestingly, with rapid growth over the past half century, East Asian countries have now climbed considerably, reaching the middle of our sample of countries and clearly rising above the middle for the entire world. However, Latin American countries have fallen within our sampled countries and remain low by world standards. (Because of our interest in Latin America—which we expand upon in the next chapter—we use specific tests for the region to bring the sample of countries there from seven to sixteen and the total of countries in our analysis from fifty to fifty-nine. See the discussion in chapter 5 for details.)

Table 4.4 reports the results on the share of the cross-country variation in GDP per capita in 2000 that is attributable to variation in human capital in various development accounting comparisons. In the first line, the covariance measure is used to decompose the variation of all fifty-nine countries. While 24 percent of the variation in GDP per capita is attributable to differences in school attainment (i.e., when $\gamma = 0$ in equation 4.6; column 1), the share attributable to total human capital rises to 39 percent when cognitive skills are considered (and valued at our preferred return of $\gamma = 0.20$; column 2).

Table 4.4
Development accounting: share of variation in GDP per capita attributed to variation in human capital

	Considering only years of schooling (1)	Considering years of schooling and cognitive skills			Relative GDP per capita (5)	Relative human capital ($\gamma = 0.20$) (6)
		$\gamma = 0.20$ (2)	$\gamma = 0.15$ (3)	$\gamma = 0.25$ (4)		
Covariance measure	0.24	0.39	0.35	0.43		
Comparing OECD countries to others:					Other group divided by OECD	
Non-OECD countries	0.28	0.43	0.40	0.47	28.1%	57.7%
Latin America	0.28	0.50	0.45	0.56	26.1%	50.9%
East Asia	0.25	0.27	0.26	0.27	51.7%	83.8%
Comparing Latin America to others:					Latin America divided by other group	
Non-Latin America countries	0.28	0.59	0.51	0.67	44.5%	61.9%
East Asia	0.30	0.73	0.62	0.84	50.5%	60.7%

Notes: Results of development accounting analyses for GDP per capita in 2000 in the 59-country sample. The parameter γ refers to the income return to a standard deviation in test scores in Mincer earnings functions. Covariance measure is based on the decomposition $\text{cov}(\ln(y), \ln(b))/\text{var}(\ln(y))$. Decompositions between any two groups of countries are based on $\ln(b_{group1}/b_{group2})/\ln(y_{group1}/y_{group2})$, where countries within each group are averaged geometrically. See text for details.

The parameterization of $\gamma = 0.20$ assumes that the microeconomic return to cognitive skills on the labor market captures their full macroeconomic effect. As discussed in the previous section, however, the social return to skills may be higher than the private return if there are externalities, as in endogenous growth models. This may mean the macro return to skills is substantially higher than indicated by the parameter value of $\gamma = 0.20$. Yet some of the labor market studies reviewed above suggest the return to test scores may be somewhat lower. Therefore we show in columns 3 and 4 the results of our development accounting analyses for parameter values of $\gamma = 0.15$ and $\gamma = 0.25$, respectively. If the macroeconomic return to skills lies in this range, the share of variation in GDP per capita that can be attributed to human capital differences ranges from 35 to 43 percent.

Just as interesting in terms of our overall investigation is the look at how income levels vary across regions—particularly for comparisons of rich and poor regions. We begin by comparing OECD countries to other groupings and then turn to the special situations of Latin America and East Asia. When human capital is measured only by years of schooling, 28 percent of the income variation between OECD and non-OECD is attributed to human capital in the development accounting analysis. Once we include differences in cognitive skills as part of the human capital variation, however, the share attributed to human capital increases to 43 percent. As described in the last two columns of table 4.4, this follows from non-OECD countries' having just 28 percent of the income of OECD countries but human capital equaling 58 percent that of the OECD countries $(0.43 = \ln(0.577)/\ln(0.281))$.

The share of differences in GDP per capita attributable to total human capital rises to 50 percent in the comparison between OECD and Latin American countries, reflecting the larger difference in human capital between these regions. But the human capital share of the OECD-East Asian income difference is noticeably less, at 27 percent. Little of this difference comes from cognitive skills because the test scores of the two regions are very similar, and the average total human capital is just 16 percent lower in East Asian countries than in the OECD.[50]

The comparisons of Latin America and East Asia are especially interesting. In 1960, the income levels in East Asia were substantially below those of Latin America, but by 2000, the reverse was true. By our decomposition, almost three-quarters of the income difference in 2000 can be attributed to differences in human capital, most of which come from differences in cognitive skills.

These development accounting results derive structure from assuming a known production function with well-identified parameters on the income returns to cognitive skills from the micro literature. They indicate differences in cognitive skills are indeed significant enough to account for major parts of the differences in per-capita income around the world, and in particular between the outlying growth regions of Latin America and East Asia. The approach eliminates major (though obviously not all) sources of endogeneity bias because it is not subject to the kind of bias from omitted variables or reverse causation that has apparently plagued prior cross-country growth regressions. The evidence is consistent with and complementary to our growth regression results.

4.5   Conclusions on Causality

Myriad empirical estimates of cross-country growth models exist. The general criticism of these is they provide little confidence to satisfactorily identify the causal impact of their included determinants of growth. A related criticism is they cannot then provide any real policy guidance.

We have focused on the role of cognitive skills in determining economic growth and taken seriously the quest for policy guidance. We have investigated a set of models that approach identification from different vantage points. Individually, as discussed, these approaches do require maintaining certain assumptions, but importantly, each approach is subject to different questions and would fail for very different reasons. While other threats to identification remain that cannot be ruled out in our samples, the alternative analytical perspectives narrow the range of possible opposing explanations for the stylized facts based on omitted variables, reverse causation, economic and social institutions, and cultural influences.

The development accounting reinforces this analysis. We find differences in human capital can account for substantial portions of income variation across countries and regions in a simple neoclassical macro model that takes its parameters from the micro literature.

Our analysis is further reinforced by the analysis in Ciccone and Papaioannou (2009), who found that countries with more skilled labor forces—according to the Hanushek and Kimko (2000) test measures—experienced faster growth in skill-intensive industries during the 1980s and 1990s. This evidence, which is derived from within-country analysis of development outcomes, strengthens our interpretation that more skilled people contribute to faster adoption of new technologies and production processes—a central element of both endogenous growth models that stress innovation and ideas (Romer 1990a) and models of technological diffusion and growth (Nelson and Phelps 1966). By using country and industry fixed effects, their analysis also excludes a variety of concerns about endogeneity due to variations in institutions and cultures that tend to affect sectors uniformly.

The simple conclusion from the combined evidence is that differences in cognitive skills lead to economically significant differences in prosperity. Moreover, since the tests concentrate on the impact of schools, the evidence suggests school policy can, if effective in raising cognitive skills, be an important force in economic development. Thus it would be inappropriate to interpret the test differences as a simple reflection of ability or family differences—factors that might be very impervious to policy changes.

Appendix 4A: Descriptive Statistics for Causation Analyses

Table 4A.1

Descriptive statistics for the changes-in-growth-paths models

	Mean	Std. dev.	Min	Max
Trend in growth rate of GDP per capita (1975–2000)	-0.007	0.071	-0.118	0.106
Trend in cognitive skills	0.409	0.546	-0.630	1.420
Average annual growth rate in GDP per capita (1975–2000)	2.318	1.106	0.855	5.978
GDP per capita (1975)	13,884	3,217	3,720	18,175
Change in years of schooling (1975–2000)	1.994	0.895	0.899	4.376

Notes: Descriptive statistics for variables used in table 4.2, 15 country observations. See main text for data sources.

Table 4A.2

Changes in cognitive skills and changes in growth paths with updated data series on economic growth

Period of trend in growth	1975–2000	1975–2007	1985–2007
	(1)	(2)	(3)
Trend in cognitive skills	0.072**	0.072***	0.115***
	(2.61)	(2.92)	(2.94)
Average annual growth rate	-0.017	-0.022	-0.067***
in GDP per capita over period	(1.30)	(1.69)	(3.16)
Number of countries	15	15	15
R^2 (adj.)	0.316	0.387	0.516

Notes: Dependent variable: trend in the annual growth rate of GDP per capita over the period shown in the header, based on PWT version 7.0. Regressions include a constant. Sample: OECD countries with test-score data both before 1985 and up to 2003. Cognitive-skill measure refers to average of math and science. t-Statistics in parentheses: statistical significance at * 10 percent, ** 5 percent, *** 1 percent.

Table 4A.3

Descriptive statistics for the US immigrant models

	Mean	Std. dev.	Min	Max
Annual earnings	33,243	40,983	1,000	385,000
Cognitive skills	4.334	0.535	3.089	5.452
Educated in country of origin	0.837	0.370	0	1
Years of schooling	11.558	5.006	0	20
Potential experience	24.841	11.966	0	87

Notes: Descriptive statistics for variables used in table 4.3, 309,574 observations. See main text for data sources.

5

Developing Countries

As we look at the impoverishment of the developing countries of the world, it is difficult to argue against a strategy of "education for all." Several decades of thought about human capital—and centuries of general attention to education in the more advanced countries—have led naturally to a belief that a productive development strategy would be to raise the schooling levels of the population. But the previous chapters foreshadow the need for a significantly altered strategy.

For a variety of reasons the consensus behind a development strategy of expanded schooling has been breaking down over recent decades, but the message has been confused and the appropriate alternative not entirely clear. Somewhat conflicting observations drive the confusion. First, developed and developing countries differ in countless ways other than schooling levels, which may be distorting the observed outcomes. Second, a number of developing countries—both on their own and with the assistance of others—have expanded schooling opportunities without seeing any dramatic catch-up with developed countries in terms of economic well-being. Third, countries that do not function well in general might not be any more able to mount effective education programs than they are to pursue other societal goals. Fourth, even when schooling policy is made a focal point, many of the approaches undertaken do not seem very effective and do not lead to the anticipated student outcomes. In sum, is it obvious that education is the driving force behind development, or is it merely one of several factors correlated with more fundamental forces?

Our message is simple and straightforward. We have come to conclude—particularly in assessing policies related to developing countries—that *the* key issue is cognitive skills. It is both conventional and convenient in policy discussions to concentrate on such things as years of school attainment or enrollment rates that are readily observed and measured.

They appear in administrative data, they are published on a consistent basis in virtually all countries—and they are very misleading in the policy debates.

In this chapter, building on the previous chapters, we look more closely at the history of developing countries. Specifically, we focus on one success story—East Asia—and one failure—Latin America. A great many studies and books written about each case have produced a variety of stories about their development histories. Our own version is simple: a single explanation unifies the development patterns of both regions. One invested in knowledge capital, and one did not.

We start with an overview of the broad facts of human capital development in developing countries (section 5.1). We then turn to general cases that have been treated as puzzles, albeit for opposite reasons: Latin America with its inexplicably slow growth (section 5.2) and East Asia with its stunningly rapid growth (section 5.3). We show here that nothing is special in terms of growth and development about either experience.[1]

By ignoring differences in what students actually know, the existing literature very significantly misses the true importance of human capital for economic growth in both East Asia and Latin America. Our results reveal school attainment is associated with economic growth only insofar as it entails cognitive skills—which in Latin America is the case to a much lesser extent than elsewhere and in East Asia to a much greater extent.

5.1   Where Does the Developing World Stand?

Documenting how the developing countries fare in terms of human capital development is telling. In the following, we document both the quantity of schooling and the cognitive skills achieved by developing countries from an international perspective—an undertaking that vividly illustrates the magnitude of the task at hand.[2]

Lack of Quantity of Schooling

The historic disadvantages of less developed countries in terms of educational enrollment and attainment have been well documented and are well known. As noted earlier, current international policy initiatives—the Millennium Development Goals and the Education for All initiative—focus on the importance of expanded school attainment in developing countries. And the expansion of schooling in the developing world has happened, and it has led toward convergence of schooling across countries of differing income levels. To provide an aggregate picture, figure 5.1

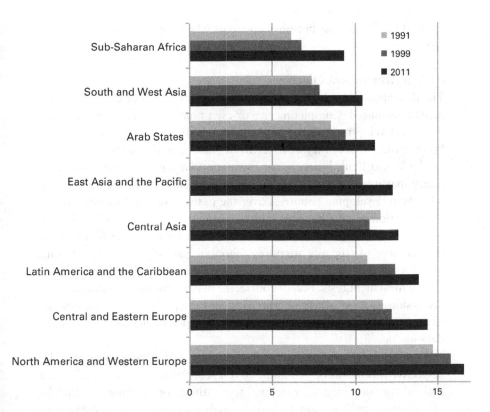

Figure 5.1

Lack of school attainment in developing countries

Notes: School life expectancy, given by the expected number of years of formal schooling from primary to tertiary education. Data source: UNESCO (2014).

plots the UNESCO (2014) calculations of the expected number of years of formal schooling for different regions over the past two decades.[3]

Three conclusions follow from this figure. First, schooling levels have risen in all parts of the world in the past twenty years. Second, while gaps in attainment—say, between North America and Europe, on the one hand, and less developed regions, on the other—remain, they have closed some over this time. Third, the remaining gaps are significant.

Focusing on this dimension of schooling quantity, many policy initiatives of national governments and international development agencies have tried to increase the educational attainment of the population. The evidence suggests they are succeeding at least partially. Our view, as should be apparent by now, is that this picture significantly understates the real challenge that becomes apparent when cognitive achievement is also considered.

Lack of Achievement Outcomes

The description of school completion ignores the level of cognitive skills actually acquired. Completing five or even nine years of schooling in the average developing country does not necessarily mean the students have become functionally literate in terms of basic cognitive skills. As a report by the World Bank Independent Evaluation Group (2006) documented, policy makers accorded high priority to increasing enrollment in primary schools in developing countries over the past decades but directed much less attention to whether the children were learning adequately. We have already documented in figure 2.3 the particularly low levels of mean performance of students attending school in basically all the developing countries that have participated in at least one of the international student achievement tests. But, of course, mean performance can hide a lot of dispersion that exists within countries, and the prior analyses of growth have shown separate information at different percentiles of the test score data (section 3.3).

Figure 5.2 depicts the shares of students in a country who surpass the respective thresholds of 400 and 600 test score points on the transformed scale of the combined international tests—the same measure and thresholds we used in the section 3.3 growth analyses. Panel A shows the sample of fifty countries on which we base our growth analyses, and panel B shows the remaining twenty-seven countries, each of which participated in one of the international student achievement tests but lacks internationally comparable GDP data for the 1960 to 2000 period that would allow it to be included in the growth analyses (see appendix table 2A.1).

When considering the basic educational achievement of students, we are interested in the share that surpasses the threshold of 400 test score points, which may be viewed as a rough threshold of basic literacy in mathematics and science. As the figure makes evident, this share varies immensely across countries. In Japan, the Netherlands, Korea, Taiwan, and Finland, for instance, less than 5 percent of tested students fall below this literacy threshold. By contrast, in many of the developing countries participating in the international achievement tests, more than half of the tested students do not reach it. The countries with the largest shares of test-taking students who are functionally illiterate by this definition are Peru (82 percent), Saudi Arabia (67 percent), Brazil (66 percent), Morocco (66 percent), South Africa (65 percent), Botswana (63 percent),

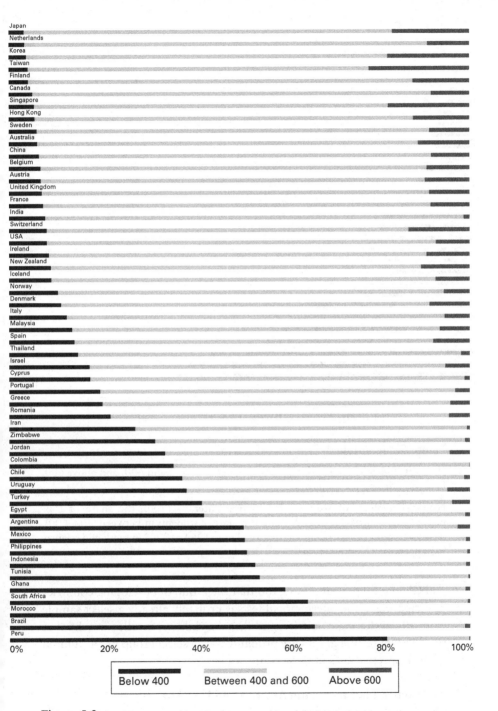

Figure 5.2

Share of students below 400 ("illiterate"), between 400 and 600, and above 600.
Panel A: countries in growth analysis.

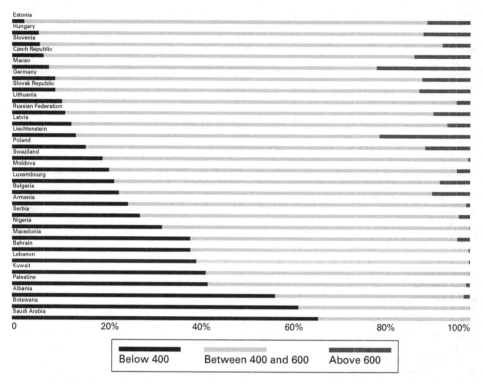

Figure 5.2 (continued)

Share of students below 400 ("illiterate"), between 400 and 600, and above 600. Panel B: other tested countries.

Notes: The share of students below basic literacy (400), the share of top-performing students (above 600), and the share of students in-between (400–600), based on average score on all international tests 1964 to 2003 in math and science. See appendix 2A and section 3.3 for details.

and Ghana (60 percent). Note too that the group of developing countries participating in the international tests is probably already a select sample from all developing countries, and that the children enrolled in school at the different testing grades are probably only a select group of all children of the respective ages in these countries.[4]

The Contrast between Latin America and East Asia

The overall picture of attainment and performance, however, masks important differences across both countries and regions. The remainder of this chapter highlights some informative variations in this overall picture.

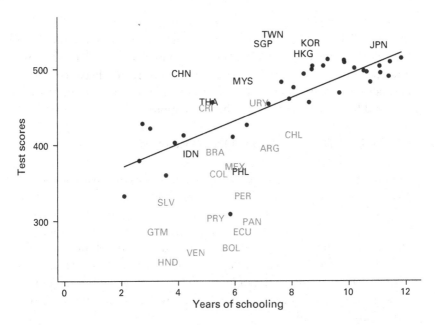

Figure 5.3

Years of schooling and educational achievement: Latin America, East Asia, and the rest of the world

Notes: Scatter plot of average years of schooling (average of 1960 and 2000) and average scores on international student achievement tests (extended with Latin American regional test measures). Latin American countries have gray letter codes, East Asian countries black letter codes, all other countries dots. Regression line relates to countries outside of Latin America and East Asia only. Authors' calculations. See tables 2A.1 and 5A.1 for country letter codes.

The conventional argument behind policies focused on school attainment is quite simple: improving educational outcomes requires students to be in school; while attendance might not be sufficient, it is necessary. But this position has led to very different student outcomes, depending on countries and policies.

Replicating the general pattern of figure 2.4 above, figure 5.3 plots years of schooling (the average attainment in 1960 and 2000) against our measure of cognitive skills. We identify the position of each of the ten East Asian countries (in black) and the sixteen Latin American countries (in gray) by country code.[5] The black circles denote the remaining countries in our sample, and the line shows the strong correlation for these remaining countries between attainment and achievement ($r = 0.83$).

No statistical analysis is needed to see regional performance is very different. All East Asian countries except Indonesia and the Philippines fall well above the line; all Latin American countries except Uruguay and Costa Rica fall far below it. It is precisely this divergence between school attainment and achievement that we think fully explains the apparent puzzling difference in fortunes of the two regions.

5.2   The Latin American Growth Puzzle Resolved

The Latin American growth puzzle served as a basic motivation for our entire exercise. As noted in section 1.1, an observer transported back to 1960 might well have expected Latin America to be on the verge of significant economic growth. Both its level of school attainment and its income level were well ahead of those of East Asia and other developing regions. But by 2000, Latin America was left with sub-Saharan Africa at the bottom of the global league tables of long-run economic growth rates and, as a consequence, of incomes per capita. We now turn to investigating this puzzle in greater detail.[6]

Latin American Achievement on Worldwide Tests

The existing data from worldwide student achievement tests paint a bleak picture of performance in Latin America.[7] Although Latin American countries have not participated frequently in the testing, we can see from the data we have that their performance is uniformly uncompetitive, both with developed and many developing countries.

Latin American participation in international testing has been very light and spotty. As noted in chapter 2, international agencies developed and deployed a total of thirty-six different international student achievement tests in math, science, or reading on twelve separate international testing occasions between 1964 and 2003, with several testing in more than one subject and at more than one age level. Yet only seven Latin American countries ever participated in any of the international math or science tests: Argentina, Brazil, Chile, Colombia, Mexico, Peru, and Uruguay.[8]

Before 2000, only Chile and Colombia participated in the IEA math or science tests. Their performance was at the bottom (ranking between second and fourth from last on five different occasions that included between twelve and thirty-nine participating countries), and they only outperformed a handful of countries, such as India, Iran, Malawi, and South Africa. In IEA assessments after 2000, other Latin American countries also established positions near the bottom. Argentina and Colombia, for example, were fifth and sixth from last (with only Belize, Morocco, Kuwait, and Iran, in that order, below them) in the 2001 Progress in International Reading Literacy Study (PIRLS) of fourth-graders.

Even with the expansion of international testing in 2000 with the OECD PISA tests, by 2003, only six Latin American countries had participated in any of the PISA rounds. The results mirrored the earlier testing. In 2000 and 2003, Indonesia and Tunisia were the only countries to keep Brazil and Mexico off the bottom of the list of thirty-one participants in the three tested subjects. In 2002, an additional ten countries took the 2000 PISA test. Peru came out last, at an amazing distance from those above it, among the combined sample of forty-one countries, while Argentina and Chile performed between sixth and eighth from the bottom on the three subjects (outside Latin America followed only by Albania, Indonesia, and Macedonia).

To summarize simply, for the forty occasions until 2003 on which a Latin American country participated in an international student achievement test (counting different subjects and age groups separately), the average rank was 31.8 among an average of 34.5 participants (where a significant portion of the ranks below each Latin American country were taken up by other Latin American countries).[9]

The picture has not improved since. Of the six Latin American countries participating in the PISA 2006 cycle, four were among the bottom ten of the fifty-seven participating countries in math and science. The only Latin American country ever making it to the "top forty" of the fifty-seven countries was Chile (ranking thirty-ninth in reading). Eight Latin American countries were among the sixty-five countries participating in PISA 2009 and 2012. In PISA 2009, Uruguay achieved the highest rank of the eight in math at forty-eighth and Chile in science and reading at forty-fourth. Panama came out second from the bottom in math and Peru in science, followed only by Kyrgyzstan. In PISA 2012, Chile achieved the highest rank of the participating Latin American countries at fifty-first in math, forty-sixth in science, and forty-seventh in reading. Peru came out last of the sixty-five participating countries in math and science.

The bottom line of Latin American performance on the worldwide tests is truly dismal: the average cognitive skills of Latin American students in the participating countries are consistently near or at the bottom of the international distribution, and only a very small fraction of each young cohort reaches a level of even the most basic cognitive skills by international standards.

Regional Achievement Tests in Latin America

We expand on the assessments for Latin American countries described in chapter 2 for two reasons. First, going beyond the seven Latin American countries that volunteered to participate in the international testing through 2003 would help us get a full picture of the economic situation. Second, the poor performance raises questions about the reliability of the international test information, particularly for any comparisons we make across the region itself. Thus, before undertaking our analysis of growth within the region, we consider using regional tests to expand the information on cognitive skills.

The international tests are designed primarily for developed countries (which provide most of the financial support for the testing). They can accurately place student performance near the OECD mean but are thin in questions that would allow us to discriminate among performances in the tails of the distribution. As a result they may be unable to distinguish reliably among varying levels of learning of Latin American students. At the very least, the differences recorded among Latin American countries undoubtedly contain considerable noise, even though several thousand students take the tests in each.

These limitations of the worldwide tests lead us to turn to two regional achievement tests specifically designed for the Latin American countries. Starting in the 1990s and aided by UNESCO, Latin American countries developed tests of math and reading skills that could be applied across the region. In 1997, the Latin American Laboratory for the Assessment of Quality in Education—Laboratorio Latinoamericano de Evaluación de la Calidad de la Educación (LLECE)—carried out the "First International Comparative Study in Language, Mathematics, and Associated Factors in the Third and Fourth Grades of Primary Education" (Primer Estudio Internacional Comparativo), specifically designed to test cognitive skills in Latin American countries.[10] For ease of reference we refer to this study as "LLECE" in the following. LLECE provides data on educational performance for nine Latin American countries that also have internationally comparable GDP data.

LLECE tested the performance in math and reading of representative samples of primary school students in each participating country. The study released country medians in each grade and subject; in our analyses, we use performance of the older (fourth-grade) students (see appendix table 5A.1, column 6). The LLECE scores are standardized to have a mean of 250 test score points and a standard deviation of 50 among participating countries. Median math performance ranges from

226 in Venezuela to 269 in Argentina and Brazil and median reading performance from 233 in Bolivia to 286 in Chile. In other words, student performance on the tests differs across countries by around one standard deviation—a huge within-region variation.

In 2006, the Latin American bureau of UNESCO also conducted the "Second Regional Comparative and Explanatory Study" (Segundo Estudio Regional Comparativo Explicativo, or SERCE) designed for Latin American countries.[11] It covered thirteen countries usable in our subsequent growth analyses.[12] Combining the LLECE and SERCE studies provides cognitive skills assessments for a total of sixteen Latin American countries, all with populations greater than one million and without Communist backgrounds.[13]

SERCE tested the performance in math and reading of representative samples of students in the third and sixth grades, reporting country medians in each grade and subject. In our analyses, we again use the performance of the older (sixth-grade) students (see appendix table 5A.1, column 7). The SERCE scores are standardized to have an international mean of 500 test score points and a standard deviation of 100 among participating countries. Across the thirteen countries, median performance (averaged across math and reading) ranges from about 454 in Ecuador and Guatemala to 560 in Uruguay, again revealing a within-regional difference of median performance of more than one standard deviation.

Splicing the Regional into the Worldwide Tests

To place the whole Latin American region in the worldwide analysis, we need to place the regional tests on the scale of the worldwide tests. As noted, the performance of the seven Latin American countries that ever participated in a worldwide test is very far down on such tests as TIMSS and PISA. This raises questions about how informative the variation in performance is on these tests across individuals and schools in each country, as well as across countries in the region. Across the five Latin American countries that participated both in LLECE and some worldwide achievement tests, no significant correlation occurs between the two sets of scores. The range of the average international scores across the five is 364 to 415 points, however (and remember that only the lowest 16 percent of students in OECD countries perform below 400). We attempt to improve upon the information on Latin American performance on the global scale by using the more reliable information about intraregional variations in performance from tests designed for the region. This also allows us to expand the sample of Latin American countries used in the worldwide growth analysis.

Splicing the regional tests into the world picture involves a number of steps. First, we combine the two regional tests on a common scale using the sample of countries that have taken both assessments. Specifically, using the average of math and reading performance of the older cohort in both LLECE and SERCE, we first standardize both tests to have mean zero and standard deviation one among the six countries participating in both tests. The combined score on the two regional tests is then given by the simple mean of a country's performance on these two rescaled test metrics.

Second, we presume that the regional mean observed for the Latin American participants on the worldwide tests provides a reasonable scale for the level of average regional performance on the global scale. Therefore we rescale the mean of the combined regional test so the seven Latin American countries that also participated in the worldwide tests have the same average performance they have on our basic scaling in chapter 2.

Third, we take the view that the within-region placement of individual Latin American countries found in the worldwide tests is not reliable. This leads us to rely on the individual country performance in Latin America from the regional rather than worldwide tests (even for the seven countries participating in the worldwide tests).

Finally, splicing the regional Latin American tests into the worldwide test metric requires an assumption about the size of the within-regional variation on the worldwide scale. Here we again take the broad metric from the global scale and rescale the combined regional test so the seven Latin American countries that also participated in the worldwide tests have the same cross-country standard deviation they have on the worldwide tests. This method effectively superimposes the distributional information from the international tests onto the Latin American regional tests, but uses the regional test information to place the individual Latin American countries more accurately within the region. The result is an expanded sample that includes all large mainland Latin American countries. The ensuing regional test-based performance measure of the Latin American countries, expressed on our prior combined scale of the worldwide tests, is shown in column 8 of appendix table 5A.1.

The scatter plot in figure 5.3 incorporates our expanded set of countries and reveals a central message of this analysis: in virtually all Latin American countries, the average student gets much less learning for each year of schooling than the average student in the rest of the world. This is the crucial element in our resolution of the Latin American growth puzzle.

Schooling, Knowledge Capital, and Latin American Growth

We can now look in detail at the growth performance of Latin American countries. We begin by showing that Latin America does not stand out from the rest of the world in the basic growth models of chapter 3. In the next subsection we proceed to use the expanded data for Latin America to show that differences in knowledge capital within the region can explain the within-region growth differences since 1960. Finally, we add the expanded group of Latin American countries into the world growth picture and find the picture of chapter 3 remains fully intact.

Can the low levels of cognitive skills in Latin American countries account for their poor record of economic growth? To answer this question, we start with the sample of fifty countries that have ever participated in worldwide achievement tests and have internationally comparable data on GDP growth. (This sample, as noted, includes just seven Latin American countries.)

The "Latin American growth puzzle" motivating this analysis is evident from the first two columns of table 5.1. Economic growth in 1960 to 2000 was significantly lower in Latin America than in the rest of the world. A significant negative bivariate correlation exists between growth and an indicator for Latin American countries which is hardly affected by controlling for initial income and initial education in the form of average years of schooling. We find that over this entire period, Latin American countries on average grew by 1.3 percent per year less than the rest of the sampled countries, even after allowing for starting income levels. As discussed in section 1.2, this is an enormous difference in growth over such a long period, and it has naturally led to many attempts to understand the "why."

This puzzle is resolved once differences in cognitive skills, our more encompassing measure of knowledge capital, are taken into account. Column 3 of table 5.1 shows that conditional on cognitive skills, the Latin American countries do *not* show significantly different long-run growth than the rest of the world. And, as before, the coefficient on years of schooling becomes insignificant and drops to close to zero. Conditional on test scores—that is, on what students know—additional years of schooling do not show a significant association with economic growth.

Table 5.1
Latin America in worldwide growth regressions: worldwide test measures

	(1)	(2)	(3)	(4)	(5)
Latin America	-1.328**	-1.380***	-0.095	-0.055	-0.577
	(2.47)	(3.04)	(0.28)	(0.18)	(0.58)
Cognitive skills			1.947***		
			(7.77)		
Cognitive skills (exponential)				2.135***	2.151***
				(9.20)	(9.13)
Cognitive skills (exp.) × Latin America					-0.854
					(0.56)
Initial years of schooling (1960)		0.350***	0.031	-0.006	-0.009
		(3.32)	(0.38)	(0.08)	(0.12)
Initial GDP per capita (1960)		-0.378***	-0.303***	-0.278***	-0.276***
		(4.59)	(5.49)	(5.52)	(5.43)
Constant	3.089***	3.080***	4.262***	4.330***	4.335***
	(15.34)	(8.56)	(15.11)	(17.06)	(16.94)
Number of countries	50	50	50	50	50
R^2 (adj.)	0.094	0.364	0.723	0.774	0.771
F (Latin America and interaction)					0.17
Prob > F					(0.844)

Notes: Dependent variable: average annual growth rate in GDP per capita, 1960 to 2000. Cognitive skill measure refers to average score on all international tests 1964 to 2003 in math and science. In the interacted model, cognitive skills are de-meaned. t-Statistics in parentheses: statistical significance at * 10 percent, ** 5 percent, *** 1 percent.

In other words, school attainment, which is positively correlated with test scores (see figure 5.3), only matters for economic growth inasmuch as it is related to better skills among the students.

The previous specification, consistent with the estimation in chapter 3, assumes a linear relationship exists between growth and the international test scores. Although not stressed previously, however, the shape of the scaling of test performance is ultimately arbitrary, and casual inspection of the conditional association between growth and the test score measure indicates some curvilinear pattern. Therefore the specification of column 4 enters our test score measure in exponential form. The results reveal such a specification provides a considerably better fit to the data, while the Latin American dummy continues to be very small and statistically insignificant.[14] The exponential form of the test score–growth relationship ultimately reflects arbitrary scaling choices for the underlying achievement tests, but it means that the same absolute increase in test scores—when measured on the standard international PISA scale—is related to larger absolute increases in economic growth rates at higher levels of the test metric than at lower. For example, according to this specification, a 10-point increase from 400 to 410 on the PISA scale is related to a 0.13 percentage point increase in the economic growth rate, whereas a 10-point increase from 500 to 510 is related to 0.35 percentage points higher growth.

In the final column, we allow the test score effect to differ between the seven Latin American countries and the rest of the world. The interaction term, either individually or jointly with the Latin American dummy, is not statistically significant, suggesting the relationship between cognitive skills and growth is not different in Latin America than in the rest of the world. (This result holds if interactions of the Latin American dummy with years of schooling and initial GDP, which are insignificant, are included.) This analysis is, however, restricted by the limited number of Latin American countries participating in the worldwide tests, as well as the tests' relatively low informational content for Latin American countries. We therefore turn next to our extension to the regional Latin American tests.

Knowledge Capital and Growth within Latin America
Both skill levels and economic performance have varied greatly across the sixteen Latin American countries. Even on the worldwide tests, for example, more than a whole standard deviation distinguishes the average cognitive skills in Peru (312) from those in Uruguay (430). In 1960 people

in Guatemala, Honduras, and El Salvador averaged a mere two years of schooling, as opposed to more than six years in Chile and Argentina.

Likewise economic performance has varied substantially among the Latin American countries. GDP per capita in 1960 ranged from below $2,000 in Honduras and Ecuador to more than $7,000 in Venezuela and Argentina—close to the mean of European countries.

Finally, the growth experience between 1960 and 2000 ranged from negative in Venezuela to almost 3 percent per year in Brazil. As a consequence of the differing initial income levels and growth experiences, GDP per capita in 2000 ranged from about $2,000 in Honduras to more than $10,000 in Argentina.

As figure 5.4 shows, differences in growth performance are closely related to cognitive skills just within the region. Using the LLECE and SERCE measures confirms that Latin American countries with higher

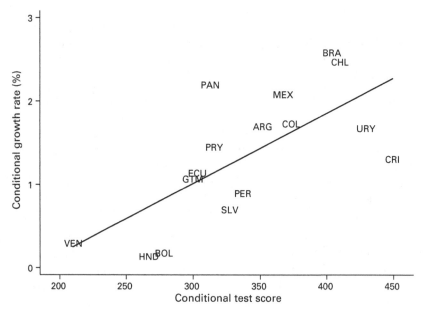

Figure 5.4

Educational achievement and economic growth: Latin America

Notes: Added-variable plot of a regression of the average annual rate of growth (in percent) of real GDP per capita in 1960 to 2000 on average test scores on Latin American student achievement tests and initial level of real GDP per capita in 1960 (mean of unconditional variables added to each axis). Authors' calculations; see table 5.2, column 6. See table 5A.1 in appendix 5A for country letter codes.

cognitive skills have experienced faster economic growth over the long run. Although analyses within this small sample of countries are limited by their degrees of freedom, within-region regressions, reported in table 5.2, descriptively confirm the general pattern of the worldwide regressions. Cognitive skills as measured by the LLECE and SERCE data enter significantly in intraregional growth regressions, increase their explanatory power substantially, and render years of schooling insignificant.[15] This pattern clearly illustrates the potential of cognitive skills to explain growth differences within the region.

Such an analysis does, of course, raise concerns. While the LLECE and SERCE tests provide a reliable measure of performance differences among Latin American countries, they refer to performance at relatively early school grades, necessitating an assumption that such early performance is a reasonable index of performance throughout the schooling system. Additionally the tests were administered toward the end of the observed growth period, necessitating an assumption that performance differences were relatively stable over the prior decades.

Combining Regional and Worldwide Tests

We now employ the new dataset that splices the regional Latin American tests into the global test score measure in our cross-country growth regressions. Results reported in table 5.3 retain the exponential form of the test score measure in the worldwide setting derived above. The first four columns mirror the analyses based on just the worldwide tests (table 5.1).

In the expanded fifty-nine-country sample, which now includes the entire set of sixteen Latin American countries, a Latin American dummy is strongly negative in models without cognitive skills but becomes very small and statistically insignificant once cognitive skills are controlled for. The point estimate on cognitive skills is slightly smaller than in the previous analyses. Column 5, which reverts to the original fifty-country sample except with the new test information, shows this slight reduction is not due to the additional Latin American countries in the expanded sample but rather to the substitution of the regional for the global test data for the Latin American countries. Again, no significant interaction takes place between test scores and the indicator for Latin American countries.

In sum, there is no Latin American growth puzzle. Once one considers that the learning per year is so low across the region, the historically poor growth performance falls right in line with that of the rest of the world.

Table 5.2
Cognitive skills and economic growth within Latin America: evidence from regional achievement tests

	LLECE			LLECE + SERCE		
	(1)	(2)	(3)	(4)	(5)	(6)
Cognitive skills		2.910**	2.669***		0.641**	0.844***
		(3.68)	(5.44)		(2.50)	(3.46)
Initial years of schooling (1960)	0.469*	-0.083		0.377**	0.225	
	(1.98)	(0.41)		(2.73)	(1.71)	
Initial GDP per capita (1960)	-0.319*	-0.247**	-0.262**	-0.290**	-0.319***	-0.277***
	(2.15)	(-2.84)	(3.59)	(-2.88)	(3.71)	(3.14)
Constant	0.716	-8.161**	-7.536***	0.938	-0.556	-0.537
	(0.77)	(3.31)	(4.18)	(1.76)	(0.74)	(0.67)
Number of countries	9	9	9	16	16	16
R^2 (adj.)	0.339	0.786	0.816	0.382	0.559	0.494

Notes: Dependent variable: average annual growth rate in GDP per capita, 1960 to 2000. Cognitive skill measure refers to average score on the LLECE and SERCE regional tests as indicated in headers. t-Statistics in parentheses: statistical significance at * 10 percent, ** 5 percent, *** 1 percent.

Table 5.3
Latin America in worldwide growth regressions: extension with regional test measures

	(1)	(2)	(3)	(4)	(5)ª	(6)
Latin America	-1.744***	-1.713***	-0.373	-0.624	-0.585	
	(4.70)	(5.34)	(1.47)	(1.39)	(0.93)	
Cognitive skills			1.591***	1.625***	1.705***	1.745***
			(8.97)	(8.79)	(9.15)	(12.05)
Cognitive skills × Latin America				-0.351	-0.870	
				(0.68)	(0.92)	
Initial years of schooling (1960)		0.348***	0.048	0.045	-0.009	0.034
		(5.34)	(0.73)	(0.67)	(0.13)	(0.51)
Initial GDP per capita (1960)		-0.369***	-0.305***	-0.304***	-0.276***	-0.302***
		(5.26)	(6.71)	(6.64)	(5.45)	(6.58)
Constant	3.089***	3.041***	3.903***	3.905***	4.046***	3.862***
	(15.99)	(9.19)	(16.79)	(16.71)	(16.84)	(16.56)
Number of countries	59	59	59	59	50	59
R^2 (adj.)	0.267	0.498	0.795	0.793	0.771	0.790
F (Latin America and interaction)				1.30	0.46	
Prob > F				(0.281)	(0.636)	

Notes: Dependent variable: average annual growth rate in GDP per capita, 1960 to 2000. Cognitive skill measure refers to average exponential score on all international tests 1964 to 2003 in math and science, extended with Latin American regional tests. In the interacted models, cognitive skills are de-meaned. t-Statistics in parentheses: statistical significance at * 10 percent, ** 5 percent, *** 1 percent. a. Country sample as in tables 3.1 and 5.1.

The importance of educational achievement has not been missed by some Latin American countries that have shown strong improvements in recent years. In terms of trends for lower secondary school students over the most recent cycles of international achievement tests, Brazil and Chile in particular show considerable improvements (Hanushek, Peterson, and Woessmann 2013: ch. 6). These changes support our basic perspective, indicated in chapter 4 above and elaborated upon in chapter 8 below, that achievement can be improved through governmental policies. They also suggest that Latin American countries are not necessarily destined to remain at the bottom of the economic distribution.

5.3   The East Asian Miracle Demystified

Virtually everybody in the world recognizes the exceptional growth seen in the East Asian economies. Today East Asia is not generally placed in the "developing countries needing help" category. As indicated in our introduction, however, this would not have been obvious in 1960. The level of economic prosperity in East Asia at the time was in fact substantially below that of Latin America and even sub-Saharan Africa (see table 1A.1 in appendix 1A). Disregarding Japan, years of schooling were also just roughly at the level of sub-Saharan Africa and far below Latin America.

The perception of the growth record of the region has changed dramatically over the past half century. As far back as the early 1990s, the World Bank (1993) tried to see what could be extracted from the East Asian experience—particularly, what could be disseminated to other developing countries. "East Asia," its researchers reported in their framing of the issue,

has a remarkable record of high and sustained economic growth. From 1965 to 1990 the twenty-three economies of East Asia grew faster than all other regions of the world ... Most of this achievement is attributable to seemingly miraculous growth in just eight economies: Japan; the "Four Tigers"—Hong Kong, the Republic of Korea, Singapore, and Taiwan, China; and the three newly industrializing economies (NIEs) of Southeast Asia, Indonesia, Malaysia, and Thailand. (World Bank 1993: 1)

The researchers made "these eight high-performing Asian economies (HPAEs)" the subject of their study.

Looking at this "East Asian Miracle" through the World Bank analysis, however, does not yield much in the way of a simple and coherent conclusion about how the region leapfrogged as far ahead as is shown in figure 1.1—and researchers have done little since to solve the mystery.

We provide such a simple and coherent explanation here, rooted in a very straightforward empirical analysis and falling perfectly into our previous theme.

Cognitive Skills in East Asia
Throughout the history of international testing, the performance of East Asian students has been stellar. As early as 1964, in the First International Mathematics Study, Japanese thirteen-year-olds came out second among students the same age in eleven participating countries. Japan kept—and later topped—this high position, in several subjects: in the first science study in 1970 to 1971, its ten-year-olds came out first among those in the fourteen countries participating and its fourteen-year-olds first among those of sixteen countries. Japanese students also ranked first in the second math study in 1980 to 1982 (of thirteen-year-olds in seventeen countries) and the second science study in 1984 (of ten-year-olds in fifteen countries). Participating for the first time in the 1984 science assessment, Korean students were second only to the Japanese. Hong Kong students in their final year of secondary school took the top position among their test cohort in the 1982 math test and the second position in the 1984 science test, where Singapore was third.

The spectacular East Asian performance fully emerged by 1995, the time of the Third International Mathematics and Science Study (TIMSS). In eighth-grade math, Singapore, Korea, Japan, and Hong Kong took the first four places out of thirty-nine participating countries, a feat duplicated by their fourth-graders (among twenty-five countries). The top four ranks in eighth-grade math were taken by the "four tigers"—Singapore, Korea, Taiwan, and Hong Kong—in the 1999 TIMSS, with Japan following in fifth place, among thirty-eight participants. These five countries also took the top positions in eighth-grade math and science among the forty-six participants in TIMSS 2003. In PISA 2000, Japan and Korea were at the top of thirty-one participants in math and science, beaten only in math by Hong Kong when it took the same test two years later (together with nine other countries). In the most recent PISA wave in 2012, Shanghai, Singapore, Hong Kong, Taiwan, Korea, Macao, and Japan were the top seven out of sixty-five participants in math.

This phenomenal educational achievement in East Asia does have exceptions. Notably, in the 1984 science test, ten- and thirteen-year-olds in the Philippines came out last among fifteen and seventeen participants, respectively. In TIMSS 1995, that country was third from the bottom of thirty-eight participants in both math and science, and in TIMSS 2003, it took forty-second and forty-third places, respectively, among the forty-six participants in math and science. Indonesia's performance was similarly disappointing, as it came out thirty-fourth among thirty-eight participants in eighth-grade math in TIMSS 2009 and thirty-fifth among forty-six in TIMSS 2003. Indonesia was also third from the bottom among the forty participants in PISA 2003 in both math and science and second from the bottom among the sixty-four participants in both subjects in the most recent (2012) PISA wave.

Thailand's performance on the different tests was more middling. In the 1970 to 1971 science test, its ten- and thirteen-year-olds ranked eleventh of those in fourteen countries and its fourteen-year-olds thirteenth among those in sixteen countries. In 1995, however, Thailand came out twentieth out of thirty-nine participants in eighth-grade math, although in PISA 2002 and 2003, it was closer to the bottom, and in PISA 2012, it was fiftieth out of sixty-five participants in math. A more recent participant is Malaysia, which came out sixteenth among thirty-eight in eighth-grade math in TIMSS 1999, fourteenth among forty-six in TIMSS 2003, and fifty-second among sixty-five in math in PISA 2012. Participating in PISA that year for the first time, Vietnam came out seventeenth in math and eighth in science among the sixty-five.

In sum, Japan and the four "tiger" countries have shown outstanding performance on the international student achievement tests; the Philippines and Indonesia have regularly taken bottom places; and other East Asian countries—in particular, Malaysia and Thailand—have fallen in between.

Schooling, Knowledge Capital, and East Asian Growth

Is the educational performance of East Asian countries reflected in their growth experience? As shown in table 5.4 (which parallels the Latin America analysis), the ten East Asian countries in our sample grew, on average, 2.5 percentage points per year faster than the typical country elsewhere in the world (column 1). This falls to "just" 2 percentage points after considering initial income and school attainment (column 2). But the difference disappears altogether in column 3 when the high level of knowledge capital is included. (Note that consistent with the prior analysis, we continue to incorporate cognitive skills in exponential form, reflecting the lower marginal impact for minimal achievement and higher marginal impact at the top end relevant for most East Asian economies.) Column 4 shows these results do not depend on just the expanded sample that includes all of Latin America. Furthermore the impact of knowledge capital within the East Asian group—with its heterogeneous levels of educational achievement—is not different from that elsewhere in the world (column 5).

The final two columns put East Asia together with Latin America. Importantly, once knowledge capital is accounted for, neither East Asia nor Latin America stands out as being different from the rest of the world. Neither shows a significant average difference or a significantly different impact of cognitive skills on growth.

Figures 5.5 and 5.6 present summaries of the growth in these regions. If growth is related to school attainment (figure 5.5), other significant factors appear to come into play. East Asia as a region does noticeably better than expected (with the clear exception of the Philippines), while Latin America does noticeably worse.

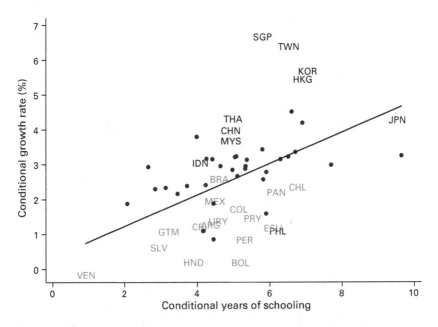

Figure 5.5

Years of schooling and economic growth rates: Latin America and East Asia

Notes: Added-variable plot of a regression of the average annual rate of growth (in percent) of real GDP per capita in 1960 to 2000 on average years of schooling in 1960 and initial level of real GDP per capita in 1960 (mean of unconditional variables added to each axis). Latin American countries have gray letter codes, East Asian countries black letter codes, all other countries dots. Authors' calculations. See appendix tables 2A.1 and 5A.1 for country letter codes.

Table 5.4
East Asia in worldwide growth regressions

	(1)	(2)	(3)	(4)ᵃ	(5)	(6)	(7)
East Asia	2.498***	2.083***	0.254	0.225	0.261	0.270	0.227
	(6.27)	(5.00)	(0.76)	(0.68)	(0.77)	(0.82)	(0.67)
Latin America						-0.379	-0.602
						(1.49)	(1.32)
Cognitive skills			1.660***	1.622***	1.680***	1.499***	1.393***
			(9.09)	(8.12)	(7.31)	(7.12)	(4.01)
Cognitive skills × East Asia					-0.046		0.211
					(0.15)		(0.54)
Cognitive skills × Latin America							-0.188
							(0.33)
Initial years of schooling (1960)		0.304***	0.036	-0.007	0.036	0.051	0.055
		(3.23)	(0.54)	(0.10)	(0.53)	(0.77)	(0.80)

Initial GDP per capita (1960)		-0.218***	-0.285***	-0.262***	-0.287***	-0.287***	-0.277***
		(2.73)	(5.58)	(4.68)	(5.31)	(5.68)	(5.02)
Constant	2.193***	1.734***	1.559***	3.923***	3.745***	3.760***	3.693***
	(13.37)	(5.65)	(7.96)	(13.29)	(11.63)	(12.93)	(11.07)
Number of countries	59	59	59	50	59	59	59
R² (adj.)	0.398	0.476	0.789	0.774	0.785	0.794	0.788
F (East Asia and interaction)					0.30	0.41	
Prob > F					(0.744)	(0.668)	
F (East Asia, Latin America, and interactions)						0.84	
Prob > F						(0.507)	

Notes: Dependent variable: average annual growth rate in GDP per capita, 1960 to 2000. Cognitive skill measure refers to average exponential score on all international tests 1964 to 2003 in math and science, extended with Latin American regional tests. In the interacted models, cognitive skills are de-meaned. t-Statistics in parentheses: statistical significance at * 10 percent, ** 5 percent, *** 1 percent.
a. Country sample as in table 3.1.

But as soon as learning (as opposed to seat time in schools) is considered, both regions fit precisely into the pattern of the rest of the world. The fact that the test score–growth connection does not differ either between Latin America and the rest of the world or between East Asia and the rest of the world is clearly evident in figure 5.6. The countries of both regions fall around a straight line that captures the conditional association between cognitive skills and economic growth everywhere. Given the exponential specification, the same absolute improvements in terms of the international PISA scale appear to be related to stronger growth improvements at higher as compared to lower test score levels, although the interpretation is not entirely clear. It could simply reflect the particular scale of our measure of cognitive skills, or it could indicate something about the impact of different levels of skills.

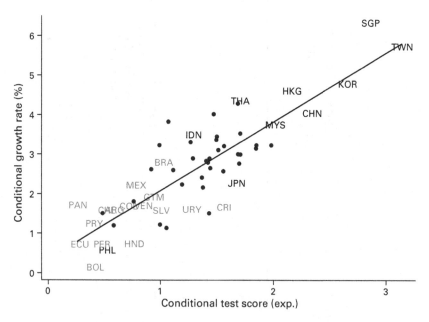

Figure 5.6

Knowledge capital and economic growth rates: Latin America and East Asia

Notes: Added-variable plot of a regression of the average annual rate of growth (in percent) of real GDP per capita in 1960 to 2000 on average test scores (exponential) on international student achievement tests, average years of schooling in 1960, and initial level of real GDP per capita in 1960 (mean of unconditional variables added to each axis). Latin American countries have gray letter codes, East Asian countries black letter codes, all other countries dots. Authors' calculations; see table 5.3, column 6. See tables 2A.1 and 5A.1 for country letter codes.

In any case, our results refute the possibility that this curvilinear pattern is specific to Latin America and to the construction of data for the extended sample. The consistency between our expanded Latin American sample and other low-scoring countries indicates that the observed growth patterns of Latin American countries do not appear to be driven by additional test errors due to the splicing of worldwide and regional tests.

Figure 5.6 also highlights the substantial heterogeneity within the East Asian group. As indicated above, not all East Asian countries have been exceptional. Note that educational achievement in Indonesia and the Philippines, which have regularly taken bottom places in test performance, in fact fell below the levels predicted by school attainment in figure 5.3. In other words, these countries did not enjoy the same extraordinary learning outcomes enjoyed by the other countries in the region. This divergence actually lies behind the search for a common way of studying the growth experience of East Asia.

Beginning with the World Bank (1993) study, researchers have commonly selected for analysis a sample of countries based on growth outcomes—the very item to be analyzed. This approach yields a focus on the four "tigers" of East Asia—Hong Kong, Korea, Singapore, and Taiwan—or the eight "miracle economies" identified by the World Bank (the four tigers plus Japan, Indonesia, Malaysia, and Thailand). Although selecting a sample based on the outcome of interest is not appropriate scientifically, we can show readily that these economies still fit within our overall growth picture. Table 5.5 shows three groupings of countries: the entire set of East Asian countries in columns 1–3, the miracle economies in columns 4–6, and the tigers in columns 7–9. Note that the average annual growth rate of the four tiger countries is close to four percentage points higher than in the rest of the world, whereas in the expanded eight miracle countries it is "only" close to three percentage points. But while the indicator for each regional grouping, considered either alone or with school attainment, suggests the group is performing better than expected, this difference disappears when we include the direct measure of cognitive skills. (As column 6 shows, only in the miracle economy grouping is the indicator significant at the 10 percent level after including cognitive skills.)

In other words, the growth experiences in East Asia, as with Latin America, are not a mystery. High growth follows high skills, while low growth follows low skills.

Table 5.5

East Asia: entire region, "miracle" countries, and "tiger" countries

	10 East Asian countries			8 "miracle" countries			4 "tiger" countries		
	(1)	(2)	(3)	(4)	(5)	(6)	(7)	(8)	(9)
East Asia	2.498***	2.083***	0.254						
	(6.27)	(5.00)	(0.76)						
Miracle countries				2.938***	2.488***	0.606*			
				(7.11)	(5.93)	(1.71)			
Tiger countries							3.916***	3.292***	0.652
							(6.84)	(5.98)	(1.34)
Cognitive skills			1.660***			1.551***			1.579***
			(9.09)			(8.51)			(8.31)
Initial years of schooling (1960)		0.304***	0.036		0.293***	0.042		0.313***	0.047
		(3.23)	(0.54)		(3.31)	(0.64)		(3.59)	(0.70)
Initial GDP per capita (1960)		-0.218***	-0.285***		-0.218***	0.269***		-0.254***	-0.283***
		(2.73)	(5.58)		(2.96)	(5.51)		(3.58)	(5.95)
Constant	2.193***	1.734***	1.559***	2.218***	1.810***	3.586***	2.351***	1.990***	3.665***
	(13.37)	(5.65)	(7.96)	(14.58)	(6.38)	(12.79)	(15.76)	(7.16)	(13.37)
Number of countries	59	59	59	59	59	59	59	59	59
R² (adj.)	0.398	0.476	0.789	0.461	0.535	0.798	0.441	0.538	0.793

Notes: Dependent variable: average annual growth rate in GDP per capita, 1960 to 2000. Cognitive skill measure refers to average exponential score on all international tests 1964–2003 in math and science, extended with Latin American regional tests. "Tiger" countries are Hong Kong, Korea, Singapore, and Taiwan. "Miracle" countries add Indonesia, Japan, Malaysia, and Thailand. The full East Asian group adds China and the Philippines. t-Statistics in parentheses: statistical significance at * 10 percent, ** 5 percent, *** 1 percent.

5.4   Conclusions on the Developing Country Challenge

We have seen that most developing countries outside East Asia are severely lacking in terms of both schooling quantity and student outcomes. Figure 5.7 shows the combination of the two. For the fourteen countries that both have reliable attainment data from household surveys and have participated in the international student achievement tests, we combine educational attainment of fifteen- to nineteen-year-olds with test scores at roughly the end of lower secondary education (eighth grade or fifteen-year-olds, depending on the specific test data) from a year close by.[16] This allows us to calculate roughly among cohorts of school-leaving age how many were never enrolled in school, how many dropped out of school by grade 5 and by grade 9, respectively, how many finished grade 9 with test score performances below 400 (which signals functional illiteracy), and, finally, how many finished grade 9 with performances above 400. Only the last group can be viewed as having reached basic literacy in cognitive skills.[17]

Figure 5.7 presents the countries in order of least to most youths mastering basic skills. In eleven of the fourteen countries, the share of fully literate youths is less than one-third. In Ghana, South Africa, and Brazil, only 5, 7, and 8 percent of a cohort, respectively, reach literacy. More than 90 percent of the respective populations are illiterate because they never enrolled in school, because they dropped out of school at the primary or early secondary level, or because even after completing lower secondary education, their grasp of basic cognitive skills is so low they must be viewed as functionally illiterate in today's world. In contrast, 55 percent of a cohort in Armenia and 63 percent in Moldova can be viewed as literate at the end of lower secondary schooling.

Perhaps most effective in illustrating the scope of the problem in developing countries is to offer an example of a basic question from one of the international achievement tests. The following was asked of eighth-grade students in TIMSS 2003:

"Alice ran a race in 49.86 seconds. Betty ran the same race in 52.30 seconds. How much longer did it take Betty to run the race than Alice? (a) 2.44 seconds, (b) 2.54 seconds, (c) 3.56 seconds, (d) 3.76 seconds."

While 88 percent of eighth-graders in Singapore, 80 percent in Hungary, and 74 percent in the United States got the correct answer (a), only 19 percent of those in Saudi Arabia, 29 percent in South Africa, and 32 percent in Ghana did. Random guessing would have yielded 25 percent correct on average.

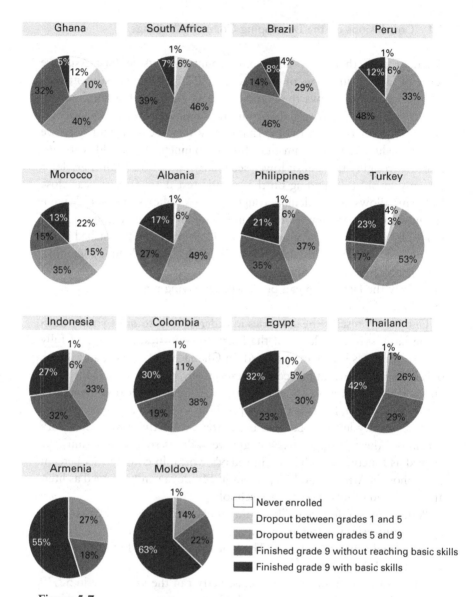

Figure 5.7

Patterns of education among 15- and19-year-olds in developing countries

Notes: Own calculations for all countries that have consistent World Bank survey data on educational attainment (Filmer 2006) along with micro data from at least one international student achievement test.

Combining data on quantitative educational attainment and cognitive skills for the countries with reliable data on both dimensions makes apparent the truly staggering nature of the task at hand in most developing countries, where the share of any cohort that completes lower secondary education and passes at least a low benchmark of basic literacy in cognitive skills is *below one person in ten*. Indeed, according to recent studies in South Asia and sub-Saharan Africa, a majority of students spend years of instruction without any noticeable progress on basic learning outcomes.[18] Thus the education deficits in developing countries seem even larger than generally appreciated. The quantity and quality of education and skills in most remain truly dismal.

Appendix 5A: Descriptive Statistics for Latin America

Table 5A.1
Income and education in Latin American countries

	GDP per capita 1960 (1)	Growth of GDP per capita 1960–2000 (2)	GDP per capita 2000 (3)	Years of schooling 1960 (4)	Measures of educational achievement			
					Worldwide tests (5)	LLECE (6)	SERCE (7)	Combined regional score (8)
ARG Argentina	7,395	1.0	10,995	6.1	392.0	275.5	509.7	395.3
BOL Bolivia	2,324	0.4	2,722	3.6	–	239	–	264.0
BRA Brazil	2,395	2.8	7,185	3.1	363.8	273	509.9	390.2
CHL Chile	3,818	2.4	9,920	6.2	404.9	275.5	531.7	412.7
COL Colombia	2,525	1.9	5,380	3.7	415.2	261.5	503.8	361.4
CRI Costa Rica	3,480	1.3	5,863	3.3	–	–	556.3	448.6
ECU Ecuador	1,974	1.4	3,467	4.3	–	–	453.5	285.2
SLV El Salvador	3,306	0.7	4,435	2.0	–	–	478.1	324.3

GTM Guatemala	2,354	1.3	3,914	1.6	–	–	453.6	285.5
HND Honduras	1,705	0.5	2,054	1.9	–	234.5	–	245.3
MEX Mexico	3,970	2.0	8,766	4.0	399.8	254	535.8	371.2
PAN Panama	2,340	2.4	6,066	4.6	–	–	461.8	298.5
PRY Paraguay	2,437	1.6	4,682	4.0	–	249.5	461.8	303.1
PER Peru	3,118	1.0	4,583	4.3	312.5	–	483.1	332.4
URY Uruguay	5,840	1.3	9,613	5.3	430.0	–	560.3	454.9
VEN Venezuela	7,751	-0.5	6,420	2.9	–	237.5	–	257.8

Sources: Heston, Summers, and Aten (2002); Cohen and Soto (2007); Laboratorio Latinoamericano de Evaluación de la Calidad de la Educación (1998, 2008a); authors' calculations.

Notes: Sample: All Latin American countries with populations greater than one million and without Communist background; see section 5.2 for details. Measures of educational achievement: column 5 shows the combined score from all international tests conducted between 1964 and 2003 on the metric developed in chapter 2; columns 6 and 7 show the scores from the regional Latin American LLECE and SERCE tests on the scale of the original tests, where LLECE refers to the average of the math and reading score in fourth grade and SERCE refers to the average of the math and reading score in sixth grade; column 8 shows the combined measure of LLECE and SERCE performance mapped on the worldwide metric, derived in section 5.2.

6

Developed Countries

Despite having surged over the past two decades, research in the economics of growth—both theoretical and empirical—has produced surprisingly few resilient findings about policies that might promote long-run growth in economically advanced countries.[1] For developed countries, most existing robust results refer to policies that affect short- to medium-term growth. Here we present evidence that improved human capital, measured by cognitive skills, fills in the picture of policies that affect the long-run economic well-being of OECD countries.[2]

The immense variation in the long-run growth experiences of developed countries has largely escaped notice. For example, from 1960 to 2000, GDP per capita grew on average by less than 1.5 percent per year in New Zealand and Switzerland but by more than 4 percent per year in Ireland, Japan, and Korea. As a consequence, the average Korean was about 10 times as well off in 2000 as in 1960, and the average Irish and Japanese about 5 times as well off. By contrast, the average New Zealander or Swiss was only 1.6 to 1.8 times as well off as forty years before. These stark differences are very visible when we compare the three fastest and three slowest growing countries highlighted (together with the United States) in figure 6.1, which plots GDP per capita in 1960 and 2000: Korea surpassed several other OECD countries, including Mexico; Japan and Ireland went from 40 to 45 percent of New Zealand's income to 131 to 140 percent; and Ireland caught up to Switzerland from initially having 35 percent of its GDP per capita.

Following the theme of the previous chapters, we investigate whether knowledge capital can explain such differences in growth among developed countries. This investigation is especially interesting and useful because only a small portion of the growth differences in the OECD can be explained by the broad economic institutions that have entered into prior analyses—openness and property rights—as the variation in them is

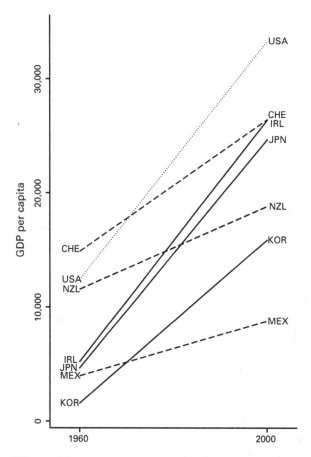

Figure 6.1

GDP per capita in fastest and slowest growing OECD countries in 1960 and 2000

Notes: GDP per capita is in constant international dollars. Authors' depiction based on data from Heston, Summers, and Aten (2002). See table 2A.1 for country letter codes.

very limited across OECD countries.[3] Thus the variations we see in figure 6.1 must come from something else.

Our analysis of growth differences in the OECD shows that long-run growth is as closely related to cognitive skills within the group of developed countries as it is in the global sample (section 6.1). Within the OECD, considerable policy discussion involves variations in more fine-grained institutional features, such as product market regulations and various forms of employment protection. Unlike the role of knowledge capital, however, a long battery of commonly identified measures of these institutions does not add to an explanation of the substantial differences in long-run growth rates across OECD countries (section 6.2).

Developed countries tend to emphasize postsecondary schooling, but there are wide differences in school attainment. Here the wide differences in the policy choices about tertiary schooling within the OECD may be more important than for nations outside of the OECD. While Australia currently has 87 percent of a cohort entering tertiary education, Norway has 71 percent, and Italy has 51 percent (Organisation for Economic Co-operation and Development 2010a). Nonetheless, we do not find a specific role of tertiary attainment for OECD growth once direct measures of skills are taken into consideration (section 6.3).

6.1   Basic Growth Models for OECD Countries

We begin this portion of our analysis by seeing how the OECD fits into our previous sample of fifty countries, and then we move to the separate analysis of our twenty-four OECD countries with consistent data on cognitive skills and economic growth.[4] Parallel to the treatment of Latin American and East Asian countries, we can identify differences between OECD and non-OECD countries in the education–growth connection using the full country sample, as presented in table 6.1. The first column shows that the average unconditional growth rate for the OECD countries is not statistically different from that for the non-OECD countries. Conditional on school attainment and initial income levels, annual growth appears one percentage point faster in the OECD countries (columns 2 and 3).[5] Once cognitive skills are included, however, neither the OECD dummy by itself (column 4) nor its interaction with cognitive skills (column 5) is statistically significant. In simplest terms, the OECD countries actually fit well within the rest of the world in terms of the growth impact of knowledge capital: one standard deviation higher cognitive skills are associated with two percentage points faster growth, and richer nations grow more slowly, other things equal.

The last columns in table 6.1 consider only OECD countries and show that the basic results hold there. Specifically, as seen in columns 7 and 8, the association between knowledge capital and long-run economic growth in the sample of OECD countries explains over 80 percent of the variation in growth *within* just the OECD countries.[6] (Note that in the OECD sample, the bivariate association with initial per-capita GDP

Table 6.1
Cognitive skills and long-run economic growth in OECD countries

	Full country sample					OECD sample		
	(1)	(2)	(3)	(4)	(5)	(6)	(7)	(8)
OECD	-0.121	0.969**	0.935*	-0.085	-0.063			
	(0.31)	(2.09)	(1.99)	(0.27)	(0.19)			
Cognitive skills				1.945***	1.978***		1.864***	1.966***
				(8.53)	(7.98)		(5.83)	(6.72)
Initial years of schooling		0.341***	0.396***	0.078	0.080	0.173**	0.046	
		(3.17)	(2.89)	(1.05)	(1.07)	(2.09)	(0.82)	
Initial GDP per capita		-0.417***	-0.405***	-0.317***	-0.313***	-0.293***	-0.303***	-0.285***
		(4.94)	(4.67)	(5.87)	(5.61)	(5.20)	(8.61)	(10.33)

OECD × Initial years of schooling			-0.110 (0.65)					
OECD × Cognitive skills					-0.203 (0.36)			
Constant	2.962*** (10.79)	2.909*** (8.39)	4.503*** (11.17)	-4.683*** (5.11)	4.152*** (15.68)	3.993*** (9.73)	-4.275*** (2.97)	-4.621*** (3.38)
Number of countries	50	50	50	50	50	24	24	24
F (OECD and interaction)			2.37		0.10			
R² (adj.)	-0.019	0.306	0.297	0.729	0.723	0.559	0.828	0.831

Notes: Dependent variable: average annual growth rate in GDP per capita, 1960 to 2000. Cognitive skill measure refers to average score on all international tests 1964 to 2003 in math and science. In the interacted models, initial years of schooling and cognitive skills, respectively, are de-meaned. t-Statistics in parentheses: statistical significance at * 10 percent, ** 5 percent, *** 1 percent.

accounts for 49 percent of the variance in subsequent growth, making the relative increase in our understanding of nonconvergence growth through cognitive skills substantial.)

In additional sensitivity analyses (not shown), the significant positive association of growth with cognitive skills holds in both 1960 to 1980 and 1980 to 2000, with the point estimate slightly larger in the later twenty-year period.[7] Moreover the results are hardly affected by using average years of schooling attainment across the periods instead of initial years of schooling.

Figure 6.2 depicts the fundamental association graphically, plotting growth in real per-capita GDP between 1960 and 2000 against average test scores after allowing for differences in initial GDP per capita and average years of schooling. The OECD countries align closely along the

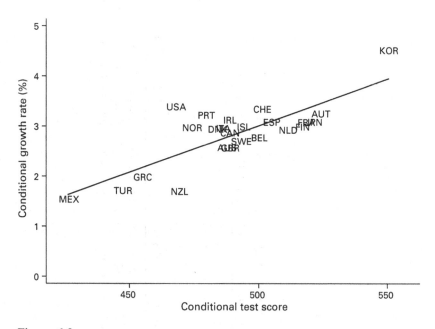

Figure 6.2

Knowledge capital and economic growth rates across OECD countries

Notes: Added-variable plot of a regression of the average annual rate of growth (in percent) of real GDP per capita in 1960 to 2000 on average test scores on international student achievement tests, average years of schooling in 1960, and initial level of real GDP per capita in 1960 (mean of unconditional variables added to each axis). Authors' calculations; see table 6.1, column 7. See table 2A.1 for country letter codes.

regression line that depicts the positive association between cognitive skills and economic growth, with the slight exceptions of New Zealand (which lies below the line) and the United States (which lies above), to which we return below.

6.2   Regulatory Environments and Growth among Rich Countries

A substantial literature has stressed the importance of how OECD countries regulate their product and labor markets. For example, Nicoletti and Scarpetta (2003) showed that short-run growth experiences across OECD countries are related to product market regulations, and Cingano et al. (2010) found employment protection legislation associated with firm-level investment and other firm outcomes across sectors and across firms with different financial constraints.

The question is, Do these factors enter into the long-run growth experiences of countries? Product market regulations affecting sectoral productivity may lead to structural change and international specialization, thereby reducing any net effects on aggregate growth rates. Similarly differences in employment protection legislation may lead to differential growth experiences in booms versus recessions that cancel out over the business cycle.

To investigate the long-run growth implications, we add a rich set of regulatory measures to our OECD growth models. Specifically, we employ the latest versions of far-ranging indicators of regulations of both product and labor markets: product market regulations (PMR) from Wölfl and others (2009), who extended previous versions from Nicoletti, Scarpetta, and Boylaud (2000); and employment protection legislation (EPL) from Venn (2009), who extended and improved upon previous versions from Organisation for Economic Co-operation and Development (1999).[8]

The results are unambiguous and telling: not one of the large battery of measures that depict product and labor market regulations comes close to being significantly related to the variation in long-run growth experiences across OECD countries (tables 6.2 and 6.3). At the same time regulatory practices do not affect the finding that knowledge capital is a powerful predictor of this variation.

The six columns of table 6.2 employ an aggregate indicator (column 1) and various subindicators of product market regulation.[9] The subindicators refer to administrative regulation, domestic economic regulation, state control, barriers to entrepreneurship, and barriers to trade and investment, respectively. The indicators of product market regulation refer

Table 6.2
Product market regulation *vs.* cognitive skills in OECD-country long-run growth models

			Type of product market regulation			
	Integrated indicator	Administrative regulation	Domestic economic regulation	State control	Barriers to entrepreneurship	Barriers to trade and investment
	(1)	(2)	(3)	(4)	(5)	(6)
Cognitive skills	1.843***	1.897***	1.840***	1.843***	1.859***	1.864***
	(5.67)	(5.92)	(5.60)	(5.66)	(5.75)	(5.67)
Initial years of schooling	0.026	0.015	0.036	0.033	0.025	0.047
	(0.41)	(0.23)	(0.60)	(0.55)	(0.40)	(0.75)
Initial GDP per capita	-0.309***	-0.310***	-0.309***	-0.311***	-0.308***	-0.303***
	(8.43)	(8.69)	(8.27)	(8.30)	(8.52)	(8.36)
Degree of regulation	-0.157	-0.178	-0.080	-0.084	-0.157	0.004
	(0.68)	(1.06)	(0.55)	(0.67)	(0.76)	(0.02)
Constant	-3.686**	-3.801**	-3.823**	-3.784**	-3.729**	-4.284**
	(2.17)	(2.52)	(2.27)	(2.32)	(2.29)	(2.77)
Number of countries	24	24	24	24	24	24
R^2 (adj.)	0.824	0.829	0.822	0.824	0.825	0.819

Notes: "Degree of regulation" refers to the specific type of product market regulation indicated in each column header. Each indicator of product market regulation is scaled from 0 to 6, with higher values reflecting more restrictions; see descriptions in Wölfl et al. (2009). Dependent variable: average annual growth rate in GDP per capita, 1960 to 2000. Sample: OECD countries. Cognitive skill measure refers to average score on all international tests 1964 to 2003 in math and science. *t*-Statistics in parentheses: statistical significance at * 10 percent, ** 5 percent, *** 1 percent.

Table 6.3
Employment protection legislation *vs.* cognitive skills in OECD-country long-run growth models

	Type of employment protection legislation				
	Summary indicator version 1	Summary indicator version 2	Dismissal regular contracts	Regulation temporary contracts	Regulation collective dismissal
	(1)	(2)	(3)	(4)	(5)
Cognitive skills	1.827***	1.788***	1.899***	1.788***	1.913***
	(5.41)	(5.06)	(5.39)	(5.00)	(5.95)
Initial years of schooling	0.027	0.025	0.034	0.036	0.071
	(0.41)	(0.37)	(0.48)	(0.58)	(1.21)
Initial GDP per capita	−0.310***	−0.307***	−0.308***	−0.307***	−0.324***
	(8.09)	(8.25)	(7.89)	(8.22)	(8.52)
Degree of protection	−0.081	−0.109	−0.051	−0.047	0.139
	(0.62)	(0.63)	(0.34)	(0.58)	(1.42)
Constant	−3.740**	−3.503*	−4.230**	−3.698*	−4.924***
	(2.16)	(1.81)	(2.79)	(2.06)	(3.26)
Number of countries	23	23	23	23	23
R^2 (adj.)	0.822	0.822	0.819	0.821	0.836

Notes: "Degree of protection" refers to the specific type of employment protection legislation indicated in each column header. Each indicator of employment protection legislation is scaled from 0 to 6, with higher values reflecting more restrictions; see descriptions in Venn (2009). Dependent variable: average annual growth rate in GDP per capita, 1960 to 2000. Sample: OECD countries. Cognitive skill measure refers to average score on all international tests 1964 to 2003 in math and science. *t*-Statistics in parentheses: statistical significance at * 10 percent, ** 5 percent, *** 1 percent.

to 1998, the first year for which they are available. While earlier measures would be preferable, under the assumption that the main institutional variation is in the cross section, these should still capture the most basic overall patterns. Furthermore results are unaffected by using the available indicators for 2003 or 2008 instead, or by taking the average over the three observations, indicating that lack of results is not driven by simple measurement error. Finally, to align the regulatory measures more closely with the period of growth observations, we perform all regressions for growth between 1980 and 2000 without affecting the results.

The five columns of table 6.3 focus on labor market regulation. Columns 1 and 2 add to the model the two versions of the aggregate employment protection index suggested by the OECD. The first version combines regulations pertaining to regular and temporary employment contracts, and the second adds to this subindexes of additional regulation of collective dismissal. Neither measure enters the model significantly nor affects the estimate on cognitive skills. The same is true when using separately the three subindicators of protection of permanent workers against (individual) dismissal, strictness of regulation on temporary forms of employment, and specific requirements for collective dismissal (columns 3 to 5). The indicators of employment regulation are measured as averages of the annual values between 1985 and 2000. Results are similar when the growth period is restricted to 1980 to 2000, which aligns more closely to the period of observation of the regulatory measures (not shown). Results are also robust to a new, third version of the aggregate OECD employment protection index, available only in 2008, which adds as subindicators the maximum time to make a claim of unfair dismissal, authorization and reporting requirements for temporary work agencies, and regulations requiring equal treatment of regular and agency workers at the user firm.

The robustness checks consistently document no convincing evidence that institutional or regulatory differences can account for differences in long-run growth among rich countries.[10] Instead, cognitive skills emerge as the one strong policy factor underlying growth differences in the OECD.

6.3   Different Levels of Skills and Education

An important and recurring policy question is what level of skills and education is most decisive for OECD growth. A simplified version of the question might be, should developed countries focus policy, in an egalitarian way, on decent basic skills for the whole population or, in an elitist way, on nurturing top scientists and engineers?

At a conceptual level, Vandenbussche, Aghion, and Meghir (2006) assume the innovation process is more skill-intensive than the imitation process. They present an endogenous growth model with innovation and imitation, where highly skilled labor has a greater growth-enhancing effect for countries closer to the technological frontier, while countries farther from it get greater value from what they call "unskilled human capital." While the untested underlying assumption seems reasonable, reasonable arguments can also be made for an opposite view: the innovation literature suggests many innovations emerge serendipitously, while, almost by definition, purposeful imitation processes require the work of skilled scientists.

A different conceptual extension starts from the perspective of highly skilled scientists. If these scientists were to work in a country that produces at the technological frontier, their only option would be to use their skills in the innovation of new technologies. If, by contrast, they were to work in a country that produces far below the technological frontier, they would still have the option to employ their skills in such innovative activities, but they would also have the option of using them more productively in imitating technologies at the technological frontier. These scientists will tend to work in the activity that promises the higher benefits, implying that the return to highly skilled labor may well be larger when below the technological frontier than when at it. While concentrations of highly skilled labor and spillovers across them may still be important, the alternative perspectives do introduce questions about the underlying assumptions.

We have already partially visited these issues from the perspective of cognitive skills. In section 3.3 we defined highly skilled and less skilled labor by the ends of the cognitive skill distribution (above 600 and below 400 on the PISA scale). We then looked at whether the value of skills varied with the initial income level of the country. We found that highly skilled workers were more important for growth in low-income countries—presumably those countries farther from the technological frontier (table 3.6).[11]

A different empirical approach, suggested by Vandenbussche, Aghion, and Meghir (2006), is to investigate whether countries close to the technological frontier should emphasize tertiary education. To investigate this, we make use of the Barro and Lee (2013) database, which provides average years of schooling separately at the primary, secondary, and tertiary levels. With little meaningful variation in the completion of primary education across the bulk of OECD countries, we combine the two lower levels of schooling into one category of nontertiary schooling.

In the full-country sample, the coefficients on nontertiary and tertiary schooling are both close to zero when cognitive skills are controlled for (column 1 of table 6.4). By contrast, in the OECD sample, the point estimate on years of tertiary schooling becomes larger (column 2), and it reaches marginal significance (at the 10 percent level) when years of nontertiary schooling are not included in the model (column 3). Results in column 4, however, indicate this is completely driven by the United States. Once the United States is excluded from the OECD sample, the coefficient on tertiary education is much smaller and again insignificant.

The United States is well known for its extensive tertiary education system, and figure 6.2 has already indicated it has the strongest positive residual in the growth model. While this might indicate growth-enhancing effects of its high-quality higher education system, the lack of robustness in the sample without the United States suggests it might rather be indicative of the highly skilled immigrant population the country attracts, of a particular set of economic institutions (not captured by our institutional measures), or of any other idiosyncrasy of the US economy.[12] Interestingly, years of tertiary schooling reach significance when the basic skill share is used instead of the average skill measure (column 5) but lose size and significance even in the sample that includes the United States when the top skill share is used (column 6). This pattern indicates that years of tertiary education may proxy for the share of students with high-level skills in the OECD. When the United States is disregarded, the coefficient on years of tertiary schooling again declines to close to zero in this specification (column 7).

While distinguishing the effects of different dimensions of the skill and schooling distribution is difficult in these small samples, some basic patterns are clear. First, the significant effect of cognitive skills is extremely robust to consideration of any quantitative measure of different levels of school attainment. Second, the finding of Vandenbussche, Aghion, and Meghir (2006) of a particular effect of tertiary attainment in rich countries is not robust once long-run growth experiences are the focus and knowledge capital is taken into account.

Of course, this does not mean learning beyond the secondary level does not matter. Rather, in the spirit of a life cycle interpretation where early skills facilitate the development of subsequent ones (Cunha et al. 2006), it means outcome measures of learning in school are a good predictor for

Table 6.4
Nontertiary and tertiary schooling compared

Sample:	Full (1)	OECD (2)	OECD (3)	OECD w/o USA (4)	OECD (5)	OECD (6)	OECD w/o USA (7)
Cognitive skills	1.923***	1.888***	1.912***	2.043***			
	(9.12)	(6.09)	(6.83)	(8.14)			
Years of nontertiary schooling	0.076	0.012					
	(0.94)	(0.059)					
Years of tertiary schooling	0.198	1.291	1.344*	0.543	1.685**	1.014	0.149
	(0.16)	(1.58)	(1.77)	(0.74)	(2.31)	(0.96)	(0.13)
Share of students reaching basic literacy					5.458***		
					(7.13)		
Share of top-performing students						11.597***	12.855***
						(3.93)	(4.44)
Initial GDP per capita	-0.325***	-0.323***	-0.320***	-0.323***	-0.344***	-0.264***	-0.263***
	(6.81)	(8.85)	(9.78)	(11.22)	(10.53)	(6.08)	(6.37)
Constant	-4.588***	-4.222***	-4.296***	-4.843***	0.413	3.700***	3.667***
	(5.44)	(3.02)	(3.26)	(4.12)	(0.67)	(10.27)	(10.69)
Number of countries	50	24	24	23	24	24	23
R^2 (adj.)	0.728	0.839	0.847	0.886	0.856	0.712	0.750

Notes: Dependent variable: average annual growth rate in GDP per capita, 1960 to 2000. Cognitive skill measure refers to average score on all international tests 1964 to 2003 in math and science. t-Statistics in parentheses: statistical significance at * 10 percent, ** 5 percent, *** 1 percent.

the accumulation of further skills in life and for the capacity to deploy them effectively.

6.4   Conclusions on Growth among Rich Countries

Much analysis of long-term growth depends heavily on the contrast between currently developed and currently less developed countries. This leaves open the question of what explains differences in growth among already developed countries. These differences are very large and the subject of much national policy discussion.

Our answer follows directly from the previous growth analysis. Differences in knowledge capital not only explain the differences in growth between developing and developed countries but also those among developed countries.

7

The Economic Value of Educational Reform

The preceding analyses emphasize the strong effects of cognitive skills on long-run economic growth, but they do not tell us directly the economic value of any improvements in educational outcomes. In particular, the growth rate effects do not map linearly onto the economic value of any education reform in a country, not least because different time lags are involved between successful reform in the education system today and the improvement of skills in the national workforce. Here we use the previously estimated growth models to project the economic impact of different scenarios of school improvements. To do so, we develop a basic projection model that traces out future changes in GDP triggered by knowledge improvements (section 7.1).

Importantly, the projections highlight the dynamic nature of human capital and growth. Our basic characterization of growth indicates that higher cognitive skills offer a path of continued economic improvement, so that favorable policies today have growing impacts in the future. The full ramifications of schooling outcomes will not become apparent, however, until fairly far in the future. The economic gains from education reform are surely not reaped within one or two political legislation periods. Similar to the discussion of climate policies, where considering expected outcomes that will materialize several generations from now has become customary, we argue that the formulation of education policy requires a long-run perspective that fully considers at least the time horizon of a child born today.

The historical relationships between knowledge capital and growth described above suggest that the economic impacts of improved skills would be truly astounding (section 7.2). Consider, for example, a set of school reform policies, begun today and accomplished steadily over twenty years, that lift a nation's level of skills (as measured by PISA scores) by twenty-five points (one-quarter of a standard deviation). If we trace the economic impacts suggested by the growth models over the lifetime of somebody born today, we would expect to see GDP being more than one quarter higher than without the reform by the end of the approximately eighty-year period. Over the entire period—with low initial impacts as students first have to enter the labor force—GDP would be 6 percent higher on average. This increase is roughly equivalent to an average wage increase of 12 percent for all workers over this period.

That we see such improvements in skills when we trace PISA scores of various countries over the past decade indicates they are feasible. Yet the discussions of school improvement frequently appear to understate the potential economic benefits of actually accomplishing change.

In addition to the twenty-five-PISA-point improvement scenario, we consider two country-specific reform scenarios that reflect plausible policy goals. One is bringing countries up to the level of the (former) PISA top performer, Finland. The other is bringing all students to minimum proficiency, defined as 400 points on the PISA test scale. In the projections we restrict our attention to OECD countries so as not to paint wholly unrealistic policy pictures for some of the very poorly performing countries discussed in chapter 5.[1]

Projections of economic benefits far into the future obviously depend heavily on the growth model—including not only the parameters but also the form of the relationships. Perhaps most interesting, we return in this chapter to the controversy over endogenous growth versus neoclassical growth, this time looking at it from the perspective of implications for future benefits (section 7.3). We also show how estimated impacts vary with different parameters (section 7.4).[2]

7.1   Projecting the Economic Benefits of Reform

Our economic projections involve several components. First, we calculate the time path of the annual growth rate engendered by education reform designed to move students from their current level of performance to a given new level. This pattern of economic outcomes represents the confluence of three separate dynamic processes: (1) changes in schools lead to progressive improvement in student achievement until students fully reach the new steady-state level of achievement; (2) students with better skills move into the labor force and average skills increase as new, higher achieving workers replace retiring ones; and (3) the economy responds to the progressive improvement in the average skill level of the workforce. Unlike many discussions of educational policy that implicitly assume reforms are instantaneous and the results will be seen immediately, a key element we want to emphasize in ours is that school reform takes time, and its impacts come only after students have become integrated into the workforce.

Second, based on the pattern of predicted growth rates, we model the expansion of GDP with and without the education reform.

Third, based on these projections, we calculate the total value of the reform by aggregating the discounted values of the annual differences between the GDP with reform and the GDP without reform. Appendix 7A describes in detail how the projection model permits us to simulate the economic impacts of school improvement.

Implementing the projection model requires we make a number of parameter assumptions and simplifications, most of which we subsequently subject to a sensitivity analysis. The simulation does not adopt any specific school reform package but instead focuses just on the ultimate change in achievement. For the purposes here, we assume reforms take twenty years to complete, and we take the path of increased achievement during the reform period as linear. For example, we assume an average improvement of 25 points on PISA reflects a gain in the student population of 1.25 points per year. This might be realistic when, for example, the reform relies upon a process of upgrading the skills of teachers—either by training existing teachers or changing the workforce by replacing existing teachers. This linear path dictates the quality of new cohorts of workers at each point in time.

We assume the expected work life to be forty years, which implies that each new cohort of workers comprises 2.5 percent of the workforce. Thus, even after an educational reform is fully implemented, it takes forty years until the full labor force is at the new skill level.

We anchor our projections as reforms that are assumed to begin in 2010, although changing this date has virtually no effect on our estimates. (We actually smooth over the economic changes surrounding the 2008 recession to avoid any distortions caused by specific business cycle events.) The benchmark here considers all economic returns that arise during the lifetime of a child who is born at the beginning of the reform in 2010. According to the data for 2006, a simple average of male and female life expectancy at birth over all OECD countries is seventy-nine years.[3] Therefore the baseline calculations take a time horizon until 2090, if we consider all future returns that accrue until then but neglect any that accrue afterward.

The simulations rely on the estimates of growth relationships derived from the twenty-four OECD countries with complete data. As indicated in column 7 of table 6.1, the coefficient estimate is 1.864, suggesting that, for example, a fifty-point higher average PISA score (i.e., higher by one-half standard deviation) would be associated with 0.93 percent higher annual growth in the long run in the endogenous growth projections.

The value of improvement in economic outcomes from added growth also depends, of course, on the paths of economies that would be obtained without educational improvement. The baseline analysis here takes the annual growth of OECD economies in the absence of education reform to be 1.5 percent. This is simply the average annual growth rate of potential GDP per worker of the OECD area over the past two decades: 1.5 percent in 1987 to 1996 and 1.4 percent in 1997 to 2006.[4]

Finally, more immediate benefits are both more valuable and more certain than those far in the future. To incorporate this consideration, the entire stream is converted into a present discounted value, which, in simplest terms, is the current dollar amount that would be equivalent to the future stream of returns calculated from the growth model. Specifically, if one had that amount of funds and invested it today, it would be possible to reproduce the projected stream of economic growth benefits from the principal amount and associated investment returns. Thus the calculation of present discounted value allows a relevant comparison for any other current policy actions.

In calculating the present value, the discount rate at which to adjust future benefits becomes an important parameter. A standard value of the social discount rate used in long-term projections on the sustainability of pension systems and public finance is 3 percent—see, for example, Börsch-Supan (2000) and Hagist et al. (2005)—and we follow that precedent here.[5] By contrast, the influential Stern Review report that estimates the cost of climate change uses a discount rate of only 1.4 percent, thereby giving a much higher value to future costs and benefits (Stern 2007). In our robustness analyses we will also consider such alternative discount rates.

A number of untested assumptions go into our projections. First, the projections assume skills play the same role in the future as they have in the past, so the evidence of past results provides a direct way to project future ones.

Second, while the statistical analysis has not looked at how economies adjust to improved skills, the calculations assume the experiences of other countries with greater cognitive skills provide insight into how the new skills will be absorbed into the economy.

Third, the projection of simultaneous improvement across countries presumes all countries can grow faster without detracting (or benefiting) from growth in other countries. In other words, the higher levels of human capital in each country allow it to innovate, to improve its production, and to import new technologies without affecting the growth prospects of others.[6] Furthermore the estimates ignore any other aspects of interactions, such as migration of skilled labor across borders. (Of course, one way a country could improve its human capital would be by arranging for its youth to obtain schooling in another country with better schools—that is, as long as the more educated youth return to their home country to work.)

Fourth, all countries are assumed to have a stationary population with a constant age distribution.

Fifth, we project the gross benefits of reform, and they equal net benefits only if we assume reform is costless—an assumption discussed explicitly in section 7.5.

Finally, all calculations are in real (inflation-adjusted) terms, expressed in 2010 dollars under purchasing power parity.

7.2   Baseline Reform Projections

To illustrate the benefits of school reform, we start with the results of the baseline projection model for the three education reform scenarios, each of which comes from contemporaneous policy discussions.[7]

Scenario I: Increase Average Performance by Twenty-five PISA Points

A simple starting point is to consider the economic impact on OECD countries of a 0.25 standard deviation improvement, equivalent to an increase of twenty-five points in PISA scores. The reform policy is begun in 2010 and on average yields twenty-five-point higher scores in 2030 that remain at that level for all subsequent students.

A gain of twenty-five points in average PISA scores over the next twenty years is less than has been achieved in the most rapidly improving education systems in the OECD in the past decade. Mexico gained twenty-eight points in math between 2003 and 2012, Poland gained twenty-seven, and Turkey gained twenty-five.[8] And, as shown in section 4.2, both Finland and Canada showed similar increases in scores over a period closer in length to the twenty years of the scenario. Clearly, the projected improvement is possible.[9]

Figure 7.1 provides a pictorial summary of the marginal impact on GDP of a twenty-five-point school improvement for each year into the future.[10] (Unlike in subsequent projections, this policy implies a uniform improvement in skills across countries, so the relative improvement is the same for all countries.) Although impacts will not be evident until the presence of higher achieving students starts becoming more significant in the labor market, by 2041 GDP will be more than 3 percent higher than what would be expected without improvements in human capital. (The light lines in the figure also show the relevant 95 percent confidence bounds for the regression coefficient in column 7 of table 6.1. For 2041, these bounds go from 1.9 to 4.1 percent higher GDP.) By 2090—the end of expected life for the person born in 2010—projected GDP per capita exceed the "education as usual" level by more than 26 percent.

The magnitude of such a change is best understood from an example. In the absence of changes in educational policy, France would be expected

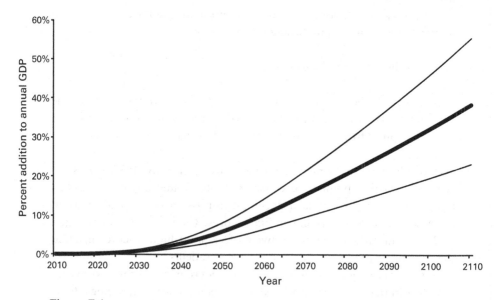

Figure 7.1

Improvement in annual GDP with scenario I (increase average achievement by one-quarter standard deviation)

Notes: GDP with reform relative to GDP without reform in each year after the reform starts. The main line gives the point estimate of scenario I. The light lines show the 95 percent confidence interval of the point estimate of the growth regression. Authors' calculations.

to have a GDP (in 2010 USD) of $3,606 billion in 2041. If, on the other hand, it achieved the improvement in cognitive skills that took it from an average PISA score of 505 to 530, total GDP would be expected to be $3,715 billion in 2041, or $108 billion higher. These calculations illustrate a simple point: while a 3 percent change may seem small, it is very large when applied to the entire GDP of any of the OECD countries.

These calculations are by themselves misleading, because the impacts of improved cognitive skills continue far into the future. The 3 percent improvement in GDP in 2041 rises to a 5.9 percent improvement in 2050, 15.3 percent in 2070, and 26.3 percent in 2090. These dynamic improvements in the economy yield ongoing gains to society, and the appropriate summary of the impact of educational improvements accumulates the value of these annual gains.

Importantly, after all people in the labor force have obtained the new and improved education (in 2070), annual growth will be 0.47 percentage points higher. This implies that each country that achieves the average improvement of one-quarter standard deviation of achievement will have a cumulative impact on the economy through 2090 equal to 288 percent of current-year GDP. The first column of table 7.1 provides these discounted values of all the future increases through 2090 for each OECD country. The dollar value for each varies by the level of GDP in 2010—but the total impact across the OECD is $123 trillion in present value.

Because these impacts are put into present value terms, they can be compared to current economic values. For example, the calculations indicate that the value of improvements through long-run growth far outstrips the cost of the recent worldwide recession and is an order of magnitude larger than the value of the worldwide fiscal stimulus efforts. They also imply that the long-run fiscal pressures facing many nations— say, because of health and retirement expenditures—would be manageable without the pain with which many nations are currently struggling.

Scenario II: Bring Each Country to Finland's Average Level (of 546 PISA Points)

The historic success of Finland on the PISA tests is well known.[11] In the second scenario we take the performance of Finnish students as a benchmark for the performance levels that are possible. The economic impact is calculated by projecting GDP growth for each OECD country, under the assumption that the country could bring itself to the top of the rankings as identified by Finland: an average PISA score of 546. (Alternatively,

Table 7.1
Baseline projections of the economic value of three education reform scenarios

| | Scenario I: Increase avg. performance by ¼ std. dev. | Scenario II: Bring each country to Finnish level of 546 points on PISA | | | | Scenario III: Bring all to minimum of 400 points on PISA | | | |
	Value of reform (billion $) (1)	Value of reform (billion $) (2)	In % of current GDP (3)	L.-r. growth increase (p.p.) (4)	Note: Increase in PISA score (5)	Value of reform (billion $) (6)	In % of current GDP (7)	L.-r. growth increase (p.p.) (8)	Share of students below minimum skills (9)
Australia	2,631	2,092	229%	0.38	20.1	2,430	266%	0.43	9.8%
Austria	969	1,545	460%	0.72	38.4	1,308	390%	0.62	13.9%
Belgium	1,208	1,586	379%	0.60	32.2	1,816	434%	0.68	15.3%
Canada	4,051	2,728	194%	0.32	17.2	3,075	219%	0.36	8.1%
Czech Rep.	830	1,177	409%	0.64	34.5	1,054	366%	0.58	13.1%
Denmark	608	1,231	584%	0.88	47.5	908	430%	0.67	15.2%
Finland	594	0	0%	0.00	0.0	255	124%	0.21	4.7%
France	6,557	11,349	499%	0.77	41.3	9,844	433%	0.68	15.3%
Germany	8,822	17,245	564%	0.86	46.0	15,166	496%	0.77	17.3%
Greece	1,047	4,253	1172%	1.59	85.2	2,943	811%	1.17	26.5%
Hungary	603	1,323	633%	0.95	51.0	972	465%	0.72	16.3%
Iceland	36	66	530%	0.81	43.6	46	371%	0.59	13.3%
Ireland	585	995	490%	0.76	40.6	664	327%	0.52	11.8%

Italy	5,526	19,353	1010%	1.41	75.6	13,503	705%	1.04	23.5%
Japan	13,280	2,871	62%	0.11	5.7	10,382	226%	0.37	8.3%
Korea, Rep.	4,120	756	53%	0.09	4.8	2,544	178%	0.30	6.7%
Luxembourg	126	421	963%	1.36	72.7	289	662%	0.99	22.3%
Mexico	4,753	39,363	2389%	2.68	143.9	29,557	1794%	2.19	49.5%
Netherlands	2,032	1,344	191%	0.31	16.9	1,779	253%	0.41	9.3%
New Zealand	361	275	220%	0.36	19.4	385	308%	0.49	11.2%
Norway	844	1,975	675%	1.00	53.9	1,391	476%	0.74	16.6%
Poland	2,119	5,320	724%	1.07	57.2	3,766	513%	0.79	17.8%
Portugal	742	2,860	1112%	1.52	81.7	1,878	730%	1.07	24.2%
Slovak Rep.	343	787	661%	0.99	52.9	549	461%	0.72	16.2%
Spain	4,496	12,332	791%	1.15	61.7	8,237	529%	0.81	18.3%
Sweden	1,080	1,761	470%	0.73	39.2	1,406	375%	0.59	13.4%
Switzerland	1,003	1,159	333%	0.53	28.6	1,263	363%	0.58	13.0%
Turkey	3,043	19,450	1844%	2.24	120.1	15,089	1430%	1.85	41.8%
United Kingdom	6,862	7,892	332%	0.53	28.5	7,669	322%	0.52	11.7%
United States	43,835	111,923	737%	1.08	58.1	86,167	567%	0.86	19.4%
OECD	123,108	275,429	645%	0.93	49.8	226,333	530%	0.80	18.0%

Notes: Discounted value of future increases in GDP until 2090, expressed in billion $ (PPP) and as percentage of current GDP. "Long-run growth increase" refers to increase in annual growth rate (in percentage points) once the whole labor force has reached higher level of educational performance. "Increase in PISA score" refers to the ultimate increase in educational performance due to reform scenario II. "Share of students below minimum skills" refers to the share of students in each country performing below the minimum skill level of 400 PISA points. See text for reform parameters. Authors' calculations.

this can be taken as moving into the score range of Korea, Japan, and a number of other East Asian countries.)

The impact on different economies varies by the size of the reform—that is, how far they are below Finland at its beginning—as well as by the size of the economies themselves. Under this scenario Finland would neither change its schools nor see any long-term economic changes. In comparison, if adopting these changes were feasible, Mexico and Turkey would see their economies completely transformed.

The country-by-country impacts of these changes are found in columns 2 to 5 of table 7.1. On average, the OECD countries see a nearly 50-point increase in performance (one-half standard deviation). While the change in Japan or Korea amounts to about 5 points, the change in Mexico is 144 points.

As discussed, some countries have experienced school improvements of twenty-five points or more (including Finland itself), but none matches the extreme cases involving more than one hundred points. Such large changes are almost inconceivable, given current knowledge of how to transform schools or cognitive skills in general, at least within the twenty years of our reform simulations. An alternative view would be to assume a number of countries would require a longer time for a reform program to yield such large changes. We show below the implications for economic benefits of stretching out the reform period.

The present value for improvements across the twenty-four OECD countries under this scenario is $275 trillion, or more than six times the current combined GDP of the OECD countries. The United States, which currently falls over fifty points behind Finland, would, based on historical growth patterns, see a present value of improved GDP of over $112 trillion, or some 40 percent of the OECD total, reflecting both the size of the country and its distance behind Finland. Germany would see a $17 trillion improvement, or more than five times current GDP.

The rankings of countries according to increases in GDP compared to current GDP are shown in figure 7.2. One way in which we can interpret this figure is that it signifies the amounts of economic leverage possible for different OECD countries from educational improvements.

Scenario III: Bring Everyone up to the Minimum Skill Level of 400 PISA Points

The final scenario considered is a "compensatory" improvement in education, whereby all students are brought up to a minimal skill level—which, as in section 3.3, is defined here as obtaining a score of 400 on the PISA

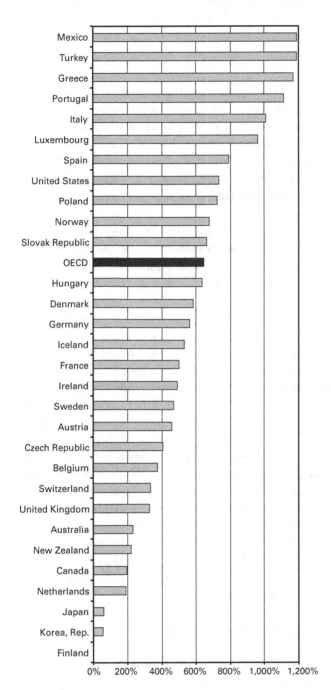

Figure 7.2

Present value of scenario II (bring each country to Finnish level) in percentage of current GDP

Notes: Discounted value of future increases in GDP until 2090 due to a reform that brings each country to the Finnish average level of 546 PISA points, expressed as percentage of current GDP. The value is 2,389 percent for Mexico and 1,844 percent for Turkey. Authors' depiction based on the projection analysis reported in table 7.1, column 3.

tests, or one standard deviation below the OECD average. While the pre-vious simulations could be thought of as shifting the entire achievement distribution, this scenario considers the implications of bringing up its bottom. To understand the implications of changing just one portion of the distribution, we employ the alternative estimation of the underlying growth models (as in table 3.6) that enter the shares of students reaching basic literacy and top-performing students rather than average cognitive skills for the OECD sample.[12]

By these calculations, all OECD countries, including Finland, have room for improvement. On average, 18 percent of students in the OECD countries score below 400. As might be expected from the average scores, the required improvements are largest in Mexico and Turkey (see the last column of table 7.1).

Columns 6 to 8 of table 7.1 display the economic outcomes, according to historical growth patterns, of bringing all OECD students up to mini-mum competence levels. The overall OECD change would be an average annual growth rate 0.8 percentage points higher after reform was accom-plished and after the full labor force had received the improved education. The total improvements for the OECD countries from achieving universal minimum proficiency would have a present value of $226 trillion. Again, the range of outcomes is wide, including relatively small improvements of 219 percent of current GDP for Canada, as compared to nine OECD countries whose benefit would be more than five times their current GDP.

The range of outcomes is depicted in figure 7.3, which ranks countries by the benefits compared to their current GDPs. Even Finland could, by these calculations, more than double its current GDP by bringing the rela-tively modest proportion of low performers (4.7 percent) up to scores of 400. Note also that the effects of these policies on the separate countries differ from those of the previous scenario, reflecting the differences in the underlying distribution of student performance.

7.3   An Alternative Neoclassical Growth Framework

The projections so far assume that higher educational achievement allows a country to keep on growing at a higher rate in the long run. Such a specification captures the basic ideas of endogenous growth theory (see section 2.1), where a better-educated workforce leads to a larger stream of new ideas that produces technological progress at a higher rate. By contrast, in the augmented neoclassical growth model, changes in test scores lead to higher steady-state levels of income but do not affect the

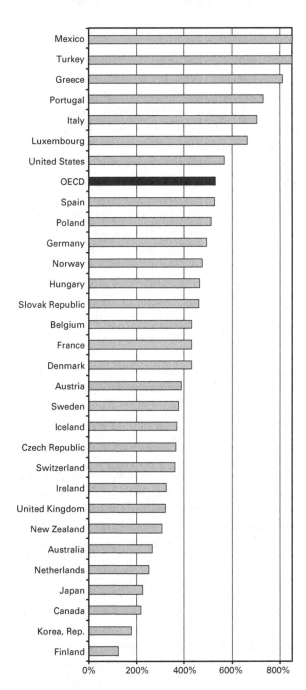

Figure 7.3

Present value of scenario III (bring everyone up to minimum skills) in percentage of current GDP

Notes: Discounted value of future increases in GDP until 2090 due to a reform that brings every individual in the country up to a minimum skill level of 400 PISA points, expressed as percentage of current GDP. The value is 1,794 percent for Mexico and 1,430 percent for Turkey. Authors' depiction based on the projection analysis reported in table 7.1, column 7.

long-run growth path. Our empirical growth model captures the conditional convergence implied by the neoclassical model—but also by a set of endogenous growth models—by including the initial GDP level as a control variable. An alternative approach for the projections is thus to interpret the model in the neoclassical rather than endogenous growth framework and have educational reforms affect the steady-state level of income but not its long-run growth.

To do so, we re-estimate our growth model with the logarithmic rather than linear initial per-capita GDP (not shown). The test score coefficient hardly changes in this specification (1.718 rather than 1.864), and the coefficient on log initial income is –1.835. This matches standard parameter assumptions in the augmented neoclassical growth model, implying that an economy moves halfway to its steady state in about thirty-eight years.[13] With convergence, projections of growth rates with and without education reform will differ only during the transition to the new balanced growth path.

To characterize growth of the world technological frontier, we assume that the GDP-weighted average of the growth rates in the three countries with the largest shares of patents in the world—the United States, Japan, and Germany—is 1.5 percent per year without reform. Together, these three countries currently account for over 70 percent of worldwide patents.[14]

In reform scenario I, where each country's test scores increase by twenty-five PISA points, the value of the reform—that is, the discounted value of the future increases in GDP—amounts to $90 trillion in present value terms, compared to our previous projection of $123 trillion. (Appendix table 7A.1 shows the results for the individual countries when the projections are based on the neoclassical model specification.) In the neoclassical projections the value of this "uniform" reform differs across countries because the projected growth rates vary with the level of GDP, but the overall OECD effect still equals 211 percent of current OECD GDP.

To illustrate the specific dynamics of the neoclassical projections, a few details of the trajectories of the projection are worth discussing. Initial growth rates (with or without reform) in 2010 to 2011 differ across countries, depending on how far away they are from their steady states. The United States is projected to grow at 1.1 percent initially, whereas the simple mean of OECD-country growth rates is higher (at 1.9 percent) because of the room many countries have for catch-up.[15] Due to the convergence process, the average growth for OECD countries is down to

1.6 percent in 2090 without the reform, ranging from 1.0 to 1.8 percent across countries. With reform, the range is 1.2 to 2.0 percent, with an average of 1.7 percent. By 2104, the average is down to 1.5 percent, and by 2130, all countries' growth rates have converged to between 1.3 and 1.6 percent without the reform and to 1.4 to 1.7 percent with the reform.

In the neoclassical projections the difference in average growth rates among the scenarios with and without reform grows to a maximum of 0.28 percentage points in about 2060 and then declines back to 0.18 percentage points in 2090 and 0.06 percentage points in 2150. (Compare this to the endogenous growth model, where the long-run growth rate stays 0.47 percentage points higher starting in 2070.) While the difference between the reform and the no-reform growth ultimately converges to zero (below 0.004 percentage points everywhere by 2300), the model underscores that this convergence process takes a very long time to take full effect.

In reform scenario II, where each country improves to the test score level of Finland, the present value of the reform amounts to $180 trillion in the neoclassical model, compared to the $275 trillion previously calculated in the endogenous growth model. Note that this scenario implies that in the *very* long run, each country converges to the same steady-state level of per-capita GDP, as test scores are the only variable influencing the steady-state level in our model. In 2090, however, the per-capita GDP of the most advanced OECD country would still be 70.6 percent higher than that of the least advanced. By 2150, this difference would be down to 19.7 percent, and by 2300 to 1.2 percent.

The present value across the OECD of reform scenario III, which brings all students to a minimum level of 400 PISA points, is $187 trillion in the neoclassical projections, rather than the $226 trillion of the endogenous growth projections.

Longer time horizons imply larger differences between the two growth models. When we estimate the neoclassical version for reform scenario II with time horizons varying between 2050 and 2150, the present value of the reform is 81 percent of the endogenous growth projection value for a time horizon through 2050, 65 percent through 2090, and 44 percent through 2150 (see columns 7 to 10 of appendix table 7A.1 for country values).

Several factors contribute to the closeness of the estimates over our time period for the two different growth models. First, our reform scenarios gradually introduce changes, reflecting the lags for the policy to become fully effective and for the new, better-educated workers to change the average skills of the labor force. Second, the biggest impacts of the differences across the alternative models occur in the distant future, and thus the impact is lessened by discounting to obtain present values and by disregarding any returns that might accrue after 2090. Third, even ignoring discounting, the estimated convergence parameters imply very long periods before any country returns to its balanced growth path following a perturbation because of policy.

7.4   Sensitivity to Alternative Parameter Choices

It is useful to consider the sensitivity of the prior projections to key parameter choices. We do this for our baseline endogenous growth-type model specification under scenario II that brings each country to the Finnish level of PISA scores. In the baseline specification the total value of the reform in the OECD amounts to $275 trillion, or 645 percent of the current GDP of OECD countries. Here we report the overall results; country-specific results for each of the sensitivity adjustments in this section are found in appendix tables 7A.2 and 7A.3.

Growth parameter: The baseline model projects 1.86 percent of additional average annual growth for a one standard deviation increase in test scores. A plausible range of alternative growth parameters takes the lowest and highest estimated parameters for cognitive skills in the different specifications related to table 6.1 for OECD countries—that is, 1.40 and 1.97.[16] With these bounds, the estimated total discounted value of the education reform for the OECD ranges between $196 trillion and $295 trillion, respectively (or 459 and 690 percent, respectively, of current aggregate GDP).

An alternative way to account for the imprecision of the growth coefficient estimate is to use the lower and upper bounds of the 95 percent confidence interval around the baseline growth coefficient. These parameter bounds imply the net present value of the education reform is between $164 trillion and $406 trillion.

Time horizon: As figure 7.1 clearly suggests, the time horizon for benefit calculations is important. While we have implicitly emphasized the importance of adopting a long-term horizon when considering education reform, even by 2050 the present value of the reform already accumulates to $36 trillion, or 85 percent of the current GDP of the OECD countries. By contrast, when adopting a time horizon until 2150, the (appropriately) discounted) value of the reform sums to a staggering $948 trillion, or more than twenty times the current GDP.

Speed of reform: The baseline scenarios assume it takes twenty years for the education reform to be fully implemented. A faster implementation (ten years) leads to an increase of the reform value to $341 trillion, whereas it is "only" $223 trillion if the reform takes thirty years to implement. Thus, while faster efforts obviously lead to substantially higher returns, even a slow (but successful) reform, if begun today, would have enormous impact.

Working life: An average working life of thirty-five, rather than forty, years appears to be a more reasonable assumption for many OECD countries. A shorter working life means the faster replacement of the workforce with better-educated individuals, so the aggregate value of the education reform increases. Assuming a thirty-five-year work life yields a projection estimate of $304 trillion for the total value of the education reform, or 10 percent greater than the baseline.

Discount rate: The rate at which future returns are discounted obviously makes a substantial difference for the net present value of reform. Discount rates of 2.5 percent or 3.5 percent result in discounted present values of the projected returns of $369 trillion and $207 trillion, respectively. For a larger band of discount rate of 2 to 4 percent, the total discounted reform value would be $497 trillion and $157 trillion, respectively. Projections of long-run effects in the area of climate change, however, have discounted the future at much lower rates. In particular (although this is highly disputed), the influential Stern Review (2007) placed a much higher value on future costs and benefits by employing a discount rate of only 1.4 percent.[17] The report also assumed a slightly lower rate of potential growth of 1.3 percent rather than 1.5 percent, as in our models. What is ultimately relevant for the projections is the difference between the discount rate and the rate of potential growth; thus, the climate change set of parameters yields an effective discount rate of 0.1 percent. If we were to adopt this discounting practice of the Stern Review, by 2090 the present value of the education reform would sum to a staggering $636 trillion, or roughly fifteen times the current GDP.

7.5   Conclusions on the Benefits and Costs of Educational Reform

The growth models suggest enormous economic gains from improvements in knowledge capital. Even with very conservative assumptions (compared to the best point estimates of impacts), improvements in school outcomes lead to added GDP growth that could dramatically change the future prosperity of a country.

Table 7.2
Summary of projection results

	Scenario I: Increase avg. performance by ¼ std. dev. (1)	Scenario II: Bring each country to Finnish level of 546 points on PISA (2)	Scenario III: Bring all to minimum of 400 points on PISA (3)
"Endogenous-growth" specification			
in billion $	123,108	275,429	226,333
in % of discounted future GDP	6.2%	13.8%	11.3%
"Neoclassical" specification			
in billion $	90,031	179,655	187,191
in % of discounted future GDP	4.3%	8.5%	8.9%

Notes: Discounted value of future increases in OECD GDP until 2090, expressed in billion $ (PPP) and as percentage of discounted value of all annual projected OECD GDPs until 2090. Authors' calculations.

The estimated dollar gains from school reform are almost unfathomably large. An alternative is to put the gains in terms of future GDP values, since GDP will grow even in the absence of reform. Table 7.2 summarizes the baseline projections of the endogenous growth model and the neoclassical growth model as compared to the discounted value of the projected future OECD GDP over the same time span (until 2090).

The value of the different reforms amounts to between 4.3 and 13.8 percent of the present value of future GDP. Independent of whether the underlying economic model is specified in endogenous growth or neoclassical terms, the projected impact of improved educational achievement on the future economic well-being of OECD countries is large.

These estimates can also be thought about in terms of average paychecks of workers. Since about half the population of each country is employed, the 6.2 percent increase in GDP per capita of the twenty-five-PISA-point reform in the endogenous growth model would translate into an average increase of more than 12 percent in incomes for all workers over the next eighty years. Achieving the cognitive skills of Finland would be equivalent to a 17 to 28 percent increase in workers' incomes, depending on whether growth is endogenous or neoclassical.

While the projections provide the gross returns to improved schools, these should be offset by the costs needed to obtain the achievement gains. Unfortunately, they are not easy to estimate. We discuss a wide range of policy options in the next chapter, although estimating the costs (or impacts) of these directly is difficult.

Some reasonable bounds might be inferred from current levels of education spending. Spending on primary and secondary schools in the OECD ranged from 2.5 percent of GDP (in the Slovak Republic) to 5.1 percent (in Iceland) in 2007, with an average of 3.6 percent.[18] Total spending, including tertiary schooling, averaged 5.7 percent. Of the primary and secondary school expenditures, about 60 percent went to teacher compensation, implying that a 50 percent increase in all teacher salaries—or, equivalently, a doubling of the salaries of half of the teachers—would amount to slightly over 1 percent of GDP.

Balanced against these input bounds, it is useful to put this discussion into the context of the benefits indicated in table 7.2. The benefits of a twenty-five-point improvement in PISA scores average 4.3 percent of GDP in the conservative neoclassical estimates. This implies that the very dramatic policy of paying all teachers 50 percent more would cost less than one-quarter of the projected benefits *if this policy led to a twenty-five-point improvement.* The latter point is important to emphasize, because many nations have put into place large spending increases, including significant increases in teacher pay, without getting the student achievement gains they had hoped for. In other words, this benefit–cost calculation only holds if the new policies reach the achievement goals.

That said, it is important to note that the most significant costs may be political. The projections clearly show the economic gains come only after a long time, involving the reform of schools and the introduction of noticeable proportions of more highly skilled workers into the labor force. This disjointedness of costs and benefits is not unusual in many public programs, but it is more extreme in this case, because the benefits come only after most current politicians have left office.

This mismatch may not be decisive. First, politicians in many countries already campaign on the possibility of improving schools. While current campaigning is often on behalf of failed programs—increases in spending or reductions in class size that have not proved successful—these efforts could perhaps be redirected to more productive areas. Second, it would not be the first time politicians have dealt with such dilemmas. In matters such as climate change, they have actively engaged in long-run activities even more mismatched in terms of timing of costs and benefits. To varying degrees, similar difficulties arise with long-run space exploration programs, military defense procurement, and others.

Appendix 7A: Technical Details of Reform Projections

The economic impact of the reform varies across four phases defined by the average quality of the labor force.

Four Phases of Economic Impact

Phase 1 (2010 to 2030): During the twenty years of the education reform program, the additional growth in GDP per capita due to the reform in year t is given by

$$\Delta^t = growth\ coefficient * \Delta PISA * \frac{1}{working\ life} * \frac{t-2010}{20} + \Delta^{t-1}, \qquad (7A.1)$$

where the *growth coefficient* comes from the regression estimations presented in chapter 3 and $\Delta PISA$ is the increase in the average PISA test score due to the reform. The working-life term indicates each cohort of new, higher-achieving students is only a fraction of the total labor force.

Phase 2 (2031 to 2050): The education reform is now fully enacted, and achievement of all subsequent students remains at the new level. But for the length of a working life from the start of reform, which in the baseline simulations is assumed to be forty years, higher achieving workers are still replacing workers with initial levels of skills who are retiring. During this phase the additional growth in GDP per capita in year t due to the reform is given by

$$\Delta^t = growth\ coefficient * \Delta PISA * \frac{1}{working\ life} + \Delta^{t-1}. \qquad (7A.2)$$

Phase 3 (2051 to 2070): During this phase the first twenty labor market cohorts—who only partially profited from the education reform—are replaced by cohorts who profited from the fully enacted reform:

$$\Delta^t = growth\ coefficient * \Delta PISA * \frac{1}{working\ life} - \left(\Delta^{t-40} - \Delta^{t-41}\right) + \Delta^{t-1}. \qquad (7A.3)$$

Phase 4 (after 2070): Finally, the whole workforce has gone through the reformed education system. The annual growth rate is now increased by the constant long-run growth effect Δ:

$$\Delta = growth\ coefficient * \Delta PISA. \qquad (7A.4)$$

Cumulative Effects of the Reform

Without reform, the economy grows at the constant growth rate of potential GDP:

$$GDP^t_{no\ reform} = GDP^{t-1}_{no\ reform} * (1 + potential\ growth). \qquad (7A.5)$$

With reform, the annual growth rate is additionally increased by the growth effect Δ^t:

$$GDP^t_{reform} = GDP^{t-1}_{reform} * (1 + potential\ growth + \Delta^t). \qquad (7A.6)$$

In the neoclassical specification an additional term ensures the growth rate is negatively affected by the (log) level of GDP reached in the previous period. As a consequence the annual growth rate without and with reform will converge to the same rate of potential growth in the long run.

The total value of any reform is given by the sum of the discounted values of the annual differences between the GDP with reform and the GDP without reform:

Total value of the reform =

$$\sum_{t=2010}^{t=2090} \left(GDP^t_{reform} - GDP^t_{no\ reform}\right) * (1 + discount\ rate)^{-(t-2010)}. \qquad (7A.7)$$

In the baseline scenario the time horizon over which future returns are considered is the lifetime of a child born at the beginning of the reform, which equals the year 2090.

Appendix 7B: Sensitivity of Economic Projections

Table 7B.1
Projection results with neoclassical model specification

	Scenario I: Increase avg. performance by ¼ std. dev.		Scenario II: Bring each country to Finnish level of 546 points on PISA		Scenario III: Bring all to minimum of 400 points on PISA		Scenario II, Time horizon 2050		Scenario II, Time horizon 2150	
	Billion $	% GDP	Billion $	% GDP	Billion $	% GDP	Billion $	% GDP	Billion $	% GDP
	(1)	(2)	(3)	(4)	(5)	(6)	(7)	(8)	(9)	(10)
Australia	2,073	227%	1,656	182%	3,826	419%	276	30%	3,696	405%
Austria	712	212%	1,120	334%	1,471	438%	186	55%	2,511	748%
Belgium	926	221%	1,207	288%	2,334	557%	200	48%	2,711	647%
Canada	3,282	234%	2,227	159%	5,209	371%	368	26%	4,984	355%
Czech Rep.	781	271%	1,095	381%	1,631	567%	169	59%	2,570	893%
Denmark	435	206%	859	407%	869	412%	143	68%	1,932	916%
Finland	560	272%	0	0%	651	316%	0	0%	0	0%
France	5,026	221%	8,552	376%	11,090	488%	1,397	61%	19,389	853%
Germany	6,521	213%	12,466	408%	15,347	502%	2,049	67%	28,191	922%
Greece	671	185%	2,548	702%	1,459	402%	417	115%	5,837	1609%
Hungary	618	296%	1,322	632%	1,302	623%	193	93%	3,213	1538%
Iceland	25	204%	46	367%	46	371%	8	61%	102	819%
Ireland	386	190%	645	318%	643	317%	111	55%	1,417	698%

Italy	3,725	194%	12,330	644%	8,102	423%	2,011	105%	28,244	1474%
Japan	12,584	273%	2,772	60%	24,595	534%	442	10%	6,329	137%
Korea, Rep.	4,489	314%	839	59%	7,094	497%	128	9%	1,969	138%
Luxembourg	46	105%	144	330%	93	214%	29	66%	291	665%
Mexico	3,451	209%	24,773	1,504%	7,160	435%	3,583	217%	62,461	3791%
Netherlands	1,623	230%	1,082	154%	2,979	423%	180	26%	2,413	342%
New Zealand	360	288%	276	221%	790	632%	42	34%	646	516%
Norway	435	149%	985	337%	855	292%	181	62%	2,088	714%
Poland	2,192	298%	5,322	725%	4,651	633%	770	105%	13,051	1777%
Portugal	579	225%	2,099	816%	1,209	470%	323	126%	4,989	1940%
Slovak Republic	337	283%	749	630%	682	573%	111	93%	1,809	1519%
Spain	3,142	202%	8,281	531%	6,275	403%	1,359	87%	18,825	1208%
Sweden	784	209%	1,259	336%	1,542	412%	210	56%	2,818	753%
Switzerland	722	208%	831	239%	1,598	460%	141	41%	1,837	528%
Turkey	2,699	256%	15,474	1,467%	6,363	603%	2,162	205%	39,523	3747%
United Kingdom	5,504	231%	6,308	265%	10,918	459%	1,032	43%	14,243	599%
United States	25,344	167%	62,386	411%	56,407	371%	10,962	72%	135,962	895%
OECD	90,031	211%	179,655	421%	187,191	439%	29,183	68%	414,050	970%

Notes: Discounted value of future increases in GDP until 2090, expressed in billion $ (PPP) and as percentage of current GDP. See text for reform parameters. Authors' calculations.

Table 7B.2
Effects of alternative parameter assumptions on growth coefficients and time horizon (scenario II)

	Lowest coefficient		Highest coefficient		Lower bound confidence		Upper bound confidence		Time horizon 2050		Time horizon 2150	
	Billion $ (1)	% GDP (2)	Billion $ (3)	% GDP (4)	Billion $ (5)	% GDP (6)	Billion $ (7)	% GDP (8)	Billion $ (9)	% GDP (10)	Billion $ (11)	% GDP (12)
Australia	1,548	170%	2,217	243%	1,317	144%	2,899	318%	308	34%	5,805	636%
Austria	1,128	336%	1,641	489%	954	284%	2,182	650%	219	65%	4,555	1,357%
Belgium	1,163	278%	1,683	402%	986	235%	2,224	531%	227	54%	4,576	1,093%
Canada	2,022	144%	2,888	206%	1,722	123%	3,767	268%	404	29%	7,497	534%
Czech Rep.	862	299%	1,249	434%	730	254%	1,655	575%	168	58%	3,423	1,189%
Denmark	893	423%	1,310	621%	753	357%	1,757	833%	171	81%	3,750	1,778%
Finland	0	0%	0	0%	0	0%	0	0%	0	0%	0	0%
France	8,268	364%	12,065	531%	6,989	308%	16,083	708%	1,596	70%	33,815	1,488%
Germany	12,519	409%	18,348	600%	10,567	346%	24,569	803%	2,400	78%	52,262	1,709%
Greece	2,993	825%	4,558	1,256%	2,493	687%	6,354	1,751%	540	149%	15,071	4,153%
Hungary	957	458%	1,409	674%	807	386%	1,896	907%	182	87%	4,084	1,954%
Iceland	48	385%	70	563%	41	325%	94	753%	9	74%	198	1,591%
Ireland	725	357%	1,057	521%	613	302%	1,409	694%	140	69%	2,957	1,457%
Italy	13,726	717%	20,702	1,081%	11,473	599%	28,562	1,491%	2,516	131%	65,827	3,436%

Japan	2,145	47%	3,034	66%	1,833	40%	3,920	85%	436	9%	7,618	165%
Korea, Rep.	565	40%	799	56%	483	34%	1,031	72%	115	8%	2,000	140%
Luxembourg	299	685%	450	1,030%	250	573%	619	1417%	55	126%	1,415	3,238%
Mexico	26,267	1,594%	42,714	2,593%	21,416	1300%	63,912	3879%	4,306	261%	186,466	11,318%
Netherlands	996	141%	1,423	202%	849	120%	1,855	263%	199	28%	3,689	524%
New Zealand	204	163%	292	233%	173	139%	381	305%	41	32%	762	610%
Norway	1,425	487%	2,104	719%	1,200	410%	2,839	971%	270	92%	6,162	2,107%
Poland	3,829	521%	5,672	772%	3,221	438%	7,679	1045%	722	98%	16,813	2,289%
Portugal	2,018	785%	3,063	1,191%	1,684	655%	4,254	1654%	366	142%	9,983	3,882%
Slovak Rep.	568	477%	838	704%	478	402%	1,130	949%	108	91%	2,445	2,054%
Spain	8,845	568%	13,158	844%	7,428	477%	17,893	1148%	1,656	106%	39,653	2,544%
Sweden	1,285	343%	1,872	500%	1,087	290%	2,490	665%	249	66%	5,208	1,391%
Switzerland	852	245%	1,229	353%	723	208%	1,619	466%	168	48%	3,304	950%
Turkey	13,273	1,258%	20,994	1,990%	10,920	1035%	30,478	2889%	2,265	215%	81,227	7,700%
United Kingdom	5,804	244%	8,372	352%	4,926	207%	11,029	464%	1,141	48%	22,498	946%
United States	80,503	530%	119,336	785%	67,686	445%	161,693	1064%	15,155	100%	354,821	2,335%
OECD	195,731	459%	294,547	690%	163,804	384%	406,270	952%	36,131	85%	947,885	2,221%

Notes: Scenario II: Bring each country to Finnish level of 546 points on PISA. Discounted value of future increases in GDP until 2090, expressed in billion $ (PPP) and as percentage of current GDP. Authors' calculations.

Table 7B.3

Effects of alternative parameter assumptions on reform duration, working life, and discount rate (Scenario II)

	10-year reform		30-year reform		Working life 35 years		Discount rate 2.5%		Discount rate 3.5%		Discount rate Stern Review	
	Billion $ (1)	% GDP (2)	Billion $ (3)	% GDP (4)	Billion $ (5)	% GDP (6)	Billion $ (7)	% GDP (8)	Billion $ (9)	% GDP (10)	Billion $ (11)	% GDP (12)
Australia	2,541	279%	1,721	189%	2,287	251%	2,788	306%	1,581	173%	4,763	522%
Austria	1,887	562%	1,263	376%	1,694	504%	2,062	614%	1,165	347%	3,533	1,052%
Belgium	1,933	462%	1,299	310%	1,736	415%	2,115	505%	1,197	286%	3,621	865%
Canada	3,310	236%	2,246	160%	2,980	212%	3,633	259%	2,062	147%	6,204	442%
Czech Rep.	1,435	499%	963	335%	1,289	448%	1,570	545%	888	309%	2,689	934%
Denmark	1,508	715%	1,004	476%	1,352	641%	1,645	780%	928	440%	2,823	1,338%
Finland	0	0%	0	0%	0	0%	0	0%	0	0%	0	0%
France	13,875	610%	9,272	408%	12,449	548%	15,152	667%	8,559	377%	25,981	1,143%
Germany	21,116	691%	14,067	460%	18,934	619%	23,034	753%	13,000	425%	39,530	1,293%
Greece	5,279	1,455%	3,421	943%	4,705	1,296%	5,703	1,572%	3,193	880%	9,855	2,716%
Hungary	1,623	777%	1,078	516%	1,454	696%	1,768	846%	997	477%	3,037	1,453%
Iceland	81	648%	54	432%	72	581%	88	707%	50	399%	151	1,213%
Ireland	1,216	599%	813	401%	1,091	538%	1,328	654%	750	370%	2,277	1,122%
Italy	23,939	1,250%	15,624	816%	21,367	1,115%	25,926	1,353%	14,545	759%	44,724	2,335%

Japan	3,472	75%	2,372	52%	3,130	68%	3,820	83%	2,173	47%	6,510	141%
Korea, Rep.	914	64%	625	44%	824	58%	1,005	70%	572	40%	1,713	120%
Luxembourg	520	1,191%	340	779%	465	1,063%	564	1,290%	317	724%	972	2,225%
Mexico	50,015	3,036%	30,929	1,877%	44,093	2,676%	53,101	3,223%	29,371	1,783%	92,736	5,629%
Netherlands	1,630	231%	1,106	157%	1,468	208%	1,790	254%	1,016	144%	3,056	434%
New Zealand	334	267%	227	181%	301	241%	367	293%	208	166%	627	501%
Norway	2,425	829%	1,607	549%	2,172	742%	2,640	903%	1,488	509%	4,537	1,551%
Poland	6,539	890%	4,323	589%	5,854	797%	7,114	969%	4,006	545%	12,233	1,665%
Portugal	3,546	1,379%	2,304	896%	3,161	1,229%	3,834	1,491%	2,148	835%	6,621	2,575%
Slovak Rep.	965	811%	640	538%	865	726%	1,051	883%	593	498%	1,807	1,518%
Spain	15,180	974%	10,005	642%	13,579	871%	16,498	1,059%	9,282	596%	28,390	1,822%
Sweden	2,152	575%	1,440	385%	1,931	516%	2,351	628%	1,329	355%	4,030	1,076%
Switzerland	1,411	406%	951	273%	1,268	365%	1,545	444%	875	252%	2,643	760%
Turkey	24,470	2,320%	15,436	1,463%	21,672	2,055%	26,174	2,481%	14,550	1,379%	45,513	4,315%
United Kingdom	9,609	404%	6,475	272%	8,638	363%	10,523	442%	5,960	251%	18,005	757%
United States	137,603	906%	90,922	598%	123,157	811%	149,676	985%	84,272	555%	257,402	1,694%
OECD	340,528	798%	222,527	521%	303,987	712%	368,864	864%	207,075	485%	635,982	1,490%

Notes: Scenario II: Bring each country to Finnish level of 546 points on PISA. Discounted value of future increases in GDP until 2090, expressed in billion $ (PPP) and as percentage of current GDP. Authors' calculations.

8

Policies to Improve Knowledge Capital

Recent history clearly shows improvements in knowledge capital are possible and within the reach of nations. Improvement is not easy, as demonstrated by the concerted but failing efforts of a number of countries. Yet the world provides substantial evidence that schools can improve and student achievement can rise by meaningful amounts. In our earlier look at average long-run changes in performance (figure 4.1) we already saw that some countries had managed to make substantial improvements through the end of the twentieth century. Finland is a well-known example, but others succeeded as well.

We extend this previous figure for selected example countries by including in our analysis the most recent international tests until 2012 and by showing more fine-grained variation, thus highlighting some very different patterns that point toward important lessons (figure 8.1).[1] Performance in several countries has remained relatively stable over a long period of time—France, as well as (with slight upward trends) the United Kingdom and the United States stick out as examples. But we also see countries can make substantial improvements even over relatively short periods, as Germany has done over the past decade and as Japan—a top performer even beforehand—has accomplished over recent years. However, just wanting to improve—a goal professed by virtually every nation in the world—is not sufficient. Some nations, notably Norway during the 1990s and Sweden during the 2000s, have shown just the opposite movement. Others have improved, only to slip back down. Finland has in fact slipped visibly over the past few years from its outstanding performance.

Our overall interpretation of figure 8.1 is that education policy is not simply settled by a once-and-for-all decision. Effective policy requires continual attention, and improved performance cannot be presumed but requires regular analysis. Already a wide variety of specific policies have been implemented within various countries without much evidence of

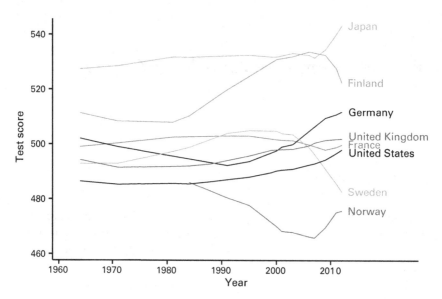

Figure 8.1

Long-run test score trends in selected countries, 1964 to 2012

Notes: Depiction of standardized data from international tests 1964 to 2003 combined with subsequently available tests to 2012, smoothing available test observations with locally weighted regressions. See note 1 to chapter 8 for details.

success in either achievement or economic terms. We believe these disappointing results generally reflect the pursuit of policies with little empirical support and no evaluation.

This chapter, drawing on relevant research and findings from a variety of sources, distills a few key conclusions concerning which broad sets of policies are promising and which are not. Indeed entire books have been written about the programs and approaches to which we draw attention here, so our intention is not to provide a detailed recipe. Instead, we wish to emphasize places where existing evidence offers support for broad policy actions, and to indicate where the evidence resides. Since much past policy action has not been very closely related to evidence on outcomes, the findings on a number of these topics stand in contrast to the policy prescriptions of many nations.

Since education is a public program in all countries, a generally appealing first-order policy for improvement is providing more public resources to the sector. Unfortunately, the evidence suggests simple resource policies have proved inconsistent and mostly ineffective (section 8.1)—a finding that, somewhat surprisingly, holds across the world, including developing countries, where available resources fall far below those in developed countries.

The existing evidence also suggests another caution: effective policies may differ by context. Particularly, some policies from developed countries, such as school autonomy, may not be equally effective in developing countries, and vice versa (section 8.2).

Available research points strongly to the essential role of high-quality teachers (section 8.3), and this evidence has clear implications for the nature of policies that are pursued. Because providing a description of the background and characteristics of effective teachers has proved highly elusive, the use of credentialing and regulations to ensure effective teachers shows little promise.

This conclusion, combined with available evidence, points to the general importance of focusing on incentives related to education outcomes, something best achieved by constructing the institutional structures of the education system to create this focus (section 8.4). While the precise details of teacher hiring, pay, and retention differ widely across nations, the evidence suggests that a general set of performance incentives is overall important. A number of education policies—notably, developing effective accountability systems, promoting choice and competition, and providing direct rewards for good performance—offer promise, supported by evidence. At the same time, just as we saw previously in terms of economic outcomes, focusing on the seemingly plausible proxies of school attendance and attainment yields disappointments in terms of student cognitive skills. The key thus is an unwavering focus on what the goal of policy is: improving student achievement.

The issues we have stressed so far in knowledge capital leave out one important dimension of education policy that is central to many countries: providing a more equitable distribution of outcomes. Just encouraging universal attendance has not been successful in expanding knowledge capital, but a variety of potentially equity-enhancing programs such as expanded preschool, delayed school tracking, and a focus on general curricula also have direct implications for overall knowledge capital in society (section 8.5). Equity may be complementary with improved performance, or it may present policy makers with a trade-off.

8.1   Resource and Input Policies

The most extensive, generally available evidence relates to the effects of resources in driving favorable outcomes. Overall, it indicates that simply providing more resources gives little assurance that student performance will improve significantly. Many policies undertaken by nations involve substantial flows of resources—in the form of direct spending, changes in teacher salaries, reductions in class size, and the like—made within the context of current school organization. The empirical evidence clearly documents the difficulties with such policies.

The easiest way to see the situation is to plot educational expenditure per student against educational achievement across countries. Again and again, such plots have shown no association between spending and outcomes across OECD countries.[2] Such a depiction can be affected by many factors, such as students' family backgrounds, that relate to both spending levels and educational outcome levels, however. Therefore, figure 8.2 plots the *change* in expenditure per student since 2000 against the *change* in the PISA reading score from 2000 to 2012 for all OECD countries

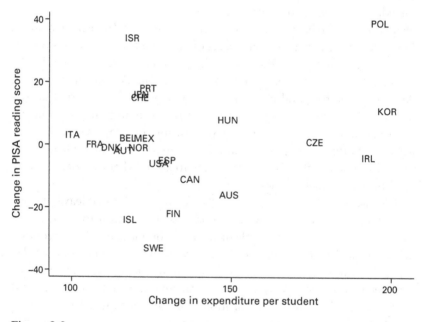

Figure 8.2

Changes in educational spending and in student achievement across countries

Notes: Scatter plot of the change in expenditure per student, 2000 to 2010 (constant prices, 2000 = 100), and the change in PISA reading score, 2000 to 2012. Authors' depiction based on data from Organisation for Economic Co-operation and Development (2013a, b). See table 2A.1 for country letter codes.

with available data. Such a depiction in changes is unaffected by cross-country differences in parental backgrounds, culture, and the like, to the extent that they have not changed significantly in a country. But, again, we see no indication whatsoever that the countries that have increased their spending the most would have seen achievement trajectories different from those without large spending increases.[3]

The underlying analyses of resources include studies within individual countries and across different countries and have been extensively reviewed elsewhere.[4] The available econometric evidence now includes hundreds of separate estimates within the United States and other developed countries. Quite uniformly, there is little evidence that *any* of the following factors has a consistently strong impact on achievement: the level of teacher education, the pupil–teacher ratio, characteristics of administration, or facilities of the school. To be sure, some individual studies show positive impacts of each of these on achievement, but the totality of evidence does not. Specifically, in aggregating results across studies, it is apparent that only a minority of estimates are statistically different from zero (at conventional levels), and those studies do not even uniformly indicate improvements in performance associated with increased resources. A second line of studies (which often do not reach the same methodological standards, though) focuses on financial inputs. Some studies simply relate spending per student to achievement or capture teacher differences by teacher salaries. These studies also fail to show a consistent relationship between financial resources and achievement.

Some of these results have been controversial,[5] especially those concerning class size reduction.[6] Long academic and policy disputes have centered on these findings, and indeed a variety of policy initiatives around the world have pursued added resource investments and reduced class sizes—but with few discernible improvements in achievement.

The current consensus is that focused policies beyond simple increases in resources are essential. A simplistic view of the results—convenient as a straw man in public debates—is that "money never matters." The research, of course, does not say that. Nor does it say that "money cannot matter." It simply underscores the fact that, historically, a set of decisions and incentives in schools has blunted any impacts of added funds, leading to inconsistent outcomes. From the available evidence, a consensus view has emerged: *how* money is spent is more important than *how much* money is spent.

Perhaps most surprising is that these general results hold equally for developing countries. It may be true, particularly with the rapid increases in spending in many developed countries, that diminishing marginal returns have set in. But many developing countries spend just a fraction of what is spent in more developed countries, and the results remain the same.[7]

The evidence on the potential impact of various resource strategies leads naturally to a consideration of incentives. Policies that mandate increases in overall resources or changes in specific resources have proved ineffective, suggesting that local circumstances strongly influence the results in terms of student outcomes. This finding also suggests that emphasizing incentives that are related to the desired outcomes rather than to how to achieve them may be more productive. We return to that below after first providing more context for the discussion.

8.2 Generalizing from Existing Evidence

Historically much of the research evidence for education policy has come from analyses in developed countries, which in turn have been heavily weighted toward studies of policies in the United States, with a frequent presumption that lessons from there can be relevant for other environments. More recently somewhat of a reversal has occurred in this source of evidence, as the rapid expansion of randomized controlled experiments in developing countries—where experimental costs generally are lower—has led to the possibility of bringing conclusions from developing country analyses to developed countries.[8]

Interpretative discussions suggest, however, that caution is needed, since some of the best strategies for improvement appear to interact with the level of development of the education system.[9] While this observation does not necessarily map directly onto the level of economic development because systemic performance differs significantly even within developed countries, it suggests the wholesale adoption of evidence across all systems may be inappropriate.

A closer look into the issues at hand is provided by the example of one policy that is frequently advocated in very different systems with very different structures for schools: permitting more autonomy or local educational decision-making. Decentralization of decision-making has been hotly debated in many countries, and prior research has left considerable uncertainty about the expected impact of allowing it.[10]

Our own analysis directly considers the interaction of autonomy and the institutional backdrop and can largely resolve the conflicting literature.[11] Our central findings are consistent with the interpretation that autonomy reforms improve student achievement in (economically and educationally) developed countries but undermine it in developing countries.

Autonomous decision-making introduces a fundamental tension. The prime argument favoring decentralization is that local decision makers have better understanding of the capacity of their schools and the demands that are placed on them by varying student populations. This knowledge in turn permits them to make better resource decisions, to improve the productivity of the schools, and to meet the varying demands of their local constituents. However, when divergent interests and asymmetric information are present in a decision-making area, agents have incentives and perhaps substantial opportunities to act in their own self-interest with little risk that such behavior will be noticed and sanctioned. In this case autonomy opens the possibility of opportunistic behavior, with negative outcomes.[12] Agents may use their greater autonomy to further goals other than advancing student achievement. Additionally the quality of decision-making may also be inferior at the local level when the technical capabilities of local decision makers to provide high-quality services are limited and when local communities lack the ability to ensure high-quality services.[13] Consequently the success of autonomy reforms may depend on the general level of human capital of the community, which affects the quality of parental monitoring.[14]

Our analysis points to the sensitivity of policies to local circumstances and raises cautions about how and when to generalize from individual microstudies to broader policy advice. The central findings from comparing outcomes of changes in the degree of local school decision-making across countries are consistent with a varying balance between the conflicting forces.[15] At low levels of economic development, increased autonomy, particularly in decision-making areas related to academic content, actually appears to hurt student outcomes. By contrast, in high-income countries, increased autonomy over academic content, personnel, and budgets exerts positive effects on achievement.[16]

This impact is shown pictorially in figure 8.3, which also shows that the entire effect of autonomous decisions is enhanced with external accountability, a complementary policy—providing more information on the outcomes of local decision-making through use of student test information for school accountability. In other words, local decision-making works better when there is also external accountability that limits any opportunistic behavior of schools.

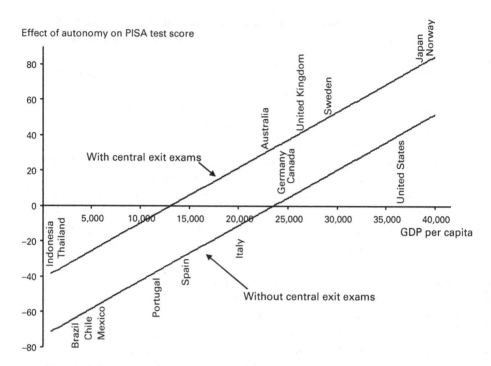

Figure 8.3

Effect of autonomy reforms on student achievement by level of development

Notes: Estimated effect of academic-content autonomy (scaled 0–1) on PISA math test score (scaled with standard deviation 100) depending on initial GDP per capita (in 2000) and on the existence of central exit exams, estimated in a panel model of PISA tests 2000 to 2009. Example countries illustrate initial level of GDP per capita. Own depiction based on Hanushek, Link, and Woessmann (2013: table 9).

The limited generalizability of findings may also be exemplified by the question of the age at which to place students into different school types—variously called tracking or streaming. As we discuss in more detail below, many studies from developed country contexts suggest early tracking may hurt students from disadvantaged backgrounds without improving the overall level of achievement. By contrast, a recent randomized evaluation study in Kenya found lower-achieving students particularly benefited from tracking because it allowed teachers to tailor instruction to their level of understanding.[17] Thus the effects of tracking may be quite opposite in settings with overly heterogeneous starting levels and generally overambitious curricula from those in more normal settings.[18]

We conclude that the impact of various incentives may vary dramatically with characteristics of the economy and the school system, and that different incentives may interact strongly. This conclusion, of course, heightens the importance of continually evaluating programs and policies within individual countries. When the precise policies that will enhance achievement are surrounded by uncertainty, there is little substitute for a program of continuing research and evaluation.

8.3   Teacher Quality

Current research suggests teacher quality is extraordinarily important and likely the most important factor in schools. The bulk of this evidence comes from developed countries and specifically the United States. But there is virtually no suggestion that the importance of quality teachers fails to generalize. Moreover the research on the determinants of teacher quality reinforces policy approaches built on expanded incentives, as described below.

The fundamental studies into teacher quality have tracked student achievement over time, concentrating on whether some teachers consistently produce more gains in achievement than others.[19] Working with extensive panel data on individual students from different US states, these studies have confirmed the existence of large differences among teachers in terms of outcomes in the classroom, after adjusting for differences in student preparation facing the teacher in the classroom. Although the work in this area, often called value-added analysis, is highly concentrated in the United States, consistency with other analyses suggests it may be generalized to elsewhere.[20]

The lessons from this research, if truly generalizable across countries, strongly conditions views on how to improve student outcomes. It turns out that easily quantifiable characteristics of teachers explain little of the variation in their effectiveness.[21] This has important implications for the development of policies designed to raise the quality of instruction and reduce unequal access to high-quality teachers. First, neither added teacher education nor additional years of experience past the initial year or two of teaching translate into significantly higher instructional effectiveness, bringing into question salary structures usually based on these variables. Second, descriptions of unequal access to high-quality teachers as measured by experience, education, certification, pedagogical training, professional development, or other quantifiable characteristics fail to portray accurately the actual differences in the quality of instruction across schools and students. Third, the failure of quantifiable characteristics to explain much of the variation in teacher effectiveness suggests that efforts to raise the quality of instruction through more stringent certification requirements for entering the profession may be misguided, particularly as they may discourage many people from becoming teachers by raising the cost of doing so.

Most important, the inability to identify specific teacher qualities associated with higher student achievement makes it difficult to regulate or legislate the presence of high-quality teachers in classrooms. Instead, it contributes to the general lesson that changes in the institutional structure and incentives of schools are fundamental to improving school outcomes.

8.4   Focusing Institutions and Incentives on Knowledge Outcomes

While being cautious about specific details, existing evidence suggests some clear general policies related to the institutional structure of school systems are important. Foremost, the performance of a system is affected by the incentives and disincentives actors receive. That is, if the actors in the education process are rewarded (extrinsically or intrinsically) for producing better student achievement, and if they are penalized for not producing high achievement, achievement is likely to improve. The incentives to produce high-quality education are in turn created by the institutions of the education system—the rules and regulations that explicitly or implicitly set rewards and penalties for the people involved in the education process.

When we look at incentive structures, three interrelated policies— some of which have already been exploited in our analyses in section 4.1—come to the forefront: developing an accountability system that identifies good school performance and leads to rewards based on it, promoting more competition so that parental demand will provide strong incentives to individual schools, and providing direct rewards for good performance. In our view, the impact of these incentive structures will, to a substantial extent, ultimately work through their effect on the quality of teaching.

School Accountability
Many countries have been moving toward increased accountability of local schools for student performance. It is difficult to imagine any

reform programs—whether based on autonomy, choice, direct performance rewards, or other concepts—working well without a good system of student testing, measurement, and accountability. Thus the ideas
about the various institutional structures are closely linked together,
since an accountability system provides for linking incentives to student
outcomes.

For example, the United Kingdom has developed an elaborate system
of "league tables" designed to give parents full information about the
performance of local schools. The United States has enacted a federal
law ("No Child Left Behind") requiring all states to have an accountability system that meets certain general guidelines. It also sets into law
a series of actions required when a school fails to bring all students up
to proficiency in core subjects. And more and more developing countries
have begun measuring student outcomes and introducing accountability
systems. Evidence on the impacts of these systems has begun to accumu-
late. The best US evidence indicates strong state accountability systems do
indeed lead to better student performance.[22]

Curriculum-based external exit exams are another means of introducing some form of accountability into school systems. They provide performance information that can hold both students and schools accountable.
Students in countries with external exit exam systems tend to outperform
systematically students in countries without them.[23] In Canada and Germany, in whose national education systems the use of external exams varies across regions, students similarly perform better in those regions that
have them.[24] As described above, external exit exams also interact with
local school autonomy by focusing local decision-making on improving
student outcomes.[25]

Choice and Competition

Promoting choice and competition with school vouchers was proposed a
half century ago by Milton Friedman (1962). The simple idea is that parents, interested in the schooling outcomes of their children, will seek out
productive schools, exerting demand-side pressure that creates incentives
for each school to produce effective education and ensure the presence of
high-quality staff in addition to good curricula.

In many school systems (with the Netherlands being the most obvious
example) privately managed schools with public funding provide alternatives for students. These schools, which often have religious affiliations,
are part of the national institutional framework. In cross-country comparisons, students in countries with larger shares of privately managed

schools perform better on average, and recent evidence corroborates the conclusion that this is due to a causal effect of private sector competition.[26]

The United States provides limited examples of private school choice, ranging from publicly funded school vouchers in Milwaukee, Cleveland, and Washington, DC, to privately financed voucher alternatives. Evaluations of these programs have generally shown that choice schools do at least as well as the regular public schools, if not better, and usually at substantially lower cost.[27] Similar positive results have been found for voucher-induced private school choice in India, for competition from publicly funded Catholic schools in Canada, and for competition from independent schools in Sweden.[28]

Perhaps most striking is the growth of low-cost private schools in developing countries. New, very inexpensive private schools have shown considerable effectiveness.[29] Evaluations have found these schools produce better student outcomes at a fraction of the cost of regular government schools.

Furthermore choice and competition are not restricted to private schooling. Depending on the circumstances, choice among public schools can also help focus attention on student outcomes.[30]

Direct Rewards

Another promising approach to improvement is aiming incentives directly at teachers. While convincing evidence on the effects of performance-related teacher pay is scarce, the more rigorous studies in terms of empirical identification tend to find a positive relationship between financial teacher incentives and student outcomes.[31]

Most evaluations of teacher performance pay systems nonetheless focus on whether existing teachers change their behavior—what is referred to as the "effort" margin. In other words, do existing teachers work harder or better because of the introduction of performance incentives? There are many reasons to believe, however, that the attraction of new teachers and the retention of the more effective teachers—the "selection" margin—are more important.[32] That is, does performance pay lead to a different group of teachers in schools? The importance of pay for selection is difficult to analyze because it generally involves considering longer-run incentives that are often at the aggregate level. For this, cross-country variation provides some indication that students perform better in countries that allow for teacher salaries to be adjusted based on teaching performance.[33]

Indirectly Focusing on Goals

The importance of incentives has been widely acknowledged, but their application has not always focused on the cognitive skills we emphasize here. The best example is efforts to encourage school attendance and attainment through the broad application of "demand-side" incentives. These are sets of incentives designed to work primarily through students and their families, as opposed to having an impact on the schools themselves.

Demand-side incentives are more commonly, but not exclusively, used in developing countries.[34] In more developed countries, the high rates of return to educational investments identified previously are often believed sufficient to motivate students and their parents. Such general market incentives may be muted in developing countries because of compressed market forces, lack of information, competing pressures, tighter credit constraints, and the like.[35]

The specific demand-side incentives that have received particular attention in developing countries involve monetary incentives (fee reduction and conditional cash transfers) and food and nutrition programs that are linked directly to school attendance. The programs examined have covered experiences in Latin America, South Asia, and sub-Saharan Africa. The conditional cash transfers, where payments are made to families if the student attends school, have been particularly broadly introduced and subjected to especially reliable analyses. The best known of these initiatives is the Progresa program in Mexico, but similar programs have been developed in Brazil, Columbia, and Nicaragua.[36]

Evaluations of these programs suggest conditional cash transfers have strong impacts on the outcome on which they are focused: school attendance.[37] Our previous evidence about economic impacts has, however, emphasized the role of cognitive skills over just school attendance and attainment. Clearly, getting students into schools is significantly different from getting them to learn something. Seat time, as we have seen, does not necessarily translate into the cognitive skills that have economic payoffs. And expanding the numbers of students in schools may even make it more difficult to mount effective programs.

Unfortunately, virtually all existing studies of demand-side programs have found that while attendance and school attainment increase, student achievement appears unaffected. The one exception was a Kenyan program that explicitly linked a scholarship for further schooling to the students' learning and knowledge.[38] In other words, incentives usually work to elicit the outcome they reward, but not necessarily different outcomes.

To improve student achievement, incentives must be linked directly to this outcome.

8.5   Equity in Knowledge Acquisition

Much of this book has focused on the average achievement of populations. As was clear when we looked at test score distributions in different countries in section 3.3, however, it is possible to arrive at a given average with quite different underlying distributions. Moreover we saw that growth benefits accrue not only from a strong group at the top of the skill distribution but also from a broad base of proficient workers at the lower end of the distribution.

Differences in the shape of the distribution are themselves the subject of policy concerns because, on equity grounds, no country wants to neglect the least skilled people in the economy. This concern is amplified when transmission of low skills is intergenerational—that is, when poorly educated parents tend to have poorly educated children, creating concerns of equality of opportunity. A fundamental issue in most policy discussions is that having a sizable population with low skills affects the distribution of income and well-being in society. Indeed some evidence, though not conclusive, shows that large variations in skills lead to large variations in incomes.[39]

As we read the available evidence, at least three policies have shown important repercussions for educational equity: those addressing early childhood education, the age of school tracking, and the type of curriculum (general versus vocational). Here we briefly discuss each in turn. Also discussed with respect to policy is the question of whether dealing with equity issues leads to a trade-off in terms of overall achievement levels—and thus in terms of overall long-run economic well-being. The evidence on whether or not trade-offs exist in terms of skill development in general is not well developed, but we can reach some clear conclusions on the three discussed policies.

Early Childhood Education

Increasingly, evidence suggests learning in the formative years before formal schooling is important for ultimate academic achievement. Consequently student achievement toward the end of compulsory schooling is related not only to features of the school system but also to preschool education.[40] This association appears both in data within developed and within developing countries and in international data.[41]

In the United States and likely many other countries, the quality of early education is closely related to the socioeconomic status of families. Upper-income families, either through education at home or formal preschool, prepare their children for entry into school better than those with lower incomes do. Thus the availability of preschool programs directly affects equity by influencing how well prepared children from more disadvantaged families are for entry to school. In line with this, the international data show equity in high school—as measured by a lower association between socioeconomic background and student achievement—is positively related to the duration of the preschool cycle and to preschool enrollment in a country (beyond an initial threshold of around 60 percent).[42]

As pointed out by James Heckman, another aspect to preschooling and preparation for school is one we discussed above: learning begets learning.[43] In other words, if children are well prepared for schooling, they will get more knowledge out of their time in school. The importance of this is that broadly providing preschool can serve equity objectives by ensuring better preparation of disadvantaged students while at the same time serving general objectives for knowledge production. Consequently, meeting equity objectives, especially through targeted preschool programs, appears to complement the production of more cognitive skills in the population. It is not a trade-off; it is reinforcing.

Tracking

Another institutional feature of education systems that has been discussed mostly in terms of the equity of student outcomes is tracking. Here tracking is meant to refer to the placement of students into different school types, hierarchically structured by (apparent) performance.[44] Besides being called tracking, such school placement policies are variously referred to as streaming, ability grouping, or selective (as opposed to comprehensive) schooling.

From a theoretical viewpoint, the effects of educational tracking are controversial. Depending on the nature of peer effects assumed, homogeneous classes may contribute to optimal learning situations for all students through focused curricula and adequate progress, or weaker groups may be systematically disadvantaged if they are separated from the stronger students early on.

Countries differ widely in the age at which they first track children into different types of schools. In most OECD countries, tracking takes place at the age of fifteen or sixteen, with no tracking until grade 9 or 10.

In contrast, countries such as Germany and Austria undertake the first tracking at the age of ten.

In simplest terms, the earlier the tracking in a country, the greater will be the impact of family background, simply because the relative time spent with parents as opposed to in school changes with the age when the decision between high- and low-track schools is made. In line with this, evidence from tracking reforms in Sweden and Finland, as well as additional evidence from the Netherlands and Germany, suggests that postponing school tracking increases equity without significant adverse effects on the average level of achievement.[45]

Very similar results emerge in cross-country analyses, which show that early tracking leads to increases in inequality of student achievement.[46] Results on achievement levels are less clear, but little overall evidence indicates early tracking increases achievement. To the contrary, some evidence suggests a negative effect of early tracking on the average achievement level. This finding holds even at the top extreme of the distribution. Moreover studies of the impact of families on achievement and earnings have suggested postponing the age of tracking lessens the impact of parents on students' achievement and subsequent earnings across the OECD countries.[47] Thus, again, neither the national nor international evidence on the impact of tracking suggests a trade-off between equity and high overall achievement levels.

Vocational versus General Curricula

A third policy concern discussed here is the extent to which curricula should be more general and academically oriented or more vocational and oriented toward skills required in specific jobs. The subject of general versus vocational education is seldom linked to either the equity or growth concerns, but we argue these linkages should receive more attention.

Conceptually, the topic of curricula is quite different from that of age of tracking: both early and late tracking can involve differently paced general curricula or differentiation between general and vocational curricula. In practice, truly vocational curricula will usually not be introduced before grades 10 or 11, so the curricular focus is quite independent of whether or not the lower secondary school system is tracked between grades 4 and 10. Still, in practice, the two are often linked, as different schools effectively offer different content and breadth of curriculum.

Most advanced economies are concerned about the ease with which young workers can make the transition from school to work. The unemployment rate for youth invariably exceeds that for the economy as a whole, contributing to a variety of social problems. One appealing way to deal with these transition problems is to link students more closely to jobs through vocational education programs and apprenticeships with firms.[48] Moreover, in developing countries, vocational education has the appeal of getting youth prepared to work in more modern production by generating the skills immediately needed.

Countries have actually adopted schooling structures that differ fundamentally in their focus on the job transition. The United States, for example, has largely eliminated vocational education as a separate track in secondary schools based on the implicit arguments that specific skills become obsolete too quickly and that people need to be given the ability to adapt to new technologies. However, many European and developing countries, led by Germany with its "dual system," provide extensive vocational education and training at the secondary level—sometimes with direct involvement of industry through apprenticeships.

These differing perspectives suggest a possible trade-off between short-term and long-term costs and benefits for both individuals and the entire society: the skills generated by vocational education may facilitate the transition into the labor market, but they may later on become obsolete at a faster rate. Even though most of the general versus vocational education debate has centered on whether vocational education is effective in facilitating the school-to-work transition for youth, existing studies have not found a universal advantage of vocational over academic education for young people's labor market outcomes even at job entry.[49] What is more, rapid technological and structural change may make it harder for workers at older ages to stay employed or get reemployed if their acquired skills are focused on occupations for which demand in the labor market has declined. Our empirical analysis in fact suggests clear losses in employment later in the life cycle may result if those with vocational education find it difficult to adjust to the changed technologies that come with economic growth.[50]

As vocational programs tend to cater to the lower end of the achievement spectrum, this creates further concerns about the long-run impacts on equity. Additionally, from an intergenerational perspective—possibly related in part to early tracking—education type is typically linked to family background: children from more disadvantaged families tend to end up in the vocational programs and those from more advantaged families in the general programs.

This individual labor market argument is related to the macroeconomic perspective of Krueger and Kumar (2004a, b), who argued that the propensity to use vocational rather than general education may be an underlying cause of growth rate differentials between the United States and Europe. This argument suggests that in economies with rapid technological and structural change that makes occupation-specific skills obsolete at a faster rate, growth might not be enhanced by favoring vocational over more general curricula.[51] In such a setting, focusing on basic general skills—as before—does not present a trade-off between equity and efficiency; rather, when it comes to the appropriate scale of the curriculum, there is a complementarity between meeting equity and growth objectives in the long run.

8.6   Conclusions on Improving Knowledge Capital

Improving educational outcomes is not a straightforward task. The evidence shows the most expensive policies—those that add resources on the input side—are generally highly ineffective. We ended the previous chapter with a discussion of how the benefits from improving achievement dwarf even radical changes in the spending of nations on their schools, but in a very real sense this calculation might encourage the wrong debates and policy deliberations.

The evidence we have reviewed indicates the most effective policies are ones that establish institutions focusing incentives on student outcomes. Most of these entail few additional resources in the long run. The costs of the suggested institutional changes appear to be mainly transition costs—the expenses of training people (including parents) in new systems, developing testing and monitoring systems, covering short-run duplicate expenditures from the introduction of new schools coupled with potential semi-fixed costs of old schools, and so forth. For sure, recruiting and retaining better teachers may involve higher salaries and added expenses, as might expanding a high-quality early childhood education sector. But, as shown before, the benefits of improvement are sufficient to pay easily the costs even of aggressive reforms—if these reforms are successful.

Of course, change carries political costs as well, not least because some current school personnel will not like any significant change in incentives. But politicians must accurately assess the implications of not changing against the well-being of current and future members of society.

In many ways this entire book is about the economic costs of *not* reforming the education system. It has a very simple message:

• In the long run, a nation's prosperity is directly related to the skills of its population.

• The relevant cognitive skills—what we call the knowledge capital of a nation—can be measured well by performance on international math and science assessments.

• As demonstrated by historical experience, relatively modest improvements in skills can be worth multiples of a country's current GDP.

• Reform is possible even if difficult.

• The most productive reform involves aligning incentives with achievement through better educational institutions.

• Nations that successfully reform will systematically pull away in economic terms from those that do not.

In short, to us the evidence points unwaveringly toward a unified theory of long-run growth based on the knowledge capital of nations.

Notes

Chapter 1

1. See Petty ([1676] 1899) and the broader account of the history of human capital by Kiker (1966, 1968).

2. See Easterly (2001) and Pritchett (2006) for examples.

3. See, for example, World Bank (1993), Fernández-Arias, Manuelli, and Blyde (2005), and Spence and Leipziger (2010).

4. Unfortunately, we have no comparable data on skills for South Asian countries, so we cannot say much about this region. The only South Asian country included in our country growth analyses is India, and if India were added to the regional picture of figure 1.1, it would fall directly on the line, as well.

5. See table 1A.1 in appendix 1A. Japan was significantly ahead of the rest of the East Asian region, but its exclusion does not change the regional ordering.

6. Even there we have a mystery in that Latin America has had considerably higher levels of school attainment than sub-Saharan Africa. While the recent growth spurt in Latin America might represent a turnaround, it may also simply be a short-run advance emanating from a commodity boom. The reality will not be confirmed for some time.

7. See, for example, Fernández-Arias, Manuelli, and Blyde (2005) and Edwards, Esquivel, and Márquez (2007). Cole et al. (2005) stated unequivocally that "Latin America's TFP [total factor productivity] gap is not plausibly accounted for by human capital differences" (69). Similarly, in a recent high-level forum on the puzzle of Mexico's disappointing growth performance, schooling got only a side mention (Hanson 2010) or no mention at all (Kehoe and Ruhl 2010).

8. Regional data come from averaging all countries in a region that have available data. The fifty countries in our analysis are not chosen to be representative but instead are exhaustive of countries that participated in international tests and for which the requisite economic data are available. Still, table 1A.1 in appendix 1A shows the average 1960 incomes for all countries in each region to be quite similar to those for our subset of countries. The division of Europe into three regions illustrates the heterogeneity within European countries, but a combined Europe also falls on the line in figure 1.1.

9. The R^2 of the underlying regression is 0.92.

10. The growth rates here, and throughout this book, refer to growth in GDP *per capita*, as opposed to growth in the total GDP of a country, which includes growth in population. Also all growth rates refer to growth in *real* rather than nominal GDP—that is, inflation is taken out so that one dollar buys the same amount of goods and services at any time.

11. This estimate is based on a comparison of future growth of 2 percent as opposed to 1.5 percent over the next fifty years, discounted at a rate of 3 percent per year; see chapter 7 for details on parameter choices for the projection model.

12. See, for example, North (1990) and Acemoglu and Robinson (2012) on the importance of economic institutions.

13. For example, Shanghai outperformed all other sixty-five participating jurisdictions by a wide margin when it first participated in an international student achievement test in math, science, and reading in 2009, and it did so again in 2012 (Organisation for Economic Co-operation and Development 2010b, 2013b).

Chapter 2

1. For introductions see, for example, Acemoglu (2009), Aghion and Howitt (1998, 2009), Barro and Sala-i-Martin (2004), and Jones and Vollrath (2013).

2. The exposition of this section draws mostly on a 2008 study by Hanushek and Woessmann, which provides additional details.

3. The form of this relationship, as noted above, has been the subject of considerable debate and controversy. As we write it, it can be consistent with both basic endogenous and neoclassical growth models. We include the initial income levels in our estimation. This allows for conditional convergence in the empirical specifications, and the parameters estimated in chapter 3 suggest very long transitional periods from any perturbations off a balanced growth path. We generally cannot adequately distinguish among alternative forms of the underlying growth process within our limited period for observing growth rates. When considering the growth implications of various policy changes in chapter 7, however, we can investigate directly the sensitivity of GDP projections to the alternative models.

4. His analysis, originally based on the United States, has been replicated across more than a hundred countries; see Psacharopoulos and Patrinos (2004) and Montegro and Patrinos (2014).

5. More precisely, the measure most commonly used in more recent analyses is average years of schooling among the working-age population, usually defined as those ages fifteen years and over, instead of the actual labor force.

6. See, for example, Barro (1991), Mankiw, Romer, and Weil (1992), and Levine and Renelt (1992). Some even earlier work—for example, Azariadis and Drazen (1990) and Romer (1990b)—used adult literacy rates, but coverage for different countries and the quality of the data were questioned. See Woessmann (2003b) for a survey of measurement and specification issues from early growth accounting to cross-country growth regressions. Historically, data on enrollment rates

reflect gross enrollment. When thought of as the flow of schooling for a population, they are subject to measurement problems due to delayed entry into school, grade retention, and changes in cohort size. Furthermore, while more accurate net enrollment rates capture the flow of schooling for the young population, the net flow for the labor force would also consider the schooling levels of those retiring and leaving the labor force.

7. See Lau, Jamison, and Louat (1991) and Nehru, Swanson, and Dubey (1995). Benhabib and Spiegel (1994) use measures of years of schooling extrapolated from enrollment rates based on regression analyses.

8. The data on school attainment have been further updated and revised; see Cohen and Soto (2007) and Barro and Lee (2001, 2013). Appendix 3A shows, however, that using the most recent attainment data leaves our results unchanged.

9. Temple and Woessmann (2006) showed that the significantly positive effect of education found by Mankiw, Romer, and Weil (1992) does not depend on their often criticized use of an education flow measure based on enrollment rates. It is replicated in their model when using years of schooling as a measure of the level of human capital.

10. For extensive reviews of the literature, see, for example, Topel (1999), Temple (2001), Krueger and Lindahl (2001), and Sianesi and Van Reenen (2003). See Delgado, Henderson, and Parmeter (2014) for a list of recent research in their table 1, as well as evidence suggesting that the link between years of schooling and growth may not prove robust in nonparametric analyses, whereas the link between cognitive skills and growth does. Gennaioli et al. (2013) found years of schooling paramount in accounting for differences in regional development across more than 1,500 subnational regions in 110 countries.

11. As discussed below, one line of investigation has been the impact of mismeasurement of the quantity of education on the estimation of growth models. The Cohen and Soto (2007) data improved upon the original quantity data by Barro and Lee (1993, 2001). Jamison, Jamison, and Hanushek (2007) supplemented the Cohen and Soto attainment series with imputed data based on the Barro and Lee series to expand the number of countries available for the growth analysis. This approach adds eight countries to the analysis.

12. Our estimates rely on version 6.1 of the Penn World Tables. Using more recent versions does not affect our conclusions (see appendix 3A). Hanousek, Hajkova, and Filer (2008) argued that growth rates are better calculated using the International Monetary Fund (IMF) International Finance Statistics. Again, our results are not significantly affected by using these alternative growth measures.

13. Called an added-variable plot, this graph shows the association between two variables after the influences of other control variables are taken out. Thus both variables in figure 2.1 are first regressed on the other controls (in this case, initial GDP per capita). Only the residuals of these regressions, which comprise the part of the variation in the two variables that cannot be accounted for by the controls, are used in the graph. Thus the graph makes sure the depicted association between the two variables is not driven by the control variables. The procedure is numerically equivalent to including the other controls in a multivariate regression

of the dependent variable (growth) on the independent variable under consideration in the graph. Note that subsequent analyses and plots of the results use a subset of countries for which we also have measures of cognitive skills.

14. See Krueger and Lindahl (2001) for a discussion of measurement error in school attainment.

15. If the omitted variables were uncorrelated with school attainment—an unlikely event—no bias would be introduced.

16. We are most concerned about the direct comparisons of achievement across countries, but these issues also enter into the estimation of earnings differences within countries. For a discussion of those issues, see Hanushek et al. (2015).

17. Some researchers have suggested test scores be thought of as a measure of school quality (q), leading to use of test scores times years of schooling as a measure of H, but this ignores the influence of family factors and other elements of equation (2.2) that have been shown to be very important in determining cognitive skills.

18. Some recent work has introduced the possibility that noncognitive skills also enter into individual economic outcomes—see, for example, Bowles, Gintis, and Osborne (2001), Heckman, Stixrud, and Urzua (2006), Cunha et al. (2006), Borghans et al. (2008), Almlund et al. (2011), and Lindqvist and Vestman (2011). Hanushek and Woessmann (2008) integrated noncognitive skills into the interpretation of general models such as the one described here and showed how this might affect the interpretation of the parameter on school attainment and other estimates. While no agreed-upon measures of noncognitive skills exist, at the aggregate level they may well be incorporated in "cultural differences," something we address in the analysis below.

19. Just as in the cross-country growth analyses described in this chapter, human capital is often proxied by quantity of schooling in within-country analyses. This is necessitated in part by what data are commonly available but justified in part by the idea that, in a given country, differences in knowledge among levels of schooling are greater than those within levels of schooling. This assumption is, however, open to question; see Hanushek et al. (2015).

20. See the "Brief History of IEA: 50 Years of Educational Research" at http://www.iea.nl/brief_history.html (accessed April 22, 2014). The exposition in this subsection is an updated version of material by Hanushek and Woessmann (2011a).

21. At the same time a number of more idiosyncratic tests have been developed, some on a regional basis. More varied in their focus, development, and quality than the IEA and OECD tests, they have, in general, been used much less frequently in analytical work. Of the ten additional testing occasions through 2010, six involved regional tests for Latin America (ECIEL, LLECE, SERCE) and Africa (SACMEQ I and II, PASEC). As discussed later in appendix 2A and chapter 5, the IEA and OECD tests may be too difficult for many students in the developing countries of these regions and thus provide unreliable information about performance variations; the regional examinations are more appropriate to these countries. Hanushek and Woessmann (2011a) provided basic information on these

assessments, and we incorporate the Latin American tests into our analysis in chapter 5. The remaining portion of this chapter concentrates on information from the IEA and OECD tests.

22. A separate analysis of coverage and testing is provided by Neidorf et al. (2006).

23. Some other studies, of foreign languages, civic education, and information technology, have also been conducted. These have involved smaller samples of countries and, in general, have not been repeated. We do not include them in our discussions, in part because they have seldom been analyzed.

24. The Second International Mathematics Study (SIMS) of the IEA had a one-year follow-up of individual students that permitted the collection of some longitudinal panel information, but this design was not repeated. Recent innovations have permitted development of panel data by individual countries; see, for example, Brunello and Rocco (2013) and Hanushek, Link, and Woessmann (2013). Recently some countries have experimented with following students tested in PISA in order to develop panel data for individuals with expanded outcomes.

25. See Mullis, Martin, Foy, and Drucker (2012), Mullis, Martin, Foy, and Arora (2012), and the Organisation for Economic Co-operation and Development (2013b) for details on the most recent of the three major ongoing international testing cycles.

26. See also Brown et al. (2007).

27. The same PISA assessments were given (to different sets of countries) in 2000 and 2002, leading us to refer to this as a single assessment—PISA 2000/02. The consistency of tests at the country level also carries over to other international assessments. The curriculum-based student tests of TIMSS and the practical examinations of the International Adult Literacy Survey (IALS) are also highly correlated at the country level (Hanushek and Zhang 2009).

28. This subsection, together with appendix 2A, draws directly on Hanushek and Woessmann (2012a).

29. The reliance on student-based measures of skills also makes clear why panel data estimation of growth models cannot be employed, even though tests are spread across almost four decades for some nations. Any panel study would require measuring the cognitive skills of the labor force at different points in time, which is not possible with the sporadic measurement of student skills. The possibility of panel estimation across countries has been suggested by the International Adult Literacy Survey (IALS) because it has tested adults rather than students (see Coulombe and Tremblay 2006; a more recent survey of adults is also available through the Programme of International Assessment of Adult Competencies [PIAAC] of the OECD). Nonetheless, such analysis requires very strong assumptions about the mapping of observed age patterns of skills onto changes in labor force skills over time. Furthermore most of the variance in growth and in test scores is found across countries, not across time within individual countries, suggesting that panel data do not deal effectively with the most acute identification and estimation issues in growth analysis.

30. The measures developed here extend earlier work by Hanushek and Kimko (2000) by adding new international tests, more countries, and intertemporal and within-country dimensions. They also deal with a set of problems that remained with the earlier calculations. Appendix 2A assesses the importance for growth modeling of the differences in the earlier measures and those developed here.

31. Ours is not the only approach to comparing international differences in achievement or attempt to do so. Lee and Barro (2001) developed an alternative early test score series for a cross-section of countries, and Barro (2001) applied it to growth models. Angrist, Patrinos, and Schlotter (2013) recently used the proposed method by Altinok and Murseli (2007) to develop a new and expanded panel data set for countries.

32. The development of aggregate scores by Hanushek and Kimko (2000) and by Barro (2001) assumed the test variances across assessments were constant, but there is no reason for this to be the case. Our approach is in the spirit of Gundlach, Woessmann, and Gmelin (2001).

33. The problems are potentially more severe with the earliest tests, but the reported information for them is insufficient for any analysis.

34. As identified in the regional growth picture of figure 1.1, the commonwealth OECD group includes developed countries that were formerly British colonies: Australia, Canada, New Zealand, and United States.

35. In the figure, years of schooling again come from the extended version of the Cohen and Soto (2007) data. For seven countries without attainment data in this database, we use data from Barro and Lee (2013), projected onto the Cohen and Soto (2007) scale by a simple linear regression among the countries with available attainment data from both sources.

36. This perspective builds on the insightful views of Nelson and Phelps (1966), Welch (1970), Schultz (1975), and Galor and Moav (2000).

37. Note that recent PISA and TIMSS assessments have been designed to be linked through standard psychometric approaches of using overlapping test items. As noted below, we make use of this linkage for some purposes such as putting together the long run trends in tests portrayed in figure 8.1.

38. The recent scaling efforts do not, however, provide any benchmarks across the two testing regimes or links with earlier testing.

39. Note that changes in NAEP testing make it difficult to use this methodology for the more recent PISA and TIMSS assessments, but it also is not crucial. On the one hand, the NAEP science tests were revised in 2009, and the new scale that was used made the data incomparable to prior years. On the other hand, recent PISA and TIMSS assessments have been designed to provide comparability of the subject surveys over time, just what was gained from the NAEP tests.

40. The standard deviations of the NAEP tests in math and science between 1977/78 and 1996 and in reading between 1984 and 1996 are reported in US Department of Education (2008). Since no standard deviation information is available for the NAEP tests preceding these and for the 1999 tests and since the available standard deviations are relatively stable over time, we take a simple

mean of the available standard deviation in each subject at each age level over time. PISA tested only fifteen-year-olds, but it has the same three subjects as the NAEP test.

41. The OSG countries are Austria, Belgium, Canada, Denmark, France, Germany, Iceland, Japan, Norway, Sweden, Switzerland, United Kingdom, and United States. The Netherlands also meets both criteria but does not have the internationally comparable PISA 2000 data we require for our standardization.

42. The sources of the underlying international test data are Beaton, Martin, et al. (1996), Beaton, Mullis, et al. (1996), Lee and Barro (2001), Martin et al. (1997), Martin et al. (2000), Martin et al. (2004), Mullis et al. (1997, 1998), Mullis et al. (2000), Mullis et al. (2003), Mullis et al. (2004), Organisation for Economic Co-operation and Development (2001, 2003b, 2004), and authors' calculations, based on the microdata of the early tests.

43. Twenty-five of the total seventy-seven countries with cognitive skill data are not included in the growth database due to lack of data on economic output or because they drop out of the sample for a standard exclusion criterion in growth analyses. These comprise fifteen former Communist countries, three countries for which oil production is the dominant industry, two small countries, three newly created countries, and two countries lacking early output data. In addition, two strong outliers, Nigeria and Botswana, are excluded in most models (see chapter 3).

44. As noted in chapter 3, direct estimation of the impacts of school selectivity and test exclusions on our growth models confirms potential testing problems do not bias our growth estimation (appendix 3B).

45. Hanushek and Kimko (2000) actually had alternative measures. Two of their three measures assumed a constant mean for all the tests, similar to what was done by Lee and Barro (2001).

46. While this indicates the intercept could be interpreted as the earnings with no schooling, in any actual empirical application the estimation samples generally consider those with at least a few years of primary schooling because the forgone earnings at no schooling are not really observed in the data. Furthermore the return parameter, r, is frequently estimated to differ by level of schooling—primary, secondary, and tertiary.

Chapter 3

1. For a sense of the instability surrounding early empirical analyses, see the early evaluations by Levine and Renelt (1992) and Levine and Zervos (1993).

2. See Organisation for Economic Co-operation and Development (2013b) and section 4.2 below, respectively.

3. See, for example, the overviews and discussions by Engerman and Sokoloff (2012) and by Acemoglu, Johnson, and Robinson (2005) and Acemoglu and Robinson (2012).

4. This chapter draws directly on Hanushek and Woessmann (2012a).

5. Contributions include, among others, studies by Barro (2001), Woessmann (2003b), Bosworth and Collins (2003), and Ciccone and Papaioannou (2009), which are discussed in detail by Hanushek and Woessmann (2011a). A recent addition is by Kaarsen (2014).

6. Because we need comparable data on economic growth over the 1960 to 2000 period, all former Communist countries are eliminated even if they have test measures. Furthermore four countries with cognitive skill data are missing a few years of economic data at the beginning or end of the period. Data for Tunisia start in 1961, while those for Cyprus and Singapore end in 1996, and those for Taiwan end in 1998. We include these countries in the growth regressions by estimating average annual growth over the available thirty-six- to thirty-nine-year period. Appendix 2A provides details on the country sample, and table 3D.1 in appendix 3D provides descriptive statistics.

7. While not the focal point of this analysis, all specifications include GDP per capita in 1960, which provides consistent evidence for conditional convergence—that is, countries with lower initial income tend to grow faster. Note that the growth impact of one year of schooling in the simplest model for our fifty-country sample (0.4) is less than that found for the ninety-three-country sample (0.6) underlying figure 2.1.

8. For ease of exposition and interpretation, we use a simple linear form of the relationship between our test-score measure and the rate of economic growth here. In chapter 5 we return to the issue of which functional form best describes this relationship.

9. A variety of people have placed extra weight on tertiary education (e.g., see Ehrlich 2007). Without building on strong basic skills, however, such investment appears to have little extra value. We investigate this topic further in chapter 6. Our analysis across both developed and developing countries finds tertiary education has little added value in explaining economic growth after consideration of cognitive skills, with the exception that US investments in higher education have signaled increased growth. The difficulty is that identifying the impact of higher education as opposed to other unmeasured determinants of economic growth in the United States is impossible.

10. This effect is equivalent to one percentage point per country-level standard deviation, thus making it virtually identical to the more limited estimates in Hanushek and Kimko (2000).

11. The specific robust regression technique reported is Stata's *rreg* command, which eliminates gross outliers with Cook's distance measure greater than one and iteratively down-weights observations with large absolute residuals. The OLS estimate of the test score effect in the fifty-two-country sample is 1.752 (*t*-statistic 5.75). Nigeria and Botswana each participated in only a single international test.

12. See, for example, Lucas (1988), Romer (1990a), and Jones (2005).

13. See, for example, Mankiw, Romer, and Weil (1992).

14. Note that the OECD division is based on the thirty countries that were members before the OECD expansion in 2010.

15. While not shown, the school attainment measures are insignificantly related to growth even among the developing countries, where schooling levels are low and cross-country variance is considerable.

16. Another way to analyze differential returns to average skills is to estimate quantile regressions. From quantile regression estimates in 5 percent steps of the effect of average test scores for percentiles of the growth distribution, it is evident that the effect is relatively constant across the whole distribution of growth residuals (see details in the working paper version of Hanushek and Woessmann 2011b). In fact all quantile regression point estimates fall within standard confidence intervals around the OLS estimate.

17. See, for example, World Bank (1993).

18. See, for example, Murnane, Willett, and Levy (1995), Katz and Autor (1999), and Goldin and Katz (2008).

19. Results using only test scores that predate the analyzed growth period are also robust when combined with our other robustness checks pursued in table 3.1 (not shown).

20. See, for example, Hanushek (2002) and Woessmann (2007a).

21. Appendix 3C discusses models that use IQ measures to assess cognitive skills.

22. For a discussion of the robustness of this approach, see Albouy (2012) and Acemoglu, Johnson, and Robinson (2012). See also Engerman and Sokoloff (2012) on different results from common colonial roots.

23. The measure of openness is the Sachs and Warner (1995) index reflecting the fraction of years between 1960 and 1998 in which a country is classified as having an economy open to international trade based on five factors, including tariffs, quotas, exchange rate controls, export controls, and whether or not its economy is socialist. Following Acemoglu, Johnson, and Robinson (2001), the measure of security of property rights is an index of the protection against expropriation risk, averaged over 1985 to 1995, from Political Risk Services, a private company that assesses the risk of investments being expropriated in different countries. Note that data limitations reduce the sample from fifty countries to forty-seven.

24. To facilitate interpretation, the test score variable is centered in the specifications that include interactions with institutions.

25. Similarly Jamison, Jamison, and Hanushek (2007) found the impact of cognitive skills on technical progress strong in countries with open trade regimes and essentially zero in closed economies.

26. This interaction between skills and openness of the economy is robust to including the measure of protection against expropriation (not shown). We find a similar positive interaction effect between test scores and openness when we specify openness as a dummy for countries that have been closed for the majority of the time (openness below 0.3).

27. To depict both ends of the distribution, we calculate the share of students reaching a basic level of literacy in the different subjects, equivalent to 400 test score points on the PISA scale, and the share reaching a top performance level, equivalent to 600 PISA test score points. We use the transformations described

in chapter 2 to translate these two thresholds into the specific metric of each separate international assessment. Using the microdata of each test, we then calculate the share of students in each country reaching the thresholds in the overall distribution of the test. The information from the different tests is again combined by taking a simple average of the shares across tests. Unfortunately, the microdata from the FIMS test do not seem to be accessible anymore, so the distributional measures draw only on the remaining international student achievement tests.

28. In fact the standard deviation in test scores does not enter our basic model significantly (in models including the mean). See Castelló and Doménech (2002) for related analyses using measures of educational inequality based on years of schooling.

29. In the joint model, the two measures are separately significant, even though they are highly correlated across countries with a simple correlation of $r = 0.73$. The mean test score used in our previous models is more highly correlated with the basic literacy share ($r = 0.96$) than the top-performing share ($r = 0.85$). If the mean test score is added to column 3, the basic literacy share becomes insignificant, but in a specification with just the mean, the mean and top-performing shares both remain significant.

30. For an alternative model of imitation and innovation that emphasizes the innovation margin, see Vandenbussche, Aghion, and Meghir (2006) and Aghion et al. (2009), as well as section 6.3. These studies, however, focused just on developed countries and missed the role of rocket scientists in the transmission of technologies to developing countries. Hanushek and Woessmann (2011b) showed that differences in basic skills are more important than differences in advanced skills in explaining growth differences among just the OECD countries.

31. The issue of skill complementarity in production has been addressed in explaining the pattern of earnings inequality. The US analysis of Autor, Katz, and Kearney (2006, 2008) suggested high-skilled workers and low-skilled workers are complements, a result that helps explain income variations across the educational spectrum.

32. As noted in section 2.2, calculation of growth rates relying on national account data rather than purchasing power parity incomes does not significantly affect our estimates.

33. This appendix draws directly on Hanushek and Woessmann (2011c). The working paper version of Hanushek and Woessmann (2011c) provides additional results, literature references and data sources, and evidence that sample selectivity also does not affect results of typical international education production functions.

34. See Organisation for Economic Co-operation and Development (2007).

35. Note, however, that, as reported in appendix 2A, changes in enrollment rates over longer periods of time are uncorrelated with trends in test scores.

36. This appendix draws directly on Hanushek and Woessmann (2011a).

37. From the policy side, it would also suggest that the growth problem is largely intractable if growth is driven by largely heritable differences in IQ. Lynn and

Vanhanen (2002: 183) conclude "the results of our study imply that it will be impossible to eradicate the gap between rich and poor nations and that there is very little hope for most poor nations ever to catch up with the rich nations."

38. Much of this recent discussion in the economics literature came in response to Herrnstein and Murray (1994), who argued that the labor market relationships to relatively fixed IQ measures had strong implications for social policy. Much of the discussion is, of course, outside of economics. While controversy is ongoing regarding the influence of genetics and environment on IQ—see, for example, the exchange by Rose (2009) and Ceci and Williams (2009)—the substantial impact environment can have on measured IQ is clear (e.g., see Turkheimer et al. 2003). Another source of discussion is the so-called Flynn effect—a rapid rise in IQ scores in many nations around the world over the course of the twentieth century noted by political scientist James Flynn. For discussions of this, see the studies by Dickens and Flynn (2001) and Flynn (2007), both of which argue that aggregate societal factors can affect the measured national data.

39. Their analyses of economic outcomes relate the level of GDP per capita to IQ scores. It is difficult to see these analyses in level form as identifying the impact of skills. Their data series, however, have been used extensively in other analyses.

40. As Hunt and Wittmann (2008) point out, concerns with the data include the fact that values for the majority of countries are derived from an unclearly specified method drawing on data from nearby countries, and that most data points are not derived from representative samples. For example, the value for Ethiopia is based on the IQ scores of a highly selected group that had emigrated to Israel, and the value for Equatorial Guinea, the lowest IQ estimate in the data, refers to a group of children in a home for the developmentally disabled in Spain.

Chapter 4

1. Aghion et al. (2009) relied on within-country variation to approach causality.

2. Sections 4.1 to 4.3 draw directly on Hanushek and Woessmann (2012a).

3. We would also be interested in sub-Saharan Africa, but the sample of countries is too thin for rigorous analysis.

4. In the next chapter we also return to an in-depth analysis of growth in Latin America and East Asia.

5. See Hanushek and Woessmann (2011a) for a review and evaluation of the micro evidence.

6. See Bishop (2006) and Hanushek and Woessmann (2011a) for reviews of the education literature. Data on external exit exams are available for forty-three countries in a study by Woessmann et al. (2009), who update Bishop's (2006) collection from reviews of comparative education studies, education encyclopedia, government documents, background papers, and interviews with national representatives. The measure refers roughly to the mid-1990s, but exam regimes are relatively stable over time for countries.

7. Note that the sample size across the different specifications varies depending on the availability of data for the specific instrumental variables in the model.

8. All models also include initial GDP per capita and a constant. The Durbin–Wu–Hausman test does not reject the exogeneity of cognitive skills at conventional levels.

9. Fuller's modification of the LIML estimator is more robust than 2SLS in the presence of weak instruments and performs relatively well in the simulations by Hahn, Hausman, and Kuersteiner (2004). We set the user-specified constant—Fuller's (1977) alpha—to a value of one, but our results are hardly affected if we set alpha to four.

10. Likewise the Anderson–Rubin χ^2 statistic (3.06) of this just-identified model indicates significance at the 8 percent level. Note that the LIML estimators, on which the Moreira bands are centered, differ from the reported 2SLS estimates only in the third digit in all our models.

11. School attainment will also be affected by enrollment in higher education, which is not explicitly modeled. The results here again suggest that international differences in cognitive skills are the dominant aspect of human capital relative to growth.

12. Note that in column 1, initial years of schooling is included as an exogenous variable in the second-stage model (the growth model), and so is also automatically included in the first-stage regression, which is why its coefficient and that for exit exams are the same in the first stage of both columns 1 and 2. In column 2, years of schooling no longer enters the second-stage equation.

13. See the review in Woessmann et al. (2009), along with West and Woessmann (2010).

14. The data on private enrollment as a percentage of total enrollment in general secondary education are from UNESCO (1998) and refer to 1985, the earliest year with consistent data. For greater consistency of the time spans, the dependent variable in this specification is economic growth in 1980 to 2000; results are robust to using growth in 1960 to 2000. Given that the results from the educational production literature mostly refer to OECD countries, we restrict the analysis to this sample, for which twenty observations are available.

15. Barrett, Kurian, and Johnson (2001) provide data on the Catholic population share of all countries in our sample for 1900 as well as for 1970.

16. These findings are entirely consistent with prior work on Catholic education. Becker and Woessmann (2009) showed that, historically, Protestant Christians were significantly more advanced educationally than Catholic Christians because of their emphasis on individuals' ability to read the Bible. West and Woessmann (2010) provided further evidence that Catholicism per se is unlikely to have a direct impact on educational achievement.

17. See Woessmann (2003a) and Hanushek, Link, and Woessmann (2013).

18. Data on the percentage of decisions made at the central level of government on the organization of instruction in public lower secondary education are available in Organisation for Economic Co-operation and Development (1998), but

only for 1998. The IV results are very similar without using years of schooling as a second instrument, and the F-statistic of the excluded instrument is already above 10. In this specification the estimated growth effect is even larger than the OLS estimate. Note, though, that the Fuller estimate is already closer to the OLS estimate and that the Moreira confidence bands include the OLS and other IV estimates.

19. See, for example, Rockoff (2004), Rivkin, Hanushek, and Kain (2005), and Hanushek and Rivkin (2010).

20. The teacher salary data come from surveys conducted by OECD and by UNESCO. Specifically, we use salaries at the top of the experience scale. A drawback of these data is that they are observed only at the end of our growth period (in 2003).

21. Relative salaries are available for thirty-four countries. Results are very similar when using the Dolton and Marcenaro-Gutierrez (2011) proxy of the percentile position of teachers' salaries in the earnings distribution, which, however, is missing for three of these countries.

22. Similarly a recent McKinsey analysis (Auguste, Kihn, and Miller 2010) highlighted relative teacher salaries as an important determinant of why some countries do better than others on the latest international tests.

23. An additional concern with the various IV models might be that the different IV models are drawing on the same source of variation in the first stage, which would make the consistency of the results obvious. However, the different instruments used in table 4.1 are in fact not statistically significantly correlated with one another, with the exception of a negative association of central exams with the 1900 Catholic share (as well as a significant negative association of initial years of schooling with centralization and with relative teacher pay), but these joint variations are not used for identification in the models that use these instruments together).

24. Relevant studies include analyses by Hausmann, Pritchett, and Rodrik (2005), who looked at episodes of "growth accelerations"; Jones and Olken (2008), who considered patterns of ten-year periods of acceleration and collapse; and Barro and Ursúa (2008), who identified events of major declines in consumption with potential implications for long-run growth. The identified periods are generally characterized by financial crisis, political instability, or war.

25. As described in chapter 2, the scaling of the individual tests uses the variance estimates from the OECD Standardization Group (OSG). To account for heteroscedasticity and for the fact that the signal-to-noise ratio will be larger the smaller the number of OSG countries that participated in a test, we weight the regression by the square root of the number of participating OSG countries.

26. All sampled countries except Canada, Korea, and Norway have in fact test scores dating back at least to 1971, so the trend estimation for each spans over thirty years.

27. A comparison of the country rankings of projected skill levels for 1975 and 2000 yields a Spearman rank correlation of 0.78—again reinforcing the validity of average country scores for the main growth analysis.

28. See appendix table 4A.1 for descriptive statistics. We also tried alternative measures of changes in growth rates, including the difference between the average rates in the first five years and the last five years; trend growth using IMF data in national currencies; and IMF national currency data for the period 1975 to 2004. The use of IMF national currency data is consistent with Nuxoll (1994) and Hanousek, Hajkova, and Filer (2008), who argued that using national accounts data when looking at growth rates is superior to relying on the price and exchange rate adjustments in the basic Penn World Tables data. In our investigation of these options, the estimates of the impact of changes in test scores remain statistically significant and quantitatively very similar, both across alternatives and compared to the estimates reported in table 4.2.

29. Alternative specifications look simply at whether the test score trend is above or below the OECD median. The impact of changes in test scores on changes in growth rates remains very stable and is always statistically significant (see Hanushek and Woessmann 2012a).

30. Results are qualitatively the same when using just the PISA tests in 2000 to 2009.

31. Column 1 of appendix table 4A.2 shows that considering the updated PWT data over the same 1975 to 2000 period hardly affects the result. Extending the growth period with the newly available data to 2007 (or to 2009, not shown) also confirms the result (column 2). Using the growth period 1985 to 2007 (column 3), so that the test score trend partly predates the growth rate trend, even strengthens the result.

32. The analysis here extends the original work by Hanushek and Kimko (2000) in several ways. Placing the analysis in the framework of a difference-in-differences model allows us to compare the earnings of late immigrants just to early immigrants from the same country. Additionally we expand dramatically both the sample of workers and the number of countries of origin for immigrants and use better test information for the comparisons. Finally, we consider a range of sensitivity analyses, such as analyses excluding Mexican immigrants and including only immigrants from English-speaking countries.

33. See Card (1999) and Heckman, Lochner, and Todd (2006) for detailed discussions of classical Mincer estimates. Hanushek et al. (2015) discuss in greater detail the extension of the Mincer equation to incorporate cognitive skills.

34. Bowles, Gintis, and Osborne (2001) provided an early survey of studies of achievement effects. Hanushek (2011) reviewed the more recent US evidence. For reviews of the international evidence, see Hanushek and Woessmann (2008, 2011a).

35. Earlier examples of US studies include those by Bishop (1989), Murnane, Willett, and Levy (1995), and Neal and Johnson (1996).

36. See, for example, Romer (1990a) and Aghion and Howitt (1998).

37. Using measures of educational attainment rather than skills, the existing literature on externalities to education is inconclusive; see, for example, Acemoglu

and Angrist (2000), Moretti (2004), Ciccone and Peri (2006), and Iranzo and Peri (2009). Beyond production externalities, substantial evidence by now exists of nonproduction benefits of education in the form of reduced crime, good citizenship, and better parenting that may partly accrue to society at large; see Lochner (2011) and Oreopoulos and Salvanes (2011) for reviews.

38. See Weiss (1995), Riley (2001), and more recently Arcidiacono, Bayer, and Hizmo (2010).

39. An immigrant is an individual born in a foreign country. The sample includes all individuals ages twenty-five or older currently in the US labor force with annual wage and salary earnings of at least $1,000 and not enrolled in school. To be included, an immigrant had to have been born in a country with international test data (see appendix table 2A.1). The number of included countries is larger than in the previous growth regressions because internationally comparable GDP data for country of origin are not needed. Appendix table 4A.3 shows descriptive statistics.

40. While our analysis uses skill differences by country of origin to infer earnings differences among immigrants in the United States, Hendricks (2002) and Schoellman (2012) went the opposite way of using earnings differences of immigrants to infer cross-country differences in human capital.

41. Immigrants educated in their home countries necessarily come to the United States at older ages than comparable immigrants educated in the United States, suggesting differential selectivity and motivation for these two groups. But the key issue for identifying the impact of cognitive skills is that any selectivity in migration is the same across countries (which would then be captured by α_3), or at least is not correlated with differences in home country cognitive skills.

42. The assignment of individuals to US schooling is based on census data indicating immigration before age six. The assignment of individuals to schooling all in the country of origin is based on age of immigration greater than years of schooling plus six. A person who moves back and forth during the schooling years could be erroneously classified as having all US or no US schooling, even though he or she is really in the partial treatment category (which is meant to be excluded from the difference-in-differences estimation).

43. Data on English language come from the CIA World Factbook. Countries are coded as English speaking if the CIA World Factbook listed English as an official language or as the most widely spoken language in the country. See https://www.cia.gov/library/publications/the-world-factbook/.

44. The full set of Mincer parameters is reported by Hanushek and Woessmann (2012a). See also Heckman, Lochner, and Todd (2008) for an interpretation of these.

45. When analyzed separately by gender, the results hold strongly for males, whereas results for females, while pointing in the same direction, mostly do not reach statistical significance, as is common in labor market analyses.

46. This section draws partly on Hanushek and Woessmann (2012c). See Caselli (2005) and Hsieh and Klenow (2010) for details on the underlying concept of

development accounting. A parallel growth accounting analysis is precluded by the lack of consistent data on variation in cognitive skills over time.

47. We return to a more detailed analysis of the growth experience of these regions in chapter 5.

48. Note that the development accounting decomposition also does not require the assumption that (unmeasured) total factor productivity is orthogonal to factor inputs, in particular to human capital.

49. For Mincer returns, see Psacharopoulos and Patrinos (2004). For returns to cognitive skills, see Hanushek and Zhang (2009) and Hanushek et al. (2015).

50. One way to interpret this finding is to say the East Asian countries are still in the process of converging to their long-run steady-state income levels.

Chapter 5

1. We would like to be able to look similarly at the experiences of the other outlying region—sub-Saharan Africa—but just three of its countries have both cognitive skills and economic data for the relevant period. As figure 1.1 shows, and additional evidence suggests, the African growth failure can also be accounted for by low levels of knowledge capital.

2. Parts of this section draw directly on Hanushek and Woessmann (2008).

3. Pritchett (2004) and Filmer (2006) argue from analysis of household survey data that these figures from administrative data may overstate the school enrollment and completion rates. See Hanushek and Woessmann (2008) for their calculations of school completion rates across developing regions.

4. As pointed out in appendix 3B, however, selectivity does not affect the growth modeling—just the perspective on how large the challenge might be.

5. This picture differs from the skills data presented in appendix table 2A.1 in that it uses the extended Latin America data series that incorporates regional data both to expand the sample and provide more meaningful within-region variation. See section 5.2.

6. This section draws directly on Hanushek and Woessmann (2012c).

7. Throughout this analysis we focus on Latin American countries with populations greater than one million. Belize, French Guiana, Guyana, and Suriname are excluded because their populations are all below one million. We also exclude Nicaragua from the analysis because of its extended period spent under Communist rule and its nonmarket conditions. Caribbean countries, while sometimes put together with Latin American countries, are not included in the analysis because no Caribbean country ever participated in the worldwide testing of math and science.

8. As discussed later in this chapter, all Latin American countries with populations over one million have participated in one or both regional testing programs conducted in 1997 and 2006. Internationally, Venezuela participated in a 1991 reading test; its student scores exceeded only those in Botswana, Nigeria, and

Zimbabwe on the test for thirteen-year-olds and no other country on the test for nine-year-olds.

9. Such a comparison of the performance of those in school will even understate the true gap in average cognitive skills between full cohorts. Enrollment in secondary school has not been universal in Latin American countries, leading to more selective test taking in these countries compared to most others in the previous figures.

10. See Laboratorio Latinoamericano de Evaluación de la Calidad de la Educación (1998, 2001, 2002) for details.

11. See Laboratorio Latinoamericano de Evaluación de la Calidad de la Educación (2005, 2008a, 2008b).

12. Bolivia, Honduras, and Venezuela participated in LLECE but not in SERCE, while Costa Rica, Ecuador, El Salvador, Guatemala, Panama, Peru, and Uruguay participated only in SERCE. Six countries (Argentina, Brazil, Chile, Colombia, Mexico, and Paraguay) participated in both tests.

13. Both tests included Cuba and the Dominican Republic, and SERCE also included Nicaragua. Nicaragua and Cuba are excluded because of their history of nonmarket economies, although Cuban students scored dramatically higher than students in the included Latin American countries. The Dominican Republic was excluded as the sole remaining Caribbean country; it turns out to be a strong outlier if included in the growth analysis, getting a weight of zero in standard robust regression techniques that down-weight outliers based on Cook's distance measure and residuals.

14. We describe this exponential relationship in terms of test scaling, but there are alternative interpretations. First, larger measurement error in the tests at the lower compared to the higher achievement levels could flatten out the relationship at the bottom. Second, returns to skills could simply be lower at very low achievement levels. We cannot distinguish among the alternative explanations.

15. Additional analyses produced results that are robust to controlling for differences in openness and property rights security (not shown).

16. Specifically, the years of the household survey data and the associated tests (where TIMSS always refers to the respective eighth-grade subtests and the first year listed always refers to attainment data) are as follows: Albania and Peru: attainment data for 2000, combined with test scores from PISA 2002; Armenia: 2000 and TIMSS 2003; Brazil: 1996 and PISA 2000; Colombia: 2000 and TIMSS 1995; Egypt, Ghana, and Morocco: 2003 and TIMSS 2003; Indonesia: 2002 and average of TIMSS 2003 and PISA 2003; Moldova: 2000 and average of TIMSS 1999 and TIMSS 2003; Philippines: 2003 and average of TIMSS 1999 and TIMSS 2003; South Africa: 1999 and TIMSS 1999; Thailand: 2002 and PISA 2003; Turkey: 1998 and TIMSS 1999.

17. See Pritchett (2004) and Woessmann (2004).

18. See Pritchett and Beatty (2012). Pritchett (2004, 2013) refers to several additional examples from different developing countries of children whose educational performance is extremely poor even after years of schooling.

Chapter 6

1. See, for example, Aghion and Howitt (2006).

2. This chapter draws directly on Hanushek and Woessmann (2011b), in which more detailed analyses are provided. Note that we do not use the set of countries added to the OECD in 2010 in these discussions, since our growth analysis focuses on an earlier period. The addition of Chile, Estonia, Israel, and Slovenia brought the total number of OECD countries up to thirty-four.

3. Most variation in expropriation risk within the OECD is driven by Mexico, Turkey, and, to a lesser extent, Greece. Variation in openness is also driven by Mexico, Turkey, and, again to a lesser extent, New Zealand. Inclusion of these institutional measures in the models for just the twenty-four OECD countries reduces the estimated effect of cognitive skills, though less than seen in section 3.2 for the full country sample. The effect is virtually identical to that of dropping the economic outliers of Mexico and Turkey. See Hanushek and Woessmann (2011b) for details.

4. From the total of thirty OECD countries that became members before 2010, the sample misses four—the Czech Republic, Hungary, Poland, and the Slovak Republic—because their Communist histories preclude their having internationally comparable economic data during the period of analysis. Moreover Germany drops out because of missing economic and test score data for its eastern parts before 1990. The exclusion of Luxembourg reflects the common practice to drop countries with populations of less than one million (see Mankiw, Romer, and Weil 1992). This also parallels our prior analysis of Latin American growth in the last chapter.

5. To maintain consistency within this chapter, all analyses in it use years of schooling data from Barro and Lee (2013), who provide the subdivision into nontertiary and tertiary schooling required in section 6.3. Results are qualitatively the same, however, with the extended Cohen and Soto (2007) data used in the previous chapters.

6. As with the results in chapter 3, the inclusion of years of schooling, which has an insignificant effect in the presence of cognitive skills, has virtually no effect.

7. See details in Hanushek and Woessmann (2011b).

8. For details on the measures of product market regulation and employment protection, see, respectively, http://www.oecd.org/economy/growth/indicatorsofproduct marketregulationhomepage.htm and www.oecd.org/employment/protection.

9. Extensive robustness checks also confirm these basic results. For example, the results hold for all underlying subindexes, including indicators of public ownership, involvement in business operations, regulatory and administrative opacity, administrative burdens on startups, barriers to competition, and explicit and other barriers to trade and investment. See details in the working paper version of Hanushek and Woessmann (2011b).

10. Added detail is provided in the working paper version of Hanushek and Woessmann (2011b).

11. If we look at the estimate of the difference in impact on growth of the top-skill share between OECD and non-OECD countries, we find a smaller impact for OECD countries that is statistically significant. See Hanushek and Woessmann (2011b).

12. For example, part of the answer for the faster than expected growth may be the range of strong, growth-supporting features of the US economy, although to explain the positive residual in figure 6.2, the US institutions must be beyond the specific measures of institutions used above. The United States, for instance, with its lower tax rates and minimal government production through nationalized industries, has generally had less government intrusion overall in the operation of the economy. The United States furthermore maintains generally much freer labor and product markets, less government regulation of firms, and less powerful trade unions than most other countries. Taken together, these characteristics of its economy encourage investment, permit the rapid development of new products and activities by firms, reward individuals for invention, and enable US workers to adjust to new opportunities.

Chapter 7

1. Hanushek and Woessmann (2012b) provided an expansion of comparable projections to the eight European Union (EU) countries that are not member states of the OECD; projection estimates for the EU as a whole; and a simulation of an additional school reform plan that is based on the official benchmark of EU policy.

2. This chapter draws directly on Hanushek and Woessmann (2011b).

3. Organisation for Economic Co-operation and Development (2009b). Note that as these life expectancy numbers are based on age-specific mortality rates prevalent in 2006, they do not include the effect of any future decline in these rates. Life expectancy at birth has increased by an average of more than ten years since 1960.

4. Organisation for Economic Co-operation and Development (2009a).

5. As a practical value for the social discount rate in cost–benefit analysis (derived from an optimal growth rate model), Moore et al. (2004) suggest using a time-declining scale of discount rates for intergenerational projects that do not crowd out private investment, starting with 3.5 percent for years 0–50 and declining to 2.5 percent for years 50–100, 1.5 percent for years 100–200, 0.5 percent for years 200–300, and 0 percent for years over 300. (The proper starting value is actually 3.3 percent, based on the parameter values they assume for the growth rate in per-capita consumption [2.3 percent], the social marginal utility of consumption with respect to per-capita consumption [1], and the utility discount rate [1 percent]).

6. Rather than necessarily being negative, spillovers of one country's human capital investments on other countries could also be positive. For example, if one country pushes out the world technological frontier by improving its human capital, others can gain from this by imitation and reach higher productivity levels. We make no attempt to consider how technological change occurs and its impact on wages and earnings. Obviously different patterns of productivity improvements

will play out differently in the labor market, as has been seen in the United States over time (Goldin and Katz 2008).

7. All calculations of PISA scores underlying the following simulations refer to the average performance in math and science (in line with the underlying growth model), averaged over the three PISA cycles 2000, 2003, and 2006 (e.g., see Organisation for Economic Co-operation and Development 2007). All underlying measures of gross domestic product (GDP) are in US dollars, measured in purchasing power parities (PPP), expressed in prices of 2010. The GDP measures were calculated from the 2007 measure of GDP in current prices and current PPPs available for all countries (extracted from http://stats.oecd.org on August 10, 2009), projected to 2010 using OECD estimates of annual changes in potential GDP and in GDP deflators (Organisation for Economic Co-operation and Development 2009a).

8. Changes in PISA scores through 2012 can be found in Organisation for Economic Co-operation and Development (2013b).

9. See, for example, Mourshed, Chijioke, and Barber (2010).

10. Note that the calculations also assume the top-ranked countries can feasibly improve their scores. Whether there is room for further improvement for them or some sort of ceiling effect in the existing tests remains in question. As an alternative, the next scenario will only assume improvements that do not go beyond the current top performer.

11. In the 2012 PISA, the scores of Finnish students slipped. Whether or not this is a long-term change is not currently known.

12. See Hanushek and Woessmann (2011b).

13. See Mankiw, Romer, and Weil (1992).

14. Patents are measured in triadic patent families; see Organisation for Economic Co-operation and Development (2008).

15. Based on our model, which depicts only effects of test scores and evolving levels of income, Luxembourg and Norway—the two countries with the highest current levels of GDP per capita—are projected to converge to a lower balanced growth path (both without and with reform) and thus initially have the lowest growth rates. If these countries can keep their current advantage in per-capita GDP relative to the other OECD countries for reasons outside our model, this would increase the projected value of their educational reforms.

16. The lower bound (not shown) comes from estimates for OECD, excluding Mexico and Turkey (see Hanushek and Woessmann 2011b).

17. See discussions in, for example, Nordhaus (2007) and Tol and Yohe (2006).

18. Organisation for Economic Co-operation and Development (2010a).

Chapter 8

1. For the depiction, we start with the age group and subject-specific standardized data from the different international tests, as described in appendix 2A. We supplement these with data from all international tests through 2012 (see table

2.1). Given that the primary and lower secondary testing cycles of TIMSS, PIRLS, and PISA are each scaled to be comparable over time, we use the following method to put them on the common scale: first, we rescale the TIMSS 2003 (PIRLS 2001) tests so the United States has the US mean and standard deviation on the PISA 2003 (2000) test in the respective subject. Second, we rescale the other TIMSS (PIRLS) waves so the difference in the US performance (mean and standard deviation) on them from TIMSS 2003 (PIRLS 2001) is simply rescaled according to the rescaled TIMSS 2003 (PIRLS 2001) scale. On this metric, the TIMSS and PIRLS tests are rescaled, so the US performance in 2003 (2001) is the same as in PISA, and the TIMSS and PIRLS trends are the original trends, with their size expressed according to the US standard deviation in PISA. For the figure, we take out age group and subject-specific trends in each country, smooth the available test observations with locally weighted regressions (using Stata's lowess command; see Cleveland 1979), and linearly interpolate among the available smoothed test observations. A previous version of this chart motivated Amanda Ripley's (2013) consideration of why some countries outperformed the United States.

2. See, for instance, Woessmann (2003a, 2007a) and Hanushek and Woessmann (2011b) for different examples.

3. In a simple first-differenced regression, the change in expenditure per student is insignificant in explaining the change in achievement; without the outlier Poland apparent in figure 8.2, the point estimate is in fact negative. We look at reading achievement here because it has been scaled in PISA to be directly comparable over the full period 2000 to 2012. Results look just the same, however, for math achievement.

4. See Hanushek (2003), Woessmann (2007a), Hanushek and Woessmann (2011a). For developing countries, see Hanushek (1995), Glewwe et al. (2014), and Kremer, Brannen, and Glennerster (2013).

5. See, for example, Burtless (1996), Greenwald, Hedges, and Laine (1996), and Hanushek (1996).

6. The US controversy has been particularly intense; see, for example, Mishel and Rothstein (2002) and Ehrenberg et al. (2001).

7. See Hanushek (1995) and Glewwe et al. (2014). Similarly, focusing just on randomized evaluations, Kremer, Brannen, and Glennerster (2013) conclude that student achievement in developing countries is generally unresponsive to adding additional inputs of the same kind, such as additional teachers or textbooks.

8. See, for example, Banerjee and Duflo (2009, 2011) and Kremer, Brannen, and Glennerster (2013).

9. See the general argument in Mourshed, Chijioke, and Barber (2010). See also Pritchett and Sandefur (2013) for the related argument that contextual factors may limit the generalizability of the impact of the same intervention across varying developing-country contexts.

10. Patrinos (2011) and Galiani and Perez-Truglia (2014) have provided thoughtful reviews of decentralized decision-making in developing countries that clearly show the results are mixed at best and may even be more negative. In their literature review Arcia et al. (2011: 3) concluded that "the empirical evidence from

Latin America shows very few cases in which SBM [school-based management] has made a significant difference in learning outcomes ..., while in Europe there is substantial evidence showing a positive impact of school autonomy on learning." Indeed, two recent studies of developed countries that paid particular attention to identification of causal impacts—by Barankay and Lockwood (2007) for Switzerland and Clark (2009) for the United Kingdom—found substantial positive effects of local autonomy. But any positive effects found for specific decentralization programs in developing countries tended either to be restricted to schools located in non-poor municipalities (Galiani, Gertler, and Schargrodsky 2008) or to originate in more comprehensive school reform programs that simultaneously raised accountability from local communities (e.g., see Jimenez and Sawada 1999; Gunnarsson et al. 2009; Gertler, Patrinos, and Rubio-Codina 2012).

11. See Hanushek, Link, and Woessmann (2013).

12. Woessmann (2005).

13. See Galiani, Gertler, and Schargrodsky (2008).

14. While we focus on issues of decision-making, there may also be technological differences. Centralization opens the possibility to exploit economies of scale, for example, in evaluation and teacher training systems.

15. Many countries have changed the locus of decision-making within their countries over the past decade—and interestingly, some have decentralized while others have centralized. We exploit this cross-country variation to investigate the impact of local autonomy on student achievement. We use the PISA data over time as a panel of country observations, and we identify the effect of school autonomy from within-country changes in the share of autonomous schools over time in a panel analysis with country (and time) fixed effects. This way each country acts as its own control. Finally, we allow the impact of autonomy of decision-making to vary with the level of economic and educational development. See Hanushek, Link, and Woessmann (2013).

16. The fundamental argument is that, at some point, more central decision-making by government becomes superior to local decision-making. The evidence presented, however, does not include broad representation of the poorest countries. It could be that local decision-making again becomes superior if central decision-making is quite dysfunctional. This idea may be supported by observations of the rapid increase of low-cost private schools in a variety of poor countries, where student outcomes appear superior to those of students in regular government schools. See Tooley and Dixon (2005), Tooley (2009), World Bank (2013), and Heyneman and Stern (2014).

17. See Duflo, Dupas, and Kremer (2011).

18. See Pritchett and Beatty (2012) for a more general discussion of the negative consequences of having overambitious curricula in developing countries.

19. See, for example, Hanushek (1971, 1992), Rockoff (2004), Rivkin, Hanushek, and Kain (2005), and a number of subsequent studies reviewed by Hanushek and Rivkin (2010, 2012). The most recent work by Chetty, Friedman, and Rockoff (2014a, b) traces teacher effects into the labor market.

20. Only relatively recently have such studies expanded to other countries and parts of the world; see, for example, Harbison and Hanushek (1992) for Brazil, Leigh (2010) for Australia, and Slater, Davies, and Burgess (2012) for England.

21. See the reviews by Hanushek and Rivkin (2006), Harris and Sass (2011), and Chingos and Peterson (2011) for the United States and by Glewwe et al. (2014) for developing countries. Virtually the only teacher characteristic more frequently found to be significantly related to student achievement is teachers' own academic skills, as measured by different test scores; see, for example, Rockoff et al. (2011) and Metzler and Woessmann (2012), as well as Wayne and Youngs (2003) and Hanushek and Rivkin (2006) for reviews of earlier studies. In addition some recent work points to the relevance of teaching methods and practices—for example, Tyler et al. (2010), Schwerdt and Wuppermann (2011), and Lavy (2011). As in our discussion in the next section, however, the crucial policy implication is probably the need to ensure incentive environments that make teachers use methods effective for their particular circumstances.

22. See Carnoy and Loeb (2002), Hanushek and Raymond (2005), Jacob (2005), and Dee and Jacob (2011); Figlio and Loeb (2011) provide a review. One institutional setup that combines accountability with parental choice gives vouchers for attending private schools to students in schools that repeatedly do badly on the accountability test. In Florida, this approach has been shown to improve school performance, particularly with respect to disadvantaged students (West and Peterson 2006; Figlio and Rouse 2006).

23. See, for example, Bishop (1997, 2006), Woessmann (2003a, 2007b), and Woessmann et al. (2009); Hanushek and Woessmann (2011a) provide a review.

24. See Bishop (1997), Jürges, Schneider, and Büchel (2005), Woessmann (2010), and Jürges et al. (2012).

25. See Woessmann (2005), Woessmann et al. (2009), and Hanushek, Link, and Woessmann (2013).

26. See Woessmann (2007b, 2009b), Woessmann et al. (2009), and West and Woessmann (2010).

27. See Rouse (1998), Howell and Peterson (2002), and Wolf et al. (2010).

28. See Muralidharan and Sundararaman (2013) for India; Card, Dooley, and Payne (2010) for Canada; and Sandström and Bergström (2005), Björklund et al. (2004), and Böhlmark and Lindahl (2012) for Sweden.

29. See Tooley (2009), Bettinger (2011), Barrera-Osorio et al. (2013), World Bank (2013), and Barber (2013).

30. See Lavy (2010) for Israel. Evidence from the United States and the United Kingdom is more mixed; see, for example, Cullen, Jacob, and Levitt (2006), Hoxby (2007), Rothstein (2007), Gibbons, Machin, and Silva (2008), and Deming et al. (2014). In the United States, charter schools—which are public schools that are free from many regulations—offer another example of increased choice among formally public schools. See, for example, the evaluations in Abdulkadiroğlu et al. (2011), Angrist, Pathak, and Walters (2013), and CREDO (2013).

31. See the surveys presented by Atkinson et al. (2009) and Podgursky and Springer (2007). Atkinson et al. (2009) found the introduction of performance-related pay had a substantial positive impact on student achievement in England. Fryer et al. (2012) found positive effects of financial teacher incentives in Chicago Heights, Illinois, when they were framed to exploit the fear of penalty rather than the hope of gain. At the school level, monetary incentives for teachers based on their students' performance were shown to improve student learning very significantly in Israel and in India (Lavy 2002, 2009; Muralidharan and Sundararaman 2011), while evidence from Kenya was less clear (Glewwe, Ilias, and Kremer 2010). Duflo, Hanna, and Ryan (2012) found that monitoring and financial incentives reduced teacher absenteeism and increased learning in India.

32. Indeed, in addressing the question of what contributes to outcomes in the best-performing countries, Barber and Mourshed (2007) emphasized both initial recruitment of teachers and the development of institutions to move ineffective teachers out of the classroom. In line with this argument, a Kenyan experimental study found that low-paid teachers hired locally on annual contracts whose renewal was conditional on performance performed substantially better than centrally hired teachers with civil service status (Duflo, Dupas, and Kremer 2012). Dee and Wyckoff (2013) find that the Washington, DC, evaluation system that permits dismissal of ineffective teachers led to higher exit rates of poor teachers from the system.

33. See Woessmann (2011).

34. One demand-side incentive found more regularly in developed countries are the systems of centralized examination discussed above. By linking tertiary school admission to exam performance, they provide direct incentives for students to perform well. In addition, experimental approaches have recently linked achievement to financial incentives for students, with somewhat mixed results; see, for example, Angrist and Lavy (2009), Fryer (2011), and Bettinger (2012).

35. See Jensen (2010) for evidence regarding the relevance of (in)accurate information on the returns to education in a developing country.

36. Kremer, Brannen, and Glennerster (2013) note that conditional cash transfer programs had been introduced in more than thirty countries by 2013.

37. See the review in Hanushek (2008), plus more recent analyses by Attanasio, Meghir, and Santiago (2012), Dubois, Janvry, and Sadoulet (2012), and Galiani and McEwan (2013), as well as the review of randomized trials by Kremer, Brannen, and Glennerster (2013).

38. Kremer, Miguel, and Thornton (2009).

39. See the discussion and review in Hanushek and Woessmann (2011a).

40. See the conceptual discussion by Cunha et al. (2006), and see Blau and Currie (2006) for a general review of the empirical literature.

41. For evidence on the two best-known US programs, see Belfield et al. (2006) and Heckman et al. (2010a, b) on the small-scale targeted Perry Preschool Program and Garces, Thomas, and Currie (2002), Ludwig and Miller (2007), and Deming (2009) on the broader Head Start program. Berlinski, Galiani, and Manacorda (2008) present evidence from Uruguay and Berlinski, Galiani,

and Gertler (2009) present evidence from Argentina. In cross-country analysis, Schuetz, Ursprung, and Woessmann (2008) found a positive association of student achievement in high school with the usual duration of the preschool cycle in a country, and Schuetz (2009) showed preprimary attendance to be positively associated with high school achievement at the individual level in most countries.

42. See Schuetz, Ursprung, and Woessmann (2008).

43. See, for example, Cunha et al. (2006) and Heckman (2006, 2008).

44. The language differs, sometimes referring to placing students into classrooms within a school on the basis of ability. Many countries, including the United States, pursue tracking within schools but not generally across schools. For more on within-school tracking, see Betts (2011).

45. See Meghir and Palme (2005) for Sweden, Pekkarinen, Uusitalo, and Kerr (2009) and Pekkala Kerr, Pekkarinen, and Uusitalo (2013) for Finland, van Elk, van der Steeg, and Webbink (2011) for the Netherlands, and Piopiunik (2014) on a Bavarian reform. See Woessmann (2009a) and Pekkarinen (2014) for reviews.

46. Hanushek and Woessmann (2006) developed an international differences-in-differences approach to identify the causal effect of early tracking in a cross-country setting. The basic idea starts with the fact that, in all countries, students are taught in a uniform school type for the first four years of schooling. This means that a comparison of the change in educational inequality between fourth grade and the end of lower secondary school between countries with and without early tracking can provide information on possible impacts of tracking.

47. See Schuetz, Ursprung, and Woessmann (2008) and Woessmann et al. (2009), chapter 7, for achievement results and Brunello and Checchi (2007) for earnings results. Ammermueller (2013) reported similar achievement effects for the number of school types (rather than the age of first tracking). See Hanushek and Woessmann (2011a) for a review of the international evidence. Pooling a sample of German states (most of which track after fourth grade, but some of which track after sixth grade) with a sample of OECD countries, Woessmann (2010) found the negative association between early tracking and inequality of educational opportunity statistically indistinguishable between the two, suggesting the international evidence does not just capture such country-level omitted factors as differences in culture, language, or legal background.

48. See Ryan (2001).

49. For examples, see Arum and Shavit (1995) and Malamud and Pop-Eleches (2010) and the reviews and discussions in Ryan (2001), Müller (2009), Wolter and Ryan (2011), and Biavaschi et al. (2012).

50. See Hanushek et al. (2014). Other examples of studies in line with our interpretation of the labor market outcomes of vocational education beyond the entry phase are Cörvers et al. (2011), Weber (2014), Hall (2013), and Golsteyn and Stenberg (2014).

51. The pattern is also in line with the model by Gould, Moav, and Weinberg (2001), in which technological progress leads to a higher depreciation of technology-specific versus general skills.

References

Abdulkadiroğlu, Atila, Joshua D. Angrist, Susan M. Dynarski, Thomas J. Kane, and Parag A. Pathak. 2011. Accountability and flexibility in public schools: Evidence from Boston's charters and pilots. *Quarterly Journal of Economics* 126 (2): 699–748.

Acemoglu, Daron. 2009. *Introduction to Modern Economic Growth*. Princeton: Princeton University Press.

Acemoglu, Daron, and Joshua D. Angrist. 2000. How large are the social returns to education? Evidence from compulsory schooling laws. In *NBER Macroeconomics Annual 2000*, ed. Ben S. Bernanke and Kenneth Rogoff, 9–59. Cambridge: MIT Press.

Acemoglu, Daron, Francisco A. Gallego, and James A. Robinson. 2014. Institutions, human capital and development. *Annual Review of Economics* 6: 875–912.

Acemoglu, Daron, Simon Johnson, and James A. Robinson. 2001. The colonial origins of comparative development: An empirical investigation. *American Economic Review* 91 (5): 1369–1401.

Acemoglu, Daron, Simon Johnson, and James A. Robinson. 2002. Reversal of fortune: Geography and institutions in the making of the modern world income distribution. *Quarterly Journal of Economics* 117 (4): 1231–94.

Acemoglu, Daron, Simon Johnson, and James A. Robinson. 2005. Institutions as a fundamental cause of long-run growth. In *Handbook of Economic Growth*, ed. Philippe Aghion and Steven N. Durlauf, 385–472. Amsterdam: North Holland.

Acemoglu, Daron, Simon Johnson, and James A. Robinson. 2012. The colonial origins of comparative development: An empirical investigation: Reply. *American Economic Review* 102 (6): 3077–3110.

Acemoglu, Daron, and James A. Robinson. 2012. *Why Nations Fail: The Origins of Power, Prosperity, and Poverty*. New York: Crown Publishers.

Aghion, Philippe, Leah Boustan, Caroline M. Hoxby, and Jérôme Vandenbussche. 2009. The causal impact of education on economic growth: Evidence from the U.S. Mimeo. Department of Economics: Harvard University (March).

Aghion, Philippe, and Peter Howitt. 1998. *Endogenous Growth Theory*. Cambridge, MA: MIT Press.

Aghion, Philippe, and Peter Howitt. 2006. Appropriate growth policy: A unifying framework. *Journal of the European Economic Association* 4 (2–3): 269–314.

Aghion, Philippe, and Peter Howitt. 2009. *The Economics of Growth*. Cambridge: MIT Press.

Albouy, David Y. 2012. The colonial origins of comparative development: An empirical investigation: Comment. *American Economic Review* 102 (6): 3059–76.

Almlund, Mathilde, Angela L. Duckworth, James Heckman, and Tim Kautz. 2011. Personality psychology and economics. In *Handbook of the Economics of Education*, vol. 4. ed. Eric A. Hanushek, Stephen Machin, and Ludger Woessmann, 1–181. Amsterdam: North Holland.

Altinok, Nadir, and Hatidje Murseli. 2007. International database on human capital quality. *Economics Letters* 96 (2): 237–44.

Ammermueller, Andreas. 2013. Institutional features of schooling systems and educational inequality: Cross-country evidence from PIRLS and PISA. *German Economic Review* 14 (2): 190–213.

Andrews, Donald R., Marcelo J. Moreira, and James H. Stock. 2007. Performance of conditional Wald tests in IV regression with weak instruments. *Journal of Econometrics* 139 (1): 116–132.

Angrist, Joshua D., Parag A. Pathak, and Christopher R. Walters. 2013. Explaining charter school effectiveness. *American Economic Journal: Applied Economics* 5 (4): 1–27.

Angrist, Joshua, and Victor Lavy. 2009. The effects of high stakes high school achievement awards: Evidence from a randomized trial. *American Economic Review* 99 (4): 1384–1414.

Angrist, Noam, Harry A. Patrinos, and Martin Schlotter. 2013. An expansion of a global data set on educational quality. Policy Research Working Paper 6536. Washington, DC: World Bank (July).

Appleton, Simon, Paul Atherton, and Michael Bleaney. 2011. Growth regressions and data revisions in Penn World Tables. *Journal of Economic Studies (Glasgow, Scotland)* 38 (3): 301–12.

Arcia, Gustavo, Kevin Macdonald, Harry A. Patrinos, and Emilio Porta. 2011. *School Autonomy and Accountability. System Assessment and Benchmarking for Education Results*. Washington, DC: World Bank.

Arcidiacono, Peter, Patrick Bayer, and Aurel Hizmo. 2010. Beyond signaling and human capital: Education and the revelation of ability. *American Economic Journal: Applied Economics* 2 (4): 76–104.

Arum, Richard, and Yossi Shavit. 1995. Secondary vocational education and the transition from school to work. *Sociology of Education* 68 (3): 187–204.

Atkinson, Adele, Simon Burgess, Bronwyn Croxson, Paul Gregg, Carol Propper, Helen Slater, and Deborah Wilson. 2009. Evaluating the impact of performance-related pay for teachers in England. *Labour Economics* 16 (3): 251–61.

Attanasio, Orazio P., Costas Meghir, and Ana Santiago. 2012. Education choices in Mexico: Using a structural model and a randomized experiment to evaluate PROGRESA. *Review of Economic Studies* 79 (1): 37–66.

Auguste, Byron, Paul Kihn, and Matt Miller. 2010. *Closing the Talent Gap: Attracting and Retaining Top-Third Graduates to Careers in Teaching*. McKinsey and Company (September).

Autor, David H., Lawrence F. Katz, and Melissa S. Kearney. 2006. The polarization of the U.S. labor market. *American Economic Review* 96 (2): 189–94.

Autor, David H., Lawrence F. Katz, and Melissa S. Kearney. 2008. Trends in U.S. wage inequality: Revising the revisionists. *Review of Economics and Statistics* 90 (2): 300–23.

Azariadis, Costas, and Allan Drazen. 1990. Threshold externalities in economic development. *Quarterly Journal of Economics* 105 (2): 501–26.

Banerjee, Abhijit V., and Esther Duflo. 2009. The experimental approach to development economics. *Annual Review of Economics* 1 (1): 151–78.

Banerjee, Abhijit V., and Esther Duflo. 2011. *Poor Economics: A Radical Rethinking of the Way to Fight Global Poverty*. New York: Public Affairs.

Barankay, Iwan, and Ben Lockwood. 2007. Decentralization and the productive efficiency of government: Evidence from Swiss cantons. *Journal of Public Economics* 91 (5–6): 1197–1218.

Barber, Michael. 2013. *The Good News from Pakistan: How a Revolutionary New Approach to Education Reform in Punjab Shows the Way Forward for Pakistan and Development Aid Everywhere*. London: Reform.

Barber, Michael, and Mona Mourshed. 2007. *How the World's Best-Performing School Systems Come out on Top*. McKinsey and Company.

Barrett, David B., George T. Kurian, and Todd M. Johnson. 2001. *World Christian Encyclopedia*, 2nd ed. Oxford: Oxford University Press.

Barro, Robert J. 1991. Economic growth in a cross section of countries. *Quarterly Journal of Economics* 106 (2): 407–43.

Barro, Robert J. 1997. *Determinants of Economic Growth: A Cross-country Empirical Study*. Cambridge: MIT Press.

Barro, Robert J. 2001. Human capital and growth. *American Economic Review* 91 (2): 12–17.

Barro, Robert J., and Jong-Wha Lee. 1993. International comparisons of educational attainment. *Journal of Monetary Economics* 32 (3): 363–94.

Barro, Robert J., and Jong-Wha Lee. 2001. International data on educational attainment: Updates and implications. *Oxford Economic Papers* 53 (3): 541–63.

Barro, Robert J., and Jong-Wha Lee. 2013. A new data set of educational attainment in the world, 1950–2010. *Journal of Development Economics* 104: 184–98.

Barro, Robert J., and Xavier Sala-i-Martin. 2004. *Economic Growth*, 2nd ed. Cambridge: MIT Press.

Barro, Robert J., and José F. Ursúa. 2008. Macroeconomic crises since 1870. *Brookings Papers on Economic Activity* 1:336–50.

Beaton, Albert E., Michael O. Martin, Ina V. S. Mullis, Eugenio J. Gonzalez, Teresa A. Smith, and Dana L. Kelly. 1996. *Science Achievement in the Middle School Years: IEA's Third International Mathematics and Science Study (TIMSS)*. Boston: Center for the Study of Testing, Evaluation, and Educational Policy, Boston College.

Beaton, Albert E., Ina V. S. Mullis, Michael O. Martin, Eugenio J. Gonzalez, Dana L. Kelly, and Teresa A. Smith. 1996. *Mathematics Achievement in the Middle School Years: IEA's Third International Mathematics and Science Study (TIMSS)*. Chestnut Hill, MA: Center for the Study of Testing, Evaluation, and Educational Policy, Boston College.

Becker, Gary S. 1964. *Human Capital: A Theoretical and Empirical Analysis, with Special Reference to Education*. New York: National Bureau of Economic Research.

Becker, Sascha O., and Ludger Woessmann. 2009. Was Weber wrong? A human capital theory of Protestant economic history. *Quarterly Journal of Economics* 124 (2): 531–96.

Belfield, Clive R., Milagros Nores, Steve W. Barnett, and Lawrence J. Schweinhart. 2006. The High/Scope Perry Preschool Program. *Journal of Human Resources* 41 (1): 162–90.

Benhabib, Jess, and Mark M. Spiegel. 1994. The role of human capital in economic development: Evidence from aggregate cross-country data. *Journal of Monetary Economics* 34 (2): 143–74.

Benhabib, Jess, and Mark M. Spiegel. 2005. Human capital and technology diffusion. In *Handbook of Economic Growth*, ed. Philippe Aghion and Steven N. Durlauf, 935–66. Amsterdam: North Holland.

Berlinski, Samuel, Sebastian Galiani, and Paul Gertler. 2009. The effect of pre-primary education on primary school performance. *Journal of Public Economics* 93 (1–2): 219–34.

Berlinski, Samuel, Sebastian Galiani, and Marco Manacorda. 2008. Giving children a better start: Preschool attendance and school-age profiles. *Journal of Public Economics* 92 (5–6): 1416–40.

Bettinger, Eric. 2011. Educational vouchers in international contexts. In *Handbook of the Economics of Education*, vol. 4, ed. Eric A. Hanushek, Stephen Machin, and Ludger Woessmann, 551–72. Amsterdam: North Holland.

Bettinger, Eric P. 2012. Paying to learn: The effect of financial incentives on elementary school test scores. *Review of Economics and Statistics* 94 (3): 686–98.

Betts, Julian R. 2011. The economics of tracking in education. In *Handbook of the Economics of Education*, vol. 3, ed. Eric A. Hanushek, Stephen Machin, and Ludger Woessmann, 341–81. Amsterdam: North Holland.

Biavaschi, Costanza, Werner Eichhorst, Corrado Giulietti, Michael J. Kendzia, Alexander Muravyev, Janneke Pieters, Núria Rodríguez-Planas, Ricarda Schmidl, and Klaus F. Zimmermann. 2012. Youth unemployment and vocational training. IZA Discussion Paper 6890. Bonn: Institute for the Study of Labor.

Bils, Mark, and Peter J. Klenow. 2000. Does schooling cause growth? *American Economic Review* 90 (5): 1160–83.

Bishop, John H. 1989. Is the test score decline responsible for the productivity growth decline? *American Economic Review* 79 (1): 178–97.

Bishop, John H. 1997. The effect of national standards and curriculum-based examinations on achievement. *American Economic Review* 87 (2): 260–64.

Bishop, John H. 2006. Drinking from the fountain of knowledge: Student incentive to study and learn - Externalities, information problems, and peer pressure. In *Handbook of the Economics of Education*, vol. 2, ed. Eric A. Hanushek and Finis Welch, 909–44. Amsterdam: North Holland.

Björklund, Anders, Per-Anders Edin, Peter Freriksson, and Alan B. Krueger. 2004. Education, equality and efficiency: An analysis of Swedish school reforms during the 1990s. In *IFAU Report 2004:1*. Uppsala: Institute for Labour Market Policy Evaluation.

Blau, David M., and Janet Currie. 2006. Pre-school, day care, and after-school care: Who's minding the kids? In *Handbook of the Economics of Education*, ed. Eric A. Hanushek and Finis Welch, 1163–1278. Amsterdam: North Holland.

Böhlmark, Anders, and Mikael Lindahl. 2012. Independent Schools and Long-Run Educational Outcomes: Evidence from Sweden's Large Scale Voucher Reform. IZA Discussion Paper 6683. Bonn: Institute for the Study of Labor.

Borghans, Lex, Angela Lee Duckworth, James J. Heckman, and Bas ter Weel. 2008. The economics and psychology of personality traits. *Journal of Human Resources* 43 (4): 972–1059.

Börsch-Supan, Axel. 2000. A model under siege: A case study of the German retirement insurance system. *Economic Journal* 110 (461): F24–F45.

Bosworth, Barry P., and Susan M. Collins. 2003. The empirics of growth: An update. *Brookings Papers on Economic Activity* (2): 113–206.

Bowles, Samuel, Herbert Gintis, and Melissa Osborne. 2001. The determinants of earnings: A behavioral approach. *Journal of Economic Literature* 39 (4): 1137–76.

Brown, Giorgina, John Micklewright, Sylke V. Schnepf, and Robert Waldmann. 2007. International surveys of educational achievement: How robust are the findings? *Journal of the Royal Statistical Society* A 170 (3): 623–46.

Brunello, Giorgio, and Daniele Checchi. 2007. Does school tracking affect equality of opportunity? New international evidence. *Economic Policy* 22 (52): 781–861.

Brunello, Giorgio, and Lorenzo Rocco. 2013. The effect of immigration on the school performance of natives: Cross country evidence using PISA test scores. *Economics of Education Review* 32 (1): 234–46.

Burtless, Gary, ed. 1996. *Does Money Matter? The Effect of School Resources on Student Achievement and Adult Success.* Washington, DC: Brookings.

Card, David. 1999. The causal effect of education on earnings. In *Handbook of Labor Economics*, ed. Orley Ashenfelter and David Card, 1801–63. Amsterdam: North Holland.

Card, David, Martin D. Dooley, and A. Abigail Payne. 2010. School competition and efficiency with publicly funded Catholic schools. *American Economic Journal: Applied Economics* 2 (4): 150–76.

Carnoy, Martin, and Susanna Loeb. 2002. Does external accountability affect student outcomes? A cross-state analysis. *Educational Evaluation and Policy Analysis* 24 (4): 305–31.

Caselli, Francesco. 2005. Accounting for cross-country income differences. In *Handbook of Economic Growth*, ed. Philippe Aghion and Steven N. Durlauf, 679–741. Amsterdam: North Holland.

Castelló, Amparo, and Rafael Doménech. 2002. Human capital inequality and economic growth: Some new evidence. *Economic Journal* 112 (478): C187–C200.

Ceci, Stephen J., and Wendy M. Williams. 2009. Should scientists study race and IQ? Yes: The scientific truth must be pursued. *Nature* 457 (February 12): 788–89.

Chetty, Raj, John N. Friedman, Nathaniel Hilger, Emmanuel Saez, Diane Whitmore Schanzenbach, and Danny Yagan. 2011. How does your kindergarten classroom affect your earnings? Evidence from Project STAR. *Quarterly Journal of Economics* 126 (4): 1593–1660.

Chetty, Raj, John N. Friedman, and Jonah Rockoff. 2014a. Measuring the impacts of teachers I: Evaluating bias in teacher value-added estimates. *American Economic Review* 104 (9): 2593–2632.

Chetty, Raj, John N. Friedman, and Jonah Rockoff. 2014b. Measuring the impacts of teachers II: Teacher value-added and the student outcomes in adulthood. *American Economic Review* 104 (9): 2633–79.

Chingos, Matthew M., and Paul E. Peterson. 2011. It's easier to pick a good teacher than to train one: Familiar and new results on the correlates of teacher effectiveness. *Economics of Education Review* 30 (3): 449–65.

Ciccone, Antonio, and Marek Jarocinski. 2010. Determinants of economic growth: Will data tell? *American Economic Journal: Macroeconomics* 2 (4): 222–46.

Ciccone, Antonio, and Elias Papaioannou. 2009. Human capital, the structure of production, and growth. *Review of Economics and Statistics* 91 (1): 66–82.

Ciccone, Antonio, and Giovanni Peri. 2006. Identifying human capital externalities: Theory with applications. *Review of Economic Studies* 73 (2): 381–412.

Cingano, Federico, Marco Leonardi, Julián Messina, and Giovanni Pica. 2010. The effects of employment protection legislation and financial market imperfections on investment: evidence from a firm-level panel of EU countries. *Economic Policy* 25 (61): 117–63.

Clark, Damon. 2009. The performance and competitive effects of school autonomy. *Journal of Political Economy* 117 (4): 745–83.

Cleveland, William S. 1979. Robust locally weighted regression and smoothing scatterplots. *Journal of the American Statistical Association* 74 (368): 829–36.

Cohen, Daniel, and Marcelo Soto. 2007. Growth and human capital: Good data, good results. *Journal of Economic Growth* 12 (1): 51–76.

Cole, Harold L., Lee E. Ohanian, Alvaro Riascos Jr., and James A. Schmitz. 2005. Latin America in the rearview mirror. *Journal of Monetary Economics* 52 (1): 69–107.

Congressional Budget Office. 2013. *The Budget and Economic Outlook: Fiscal Years 2013 to 2023.* Washington, DC: Congressional Budget Office.

Cörvers, Frank, Hans Heijke, Ben Kriechel, and Harald Pfeifer. 2011. High and steady or low and rising? Life-cycle earnings patterns in vocational and general education. ROA Research Memorandum ROA-RM-2011/7. Maastricht: Research Centre for Education and the Labour Market.

Coulombe, Serge, and Jean-François Tremblay. 2006. Literacy and growth. *Topics in Macroeconomics* 6, no. 2: Article 4.

Cullen, Julie Berry, Brian A Jacob, and Steven Levitt. 2006. The effect of school choice on participants: Evidence from randomized lotteries. *Econometrica* 74 (5): 1191–1230.

Cunha, Flavio, and James J. Heckman. 2007. The technology of skill formation. *American Economic Review* 97 (2): 31–47.

Cunha, Flavio, James J. Heckman, Lance Lochner, and Dimitriy V. Masterov. 2006. Interpreting the evidence on life cycle skill formation. In *Handbook of the Economics of Education*, ed. Eric A. Hanushek and Finis Welch, 697–812. Amsterdam: Elsevier.

Dee, Thomas S., and Brian A. Jacob. 2011. The impact of No Child Left Behind on student achievement. *Journal of Policy Analysis and Management* 30 (3): 418–46.

Dee, Thomas, and James Wyckoff. 2013. Incentives, selection, and teacher performance: Evidence from IMPACT. NBER Working Paper 19529. Cambridge, MA: National Bureau of Economic Research (October).

Delgado, Michael S., Daniel J. Henderson, and Christopher F. Parmeter. 2014. Does education matter for economic growth? *Oxford Bulletin of Economics and Statistics* 76 (3): 334–59.

Deming, David. 2009. Early childhood intervention and life-cycle skill development: Evidence from Head Start. *American Economic Journal: Applied Economics* 1 (3): 111–34.

Deming, David J., Justine S. Hastings, Thomas J. Kane, and Douglas O. Staiger. 2014. School choice, school quality and postsecondary attainment. *American Economic Review* 104 (3): 991–1013.

Dickens, William T., and James R. Flynn. 2001. Heritability estimates versus large environmental effects: The IQ paradox resolved. *Psychological Review* 108 (2): 346–69.

Dolton, Peter, and Oscar D. Marcenaro-Gutierrez. 2011. If you pay peanuts do you get monkeys? A cross country analysis of teacher pay and pupil performance. *Economic Policy* 26 (65): 7–55.

Dubois, Pierre, Alain de Janvry, and Elisabeth Sadoulet. 2012. Effects on School Enrollment and Performance of a Conditional Cash Transfer Program in Mexico. *Journal of Labor Economics* 30 (3): 555–89.

Duflo, Esther, Pascaline Dupas, and Michael Kremer. 2011. Peer effects, teacher incentives, and the impact of tracking: Evidence from a randomized evaluation in Kenya. *American Economic Review* 101 (5): 1739–74.

Duflo, Esther, Pascaline Dupas, and Michael Kremer. 2012. School governance, teacher incentives, and pupil-teacher ratios: Experimental evidence from Kenyan primary schools. NBER Working Paper 17939. Cambridge, MA: National Bureau of Economic Research.

Duflo, Esther, Rema Hanna, and Stephen P. Ryan. 2012. Incentives work: Getting teachers to come to school. *American Economic Review* 102 (4): 1241–78.

Easterly, William. 2001. *The Elusive Quest for Growth: An Economist's Adventures and Misadventures in the Tropics.* Cambridge: MIT Press.

Edwards, Sebastian, Gerardo Esquivel, and Graciela Márquez, eds. 2007. *The Decline of Latin American Economies: Growth, Institutions, and Crises.* Chicago: University of Chicago Press.

Ehrenberg, Ronald G., Dominic J. Brewer, Adam Gamoran, and J. Douglas Willms. 2001. Class size and student achievement. *Psychological Science in the Public Interest* 2 (1): 1–30.

Ehrlich, Isaac. 2007. The mystery of human capital as engine of growth, or why the US became the economic superpower in the 20th Century. NBER Working Paper 12868. Cambridge, MA: National Bureau of Economic Research (January).

Engerman, Stanley L., and Kenneth L. Sokoloff. 2012. *Economic Development in the Americas since 1500.* Cambridge, UK: Cambridge University Press.

Fernández-Arias, Eduardo, Rodolfo Manuelli, and Juan S. Blyde, eds. 2005. *Sources of Growth in Latin America: What Is Missing?* Washington, DC: Inter-American Development Bank.

Figlio, David, and Susanna Loeb. 2011. School accountability. In *Handbook of the Economics of Education,* vol. 3, ed. Eric A. Hanushek, Stephen Machin, and Ludger Woessmann, 383–421. Amsterdam: North Holland.

Figlio, David N., and Cecilia Elena Rouse. 2006. Do accountability and voucher threats improve low-performing schools? *Journal of Public Economics* 90 (1–2): 239–55.

Filmer, Deon. 2006. *Educational Attainment and Enrollment around the World.* Washington, DC: World Bank, Development Research Group. Available from econ.worldbank.org/projects/edattain.

Flynn, James R. 2007. *What Is Intelligence?: Beyond the Flynn Effect.* Cambridge, UK: Cambridge University Press.

Foshay, Arthur W. 1962. The background and the procedures of the twelve-country study. In *Educational Achievement of Thirteen-year-olds in Twelve Countries: Results of an International Research Project, 1959–61,* ed. Arthur W. Foshay, Robert L. Thorndike, Fernand Hotyat, Douglas A. Pidgeon, and David A. Walker. Hamburg: Unesco Institute for Education.

Friedman, Milton. 1962. *Capitalism and Freedom*. Chicago: University of Chicago Press.

Fryer, Roland G. 2011. Financial incentives and student achievement: Evidence from randomized trials. *Quarterly Journal of Economics* 126 (4): 1755–98.

Fryer, Roland G., Jr., Steven D. Levitt, John List, and Sally Sadoff. 2012. Enhancing the efficacy of teacher incentives through loss aversion: A field experiment. NBER Working Paper 18237. Cambridge, MA: National Bureau of Economic Research.

Fuller, Wayne A. 1977. Some properties of a modification of the limited information estimator. *Econometrica* 45 (4): 939–54.

Galiani, Sebastian, Paul Gertler, and Ernesto Schargrodsky. 2008. School decentralization: Helping the good get better, but leaving the poor behind. *Journal of Public Economics* 92 (10–11): 2106–20.

Galiani, Sebastian, and Patrick J. McEwan. 2013. The heterogeneous impact of conditional cash transfers. *Journal of Public Economics* 103 (July): 85–96.

Galiani, Sebastian, and Ricardo Perez-Truglia. 2014. School management in developing countries. In *Education Policy in Developing Countries*, ed. Paul Glewwe, 193–241. Chicago: University of Chicago Press.

Galor, Oded, and Omer Moav. 2000. Ability-biased technologoical transition, wage inequality, and economic growth. *Quarterly Journal of Economics* 115 (2): 469–97.

Garces, Eliana, Duncan Thomas, and Janet Currie. 2002. Longer-term effects of Head Start. *American Economic Review* 92 (4): 999–1012.

Gennaioli, Nicola, Rafael La Porta, Florencio Lopez-de-Silanes, and Andrei Shleifer. 2013. Human capital and regional development. *Quarterly Journal of Economics* 128 (1): 105–64.

Gertler, Paul J., Harry Anthony Patrinos, and Marta Rubio-Codina. 2012. Empowering parents to improve education: Evidence from rural Mexico. *Journal of Development Economics* 99 (1): 68–79.

Gibbons, Stephen, Stephen Machin, and Olmo Silva. 2008. Choice, competition, and pupil achievement. *Journal of the European Economic Association* 6 (4): 912–47.

Glaeser, Edward L., Rafael La Porta, Forencio Lopez-de-Silanes, and Andrei Shleifer. 2004. Do institutions cause growth? *Journal of Economic Growth* 9 (3): 271–303.

Glewwe, Paul, Eric A. Hanushek, Sarah D. Humpage, and Renato Ravina. 2014. School resources and educational outcomes in developing countries: A review of the literature from 1990 to 2010. In *Education Policy in Developing Countries*, ed. Paul Glewwe, 13–64. Chicago: University of Chicago Press.

Glewwe, Paul, Nauman Ilias, and Michael Kremer. 2010. Teacher incentives. *American Economic Journal: Applied Economics* 2 (3): 205–27.

Goldberger, Arthur S., and Charles F. Manski. 1995. Review article: The bell curve by Herrnstein and Murray. *Journal of Economic Literature* 33 (2): 762–76.

Goldin, Claudia, and Lawrence F. Katz. 2008. *The Race between Education and Technology*. Cambridge: Harvard University Press.

Golsteyn, Bart H.H., and Anders Stenberg. 2014. Comparing long term earnings trajectories of individuals with general and specific education. Paper presented at the 2014 meeting of the Society of Labor Economists.

Gould, Eric D., Omer Moav, and Bruce A. Weinberg. 2001. Precautionary demand for education, inequality, and technological progress. *Journal of Economic Growth* 6 (4): 285–315.

Greenwald, Rob, Larry V. Hedges, and Richard D. Laine. 1996. The effect of school resources on student achievement. *Review of Educational Research* 66 (3): 361–96.

Gundlach, Erich, Ludger Woessmann, and Jens Gmelin. 2001. The decline of schooling productivity in OECD countries. *Economic Journal* 111 (May): C135–C147.

Gunnarsson, Victoria, Peter F. Orazem, Mario A. Sánchez, and Aimee Verdisco. 2009. Does local school control raise student outcomes? Evidence on the roles of school autonomy and parental participation. *Economic Development and Cultural Change* 58 (1): 25–52.

Hagist, Christian, Norbert Klusen, Andreas Plate, and Bernd Raffelhüschen. 2005. Social health insurance: The major driver of unsustainable fiscal policy? CESifo Working Paper 1574. Munich: CESifo.

Hahn, Jinyong, Jerry A. Hausman, and Guido Kuersteiner. 2004. Estimation with weak instruments: Accuracy of higher-order bias and MSE approximations. *Econometrics Journal* 7 (1): 272–306.

Hall, Caroline. 2013. Does more general education reduce the risk of future unemployment? Evidence from labor market experiences during the Great Recession. IFAU Working Paper 2013:17. Upsalla, Sweden: Institute for Evaluation of Labour Market and Education Policy (July).

Hall, Robert E., and Charles I. Jones. 1999. Why do some countries produce so much more output per worker than others? *Quarterly Journal of Economics* 114 (1): 83–116.

Hanousek, Jan, Dana Hajkova, and Randall K. Filer. 2008. A rise by any other name? Sensitivity of growth regressions to data source. *Journal of Macroeconomics* 30 (3): 1188–1206.

Hanson, Gordon H. 2010. Why isn't Mexico rich? *Journal of Economic Literature* 48 (4): 987–1004.

Hanushek, Eric A. 1971. Teacher characteristics and gains in student achievement: Estimation using micro data. *American Economic Review* 60 (2): 280–88.

Hanushek, Eric A. 1992. The trade-off between child quantity and quality. *Journal of Political Economy* 100 (1): 84–117.

Hanushek, Eric A. 1995. Interpreting recent research on schooling in developing countries. *World Bank Research Observer* 10 (2): 227–46.

Hanushek, Eric A. 1996. A more complete picture of school resource policies. *Review of Educational Research* 66 (3): 397–409.

Hanushek, Eric A. 2002. Publicly provided education. In *Handbook of Public Economics*, vol. 4, ed. Alan J. Auerbach and Martin Feldstein, 2045–2141. Amsterdam: North Holland.

Hanushek, Eric A. 2003. The failure of input-based schooling policies. *Economic Journal* 113 (485): F64–F98.

Hanushek, Eric A. 2008. Incentives for efficiency and equity in the school system. *Perspektiven der Wirtschaftspolitik* 9 (special issue): 5–27.

Hanushek, Eric A. 2011. The economic value of higher teacher quality. *Economics of Education Review* 30 (3): 466–79.

Hanushek, Eric A., and Dennis D. Kimko. 2000. Schooling, labor force quality, and the growth of nations. *American Economic Review* 90 (5): 1184–1208.

Hanushek, Eric A., Susanne Link, and Ludger Woessmann. 2013. Does school autonomy make sense everywhere? Panel estimates from PISA. *Journal of Development Economics* 104 (September): 212–32.

Hanushek, Eric A., Paul E. Peterson, and Ludger Woessmann. 2013. *Endangering prosperity: A global view of the American school*. Washington, DC: Brookings Institution Press.

Hanushek, Eric A., and Margaret E. Raymond. 2005. Does school accountability lead to improved student performance? *Journal of Policy Analysis and Management* 24 (2): 297–327.

Hanushek, Eric A., and Steven G. Rivkin. 2006. Teacher quality. In *Handbook of the Economics of Education*, vol. 2, ed. Eric A. Hanushek and Finis Welch, 1051–78. Amsterdam: North Holland.

Hanushek, Eric A., and Steven G. Rivkin. 2010. Generalizations about using value-added measures of teacher quality. *American Economic Review* 100 (2): 267–71.

Hanushek, Eric A., and Steven G. Rivkin. 2012. The distribution of teacher quality and implications for policy. *Annual Review of Economics* 4:131–57.

Hanushek, Eric A., Guido Schwerdt, Simon Wiederhold, and Ludger Woessmann. 2015. Returns to skills around the world. *European Economic Review* 73:103–30.

Hanushek, Eric A., Guido Schwerdt, Ludger Woessmann, and Lei Zhang. 2014. General education, vocational education, and labor-market outcomes over the life-cycle. Revised version of NBER Working Paper 17504. Stanford University.

Hanushek, Eric A., and Ludger Woessmann. 2006. Does educational tracking affect performance and inequality? Differences-in-differences evidence across countries. *Economic Journal* 116 (510): C63–C76.

Hanushek, Eric A., and Ludger Woessmann. 2008. The role of cognitive skills in economic development. *Journal of Economic Literature* 46 (3): 607–68.

Hanushek, Eric A., and Ludger Woessmann. 2011a. The economics of international differences in educational achievement. In *Handbook of the Economics of Education*, vol. 3, ed. Eric A. Hanushek, Stephen Machin, and Ludger Woessmann, 89–200. Amsterdam: North Holland.

Hanushek, Eric A., and Ludger Woessmann. 2011b. How much do educational outcomes matter in OECD countries? *Economic Policy* 26 (67): 427–91.

Hanushek, Eric A., and Ludger Woessmann. 2011c. Sample selectivity and the validity of international student achievement tests in economic research. *Economics Letters* 110 (2): 79–82.

Hanushek, Eric A., and Ludger Woessmann. 2012a. Do better schools lead to more growth? Cognitive skills, economic outcomes, and causation. *Journal of Economic Growth* 17 (4): 267–321.

Hanushek, Eric A., and Ludger Woessmann. 2012b. The economic benefit of educational reform in the European Union. *CESifo Economic Studies* 58 (1): 73–109.

Hanushek, Eric A., and Ludger Woessmann. 2012c. Schooling, educational achievement, and the Latin American growth puzzle. *Journal of Development Economics* 99 (2): 497–512.

Hanushek, Eric A., and Lei Zhang. 2009. Quality-consistent estimates of international schooling and skill gradients. *Journal of Human Capital* 3 (2): 107–43.

Harbison, Ralph W., and Eric A. Hanushek. 1992. *Educational Performance of the Poor: Lessons from Rural Northeast Brazil.* New York: Oxford University Press.

Harris, Douglas N., and Tim R. Sass. 2011. Teacher training, teacher quality and student achievement. *Journal of Public Economics* 95 (7–8): 798–812.

Hausmann, Ricardo, Lant Pritchett, and Dani Rodrik. 2005. Growth accelerations. *Journal of Economic Growth* 10 (4): 303–29.

Heckman, James J. 1995. Lessons from the bell curve. *Journal of Political Economy* 103 (5): 1091–1120.

Heckman, James J. 2006. Skill formation and the economics of investing in disadvantaged children. *Science* 312 (5782): 1900–1902.

Heckman, James J. 2008. Schools, skills, and synapses. *Economic Inquiry* 46 (3): 289–324.

Heckman, James J., Lance J. Lochner, and Petra E. Todd. 2006. Earnings functions, rates of return and treatment effects: The Mincer equation and beyond. In *Handbook of the Economics of Education*, vol. 1, ed. Eric A. Hanushek and Finis Welch, 307–458. Amsterdam: North Holland.

Heckman, James J., Lance J. Lochner, and Petra E. Todd. 2008. Earnings functions and rates of return. *Journal of Human Capital* 2 (1): 1–31.

Heckman, James J., Seong Hyeok Moon, Rodrigo Pinto, Peter A. Savelyev, and Adam Yavitz. 2010a. Analyzing social experiments as implemented: A reexamination of the evidence from the HighScope Perry Preschool Program. *Journal of Quantitative Economics* 1 (1): 1–46.

Heckman, James J., Seong Hyeok Moon, Rodrigo Pinto, Peter A. Savelyev, and Adam Yavitz. 2010b. The rate of return to the HighScope Perry Preschool Program. *Journal of Public Economics* 94 (1–2): 114–28.

Heckman, James J., Jora Stixrud, and Sergio Urzua. 2006. The effects of cognitive and noncognitive abilities on labor market outcomes and social behavior. *Journal of Labor Economics* 24 (3): 411–82.

Hendricks, Lutz. 2002. How important is human capital for development? Evidence from immigrant earnings. *American Economic Review* 92 (1): 198–219.

Herrnstein, Richard J., and Charles A. Murray. 1994. *The Bell Curve: Intelligence and Class Structure in American Life*. New York: Free Press.

Heston, Alan, Robert Summers, and Bettina Aten. 2002. Penn World Table Version 6.1. In *Center for International Comparisons at the University of Pennsylvania (CICUP)*. Philadelphia: University of Pennsylvania.

Heston, Alan, Robert Summers, and Bettina Aten. 2011. Penn World Table Version 7.0. Center for International Comparisons of Production, Income and Prices at the University of Pennsylvania. Philadelphia: University of Pennsylvania (June 3 update).

Heyneman, Stephen P., and Jonathan M. B. Stern. 2014. Low cost private schools for the poor: What public policy is appropriate? *International Journal of Educational Development* 35: 3–15.

Howell, William G., and Paul E. Peterson. 2002. *The Education Gap: Vouchers and Urban Schools*. Washington, DC: Brookings.

Hoxby, Caroline M. 2007. Does competition among public schools benefit students and taxpayers? Reply. *American Economic Review* 97 (5): 2038–55.

Hsieh, Chang-Tai, and Peter J. Klenow. 2010. Development accounting. *American Economic Journal: Macroeconomics* 2 (1): 207–23.

Hunt, Earl, and Werner Wittmann. 2008. National intelligence and national prosperity. *Intelligence* 36 (1): 1–9.

Iranzo, Susana, and Giovanni Peri. 2009. Schooling externalities, technology, and productivity: Theory and evidence from U.S. states. *Review of Economics and Statistics* 91 (2): 420–31.

Jacob, Brian A. 2005. Accountability, incentives and behavior: The impact of high-stakes testing in the Chicago Public Schools. *Journal of Public Economics* 89 (5–6): 761–96.

Jamison, Eliot A., Dean T. Jamison, and Eric A. Hanushek. 2007. The effects of education quality on mortality decline and income growth. *Economics of Education Review* 26 (6): 772–89.

Jensen, Robert. 2010. The (perceived) returns to education and the demand for schooling. *Quarterly Journal of Economics* 125 (2): 515–48.

Jimenez, Emmanuel, and Yasuyuki Sawada. 1999. Do community-managed schools work? An evaluation of El Salvador's EDUCO program. *World Bank Economic Review* 13 (3): 415–41.

Johnson, Simon, William Larson, Chris Papageorgiou, and Arvind Subramanian. 2013. Is newer better? Penn World Table revisions and their impact on growth estimates. *Journal of Monetary Economics* 60 (2): 255–74.

Jones, Benjamin F., and Benjamin A. Olken. 2008. The anatomy of start-stop growth. *Review of Economics and Statistics* 90 (3): 582–87.

Jones, Charles I. 2005. Growth and ideas. In *Handbook of Economic Growth, Volume 1, Part B*, ed. Philippe Aghion and Steven N. Durlauf, 1063–1111. Amsterdam: Elsevier.

Jones, Charles I., and Dietrich Vollrath. 2013. *Introduction to Economic Growth*, 3rd ed. New York: Norton.

Jones, Garett, and W. Joel Schneider. 2006. Intelligence, human capital, and economic growth: A bayesian averaging of classical estimates (BACE) approach. *Journal of Economic Growth* 11 (1): 71–93.

Jones, Garett, and W. Joel Schneider. 2010. IQ in the production function: Evidence from immigrant earnings. *Economic Inquiry* 48 (3): 743–55.

Jürges, Hendrik, Kerstin Schneider, and Felix Büchel. 2005. The effect of central exit examinations on student achievement: Quasi-experimental evidence from TIMSS Germany. *Journal of the European Economic Association* 3 (5): 1134–55.

Jürges, Hendrik, Kerstin Schneider, Martin Senkbeil, and Claus H. Carstensen. 2012. Assessment drives learning: The effect of central exit exams on curricular knowledge and mathematical literacy. *Economics of Education Review* 31 (1): 56–65.

Kaarsen, Nicolai. 2014. Cross-country differences in the quality of schooling. *Journal of Development Economics* 107:215–24.

Katz, Lawrence F., and David H. Autor. 1999. Changes in the wage structure and earnings inequality. In *Handbook of Labor Economics*, ed. Orley Ashenfelter and David Card, 1463–1558. Amsterdam: Elsevier.

Kehoe, Timothy J., and Kim J. Ruhl. 2010. Why have economic reforms in Mexico not generated growth? *Journal of Economic Literature* 48 (4): 1005–27.

Kiker, B. F. 1966. The historical roots of the concept of human capital. *Journal of Political Economy* 74 (5): 481–99.

Kiker, B. F. 1968. *Human Capital: In Retrospect*. Columbia, SC: University of South Carolina.

Klenow, Peter J., and Andres Rodriquez-Clare. 1997. The neoclassical revival in growth economics: Has it gone too far? In *NBER Macroeconomics Annual 1997*, ed. Ben S. Bernancke and Julio J. Rotemberg, 83–103. Cambridge: MIT Press.

Kremer, Michael, Conner Brannen, and Rachel Glennerster. 2013. The challenge of education and learning in the developing world. *Science* 340 (6130): 297–300.

Kremer, Michael, Edward Miguel, and Rebecca Thornton. 2009. Incentives to learn. *Review of Economics and Statistics* 91 (3): 437–56.

Krueger, Alan B., and Mikael Lindahl. 2001. Education for growth: Why and for whom? *Journal of Economic Literature* 39 (4): 1101–36.

Krueger, Dirk, and Krishna B. Kumar. 2004a. Skill-specific rather than general education: A reason for US-Europe growth differences? *Journal of Economic Growth* 9 (2): 167–207.

Krueger, Dirk, and Krishna B. Kumar. 2004b. US-Europe differences in technology-driven growth: Quantifying the role of education. *Journal of Monetary Economics* 51 (1): 161–90.

Laboratorio Latinoamericano de Evaluación de la Calidad de la Educación. 1998. *First International Comparative Study of Language, Mathematics, and Associated Factors in Third and Fourth Grades.* Santiago, Chile: Latin American Educational Quality Assessment Laboratory.

Laboratorio Latinoamericano de Evaluación de la Calidad de la Educación. 2001. *Primer Estudio Internacional Comparativo sobre Lenguaje, Matemática y Factores Asociados, para Alumnos del Tercer y Cuarto Grado de la Educación Básica: Informe Técnico.* Santiago, Chile: UNECSO-Santiago, Oficina Regional de Educación para América Latina y el Caribe.

Laboratorio Latinoamericano de Evaluación de la Calidad de la Educación. 2002. *First International Comparative Study of Language, Mathematics, and Associated Factors in the Third and Fourth Grade of Primary School: Second Report.* Santiago, Chile: UNECSO-Santiago, Regional Office of Education for Latin America and the Caribbean.

Laboratorio Latinoamericano de Evaluación de la Calidad de la Educación. 2005. *Segundo Estudio Regional Comparativo Explicativo 2004–2007: Análisis Curricular.* Santiago, Chile: Oficina Regional de Educación de la UNESCO para América Latina y el Caribe (OREALC/UNESCO).

Laboratorio Latinoamericano de Evaluación de la Calidad de la Educación. 2008a. *Los Aprendizajes de los Estudiantes de América Latina y el Caribe: Primer Reporte de los Resultados del Segundo Estudio Regional Comparativo y Explicativo.* Santiago, Chile: Oficina Regional de Educación de la UNESCO para América Latina y el Caribe (OREALC/UNESCO).

Laboratorio Latinoamericano de Evaluación de la Calidad de la Educación. 2008b. *Student Achievement in Latin America and the Caribbean: Results of the Second Regional Comparative and Explanatory Study (SERCE) - Executive Summary.* Santiago, Chile: Regional Bureau for Education in Latin America and the Caribbean OREALC/UNESCO.

Lau, Lawrence J., Dean T. Jamison, and Frederic F. Louat. 1991. Education and productivity in developing countries: An aggregate production function approach. World Bank PRE Working Paper Series 612. Washington, DC: World Bank.

Lavy, Victor. 2002. Evaluating the effect of teachers' group performance incentives on pupil achievement. *Journal of Political Economy* 110 (6): 1286–1317.

Lavy, Victor. 2009. Performance pay and teachers' effort, productivity, and grading ethics. *American Economic Review* 99 (5): 1979–2011.

Lavy, Victor. 2010. Effects of free choice among public schools. *Review of Economic Studies* 77 (3): 1164–91.

Lavy, Victor. 2011. What makes an effective teacher? Quasi-experimental evidence. NBER Working Paper 16885. Cambridge, MA: National Bureau of Economic Research.

Lazear, Edward P. 2003. Teacher incentives. *Swedish Economic Policy Review* 10 (3): 179–214.

Lee, Jong-Wha, and Robert J. Barro. 2001. Schooling quality in a cross-section of countries. *Economica* 68 (272): 465–88.

Leigh, Andrew. 2010. Estimating teacher effectiveness from two-year changes in students' test scores. *Economics of Education Review* 29 (3): 480–88.

Levine, Ross, and David Renelt. 1992. A sensitivity analysis of cross-country growth regressions. *American Economic Review* 82 (4): 942–63.

Levine, Ross, and Sara J. Zervos. 1993. What we have learned about policy and growth from cross-country regressions. *American Economic Review* 83 (2): 426–30.

Lindqvist, Erik, and Roine Vestman. 2011. The labor market returns to cognitive and noncognitive ability: Evidence from the Swedish enlistment. *American Economic Journal: Applied Economics* 3 (1): 101–28.

Lochner, Lance. 2011. Nonproduction benefits of education: Crime, health, and good citizenship. In *Handbook of the Economics of Education*, vol. 4, ed. Eric A. Hanushek, Stephen Machin, and Ludger Woessmann, 183–282. Amsterdam: North Holland.

Lucas, Robert E., Jr. 1988. On the mechanics of economic development. *Journal of Monetary Economics* 22 (1): 3–42.

Lucas, Robert E., Jr. 2003. Macroeconomic priorities. *American Economic Review* 93 (1): 1–14.

Ludwig, Jens, and Douglas L. Miller. 2007. Does Head Start improve children's life chances? Evidence from a regression discontinuity design. *Quarterly Journal of Economics* 122 (1): 159–208.

Lynn, Richard, and Jaan Mikk. 2007. National differences in intelligence and educational attainment. *Intelligence* 35 (2): 115–21.

Lynn, Richard, and Jaan Mikk. 2009. National IQs predict educational attainment in math, reading and science across 56 nations. *Intelligence* 37 (3): 305–10.

Lynn, Richard, and Tatu Vanhanen. 2002. *IQ and the Wealth of Nations*. Westport, CT: Praeger Publishers.

Lynn, Richard, and Tatu Vanhanen. 2006. *IQ and Global Inequality*. Augusta, GA: Washington Summit Publishers.

Malamud, Ofer, and Cristian Pop-Eleches. 2010. General education versus vocational training: Evidence from an economy in transition. *Review of Economics and Statistics* 92 (1): 43–60.

Mankiw, N. Gregory, David Romer, and David Weil. 1992. A contribution to the empirics of economic growth. *Quarterly Journal of Economics* 107 (2): 407–37.

Martin, Michael O., Ina V. S. Mullis, Albert E. Beaton, Eugenio J. Gonzalez, Teresa A. Smith, and Dana L. Kelly. 1997. *Science Achievement in the Primary School Years: IEA's Third International Mathematics and Science Study (TIMSS)*. Boston: Center for the Study of Testing, Evaluation, And Educational Policy, Boston College.

Martin, Michael O., Ina V. S. Mullis, Eugenio J. Gonzalez, and Steven J. Chrostowski. 2004. *TIMSS 2003 International Science Report: Finding for IEA's Trends in International Mathematics and Science Study at the Fourth and Eighth Grades.* Boston: TIMSS and PIRLS International Study Center, Boston College.

Martin, Michael O., Ina V.S. Mullis, Eugenio J. Gonzalez, Kelvin D. Gregory, Teresa A. Smith, Steven J. Chrostowski, Robert A. Garden, and Kathleen M. O'Connor. 2000. *TIMSS 1999 International Science Report: Findings from IEA's Repeat of the Third International Mathematics and Science Study at the Eighth Grade.* Chestnut Hill, MA: Boston College.

McArthur, John W., and Jeffrey D. Sachs. 2001. Institutions and Geography: Comment on Acemoglu, Johnson and Robinson (2000). NBER Working Paper 8114. Cambridge, MA: National Bureau of Economic Research.

Meghir, Costas, and Mårten Palme. 2005. Educational reform, ability, and family background. *American Economic Review* 95 (1): 414–23.

Metzler, Johannes, and Ludger Woessmann. 2012. The impact of teacher subject knowledge on student achievement: Evidence from within-teacher within-student variation. *Journal of Development Economics* 99 (2): 486–96.

Mincer, Jacob. 1974. *Schooling, Experience, and Earnings.* New York: NBER.

Mishel, Lawrence, and Richard Rothstein, eds. 2002. *The Class Size Debate.* Washington, DC: Economic Policy Institute.

Montenegro, Claudio E., and Harry A. Patrinos. 2014. Comparable estimates of returns to schooling around the world. Policy Research Working Paper WPS7020. Washington, DC: World Bank (September).

Moore, Mark A., Anthony E. Boardman, Aidan R. Vining, David L. Weimer, and David Greenberg. 2004. "Just give me a number!" Practical values for the social discount rate. *Journal of Policy Analysis and Management* 23 (4): 789–812.

Moreira, Marcelo J. 2003. A conditional likelihood ratio test for structural models. *Econometrica* 71 (4): 1027–48.

Moretti, Enrico. 2004. Workers' education, spillovers, and productivity: Evidence from plant-level production functions. *American Economic Review* 94 (3): 656–90.

Mourshed, Mona, Chinezi Chijioke, and Michael Barber. 2010. *How the World's Most Improved School Systems Keep Getting Better.* McKinsey and Company.

Müller, Walter. 2009. Benefits and costs of vocational education and training. In *Raymond Boudon, a life in sociology*, vol. 3, ed. Mohamed Cherkaoui and Peter Hamilton, 123–48. Paris: Bardwell Press.

Mulligan, Casey B. 1999. Galton versus the human capital approach to inheritance. *Journal of Political Economy* 107 (6, pt. 2): S184–S224.

Mullis, Ina V. S., Michael O. Martin, Albert E. Beaton, Eugenio J. Gonzalez, Dana L. Kelly, and Teresa A. Smith. 1997. *Mathematics Achievement in the Primary School Years: IEA's Third International Mathematics and Science Study (TIMSS).* Chestnut Hill, MA: Boston College.

Mullis, Ina V. S., Michael O. Martin, Albert E. Beaton, Eugenio J. Gonzalez, Dana L. Kelly, and Teresa A. Smith. 1998. *Mathematics and Science Achievement in the*

Final Year of Secondary School: IEA's Third International Mathematics and Science Study (TIMSS). Chestnut Hill, MA: Boston College.

Mullis, Ina V. S., Michael O. Martin, Eugenio J. Gonzalez, Kelvin D. Gregory, Robert A. Garden, Kathleen M. O'Connor, Steven J. Chrostowski, and Teresa A. Smith. 2000. *TIMSS 1999 International Mathematics Report: Findings from IEA's Repeat of the Third International Mathematics and Science Study at the Eighth Grade*. Chestnut Hill, MA: Center for the Study of Testing, Evaluation, and Educational Policy, Boston College.

Mullis, Ina V.S., Michael O. Martin, Pierre Foy, and Alka Arora. 2012. *TIMSS 2011 International Results in Mathematics*. Chestnut Hill, MA: TIMSS & PIRLS International Study Center, Boston College.

Mullis, Ina V.S., Michael O. Martin, Pierre Foy, and Kathleen T. Drucker. 2012. *PIRLS 2011 International Results in Reading*. Chestnut Hill, MA: TIMSS & PIRLS International Study Center, Boston College.

Mullis, Ina V.S., Michael O. Martin, Eugenio J. Gonzalez, and Steven J. Chrostowski. 2004. *TIMSS 2003 International Mathematics Report: Findings from IEA's Trends in International Mathematics and Science Study at the Fourth and Eighth Grades*. Chestnut Hill, MA: Boston College.

Mullis, Ina V.S., Michael O. Martin, Eugenio J. Gonzalez, and Ann M. Kennedy. 2003. *PIRLS 2001 International Report: IEA's Study of Reading Literacy Achievement in Primary School in 35 Countries*. Chestnut Hill, MA: International Study Center, Boston College.

Muralidharan, Karthik, and Venkatesh Sundararaman. 2011. Teacher performance pay: Experimental evidence from India. *Journal of Political Economy* 119 (1): 39–77.

Muralidharan, Karthik, and Venkatesh Sundararaman. 2013. The aggregate effect of school choice: Evidence from a two-stage experiment in India. NBER Working Paper 19441. Cambridge, MA: National Bureau of Economic Research.

Murnane, Richard J., John B. Willett, Yves Duhaldeborde, and John H. Tyler. 2000. How important are the cognitive skills of teenagers in predicting subsequent earnings? *Journal of Policy Analysis and Management* 19 (4): 547–68.

Murnane, Richard J., John B. Willett, and Frank Levy. 1995. The growing importance of cognitive skills in wage determination. *Review of Economics and Statistics* 77 (2): 251–66.

Murphy, Kevin M., Andrei Shleifer, and Robert W. Vishny. 1991. The allocation of talent: Implications for growth. *Quarterly Journal of Economics* 106 (2): 503–30.

Neal, Derek, and William R. Johnson. 1996. The role of pre-market factors in black-white differences. *Journal of Political Economy* 104 (5): 869–95.

Nehru, Vikram, Eric Swanson, and Ashutosh Dubey. 1995. A new database on human capital stock in developing and industrial countries: Sources, methodology, and results. *Journal of Development Economics* 46 (2): 379–401.

Neidorf, Teresa S., Marilyn Binkley, Kim Gattis, and David Nohara. 2006. *Comparing mathematics content in the National Assessment of Educational Progress*

(NAEP), Trends in International Mathematics and Science Study (TIMSS), and Program for International Student Assessment (PISA) 2003 Assessments. Washington, DC: National Center for Education Statistics (May).

Nelson, Richard R., and Edmund Phelps. 1966. Investment in humans, technology diffusion and economic growth. *American Economic Review* 56 (2): 69–75.

Nicoletti, Giuseppe, and Stefano Scarpetta. 2003. Regulation, productivity, and growth: OECD evidence. *Economic Policy* 18 (1): 10–72.

Nicoletti, Giuseppe, Stefano Scarpetta, and Olivier Boylaud. 2000. Summary indicators of product market regulation with an extension to employment protection legislation. Economic Department Working Paper 226. Paris: OECD (February).

Nordhaus, William D. 2007. A review of the Stern Review on the economics of climate change. *Journal of Economic Literature* 45 (3): 686–702.

North, Douglass C. 1990. *Institutions, Institutional Change and Economic Performance.* New York: Cambridge University Press.

Nuxoll, Daniel A. 1994. Differences in relative prices and international differences in growth rates. *American Economic Review* 84 (5): 1423–36.

Oreopoulos, Philip, and Kjell G. Salvanes. 2011. Priceless: The nonpecuniary benefits of schooling. *Journal of Economic Perspectives* 25 (1): 159–84.

Organisation for Economic Co-operation and Development. 1998. *Education at a Glance: OECD Indicators.* Paris: OECD.

Organisation for Economic Co-operation and Development. 1999. *Employment Outlook.* Paris: OECD.

Organisation for Economic Co-operation and Development. 2001. *Knowledge and Skills for Life: First Results from the OECD Programme for International Student Assessment (PISA) 2000.* Paris: OECD.

Organisation for Economic Co-operation and Development. 2003a. *Education at a Glance: OECD Indicators 2003.* Paris: OECD.

Organisation for Economic Co-operation and Development. 2003b. *Literacy Skills for the World of Tomorrow: Further Results from PISA 2000.* Paris: OECD.

Organisation for Economic Co-operation and Development. 2004. *Learning for Tomorrow's World: First Results from PISA 2003.* Paris: OECD.

Organisation for Economic Co-operation and Development. 2007. *Analysis,* vol. 1. *PISA 2006: Science Competencies for Tomorrow's World.* Paris: OECD.

Organisation for Economic Co-operation and Development. 2008. *Compendium of Patent Statistics.* Paris: OECD.

Organisation for Economic Co-operation and Development. 2009a. *OECD Economic Outlook* 85 (1).

Organisation for Economic Co-operation and Development. 2009b. *Society at a Glance 2009: OECD Social Indicators.* Paris: OECD.

Organisation for Economic Co-operation and Development. 2010a. *Education at a Glance 2010: OECD Indicators.* Paris: OECD.

Organisation for Economic Co-operation and Development. 2010b. *PISA 2009 Results: What Students Know and Can Do—Student Performance in Reading, Mathematics and Science*, vol. 1. Paris: OECD.

Organisation for Economic Co-operation and Development. 2013a. *Education at a Glance 2013: OECD Indicators*. Paris: OECD.

Organisation for Economic Co-operation and Development. 2013b. *PISA 2012 Results: What Students Know and Can Do—Student Performance in Mathematics, Reading and Science*, vol. 1. Paris: OECD.

Patrinos, Harry A. 2011. School-Based Management. In *Making Schools Work: New Evidence on Accountability Reforms*, ed. Barbara Bruns, Deon Filmer, and Harry A. Patrinos, 87–140. Washington, DC: World Bank.

Pekkala, Kerr, Tuomas Pekkarinen Sari, and Roope Uusitalo. 2013. School tracking and development of cognitive skills. *Journal of Labor Economics* 31 (3): 577–602.

Pekkarinen, Tuomas. 2014. School tracking and intergenerational social mobility. *IZA World of Labor* 214:56. doi:10.15185/izawol.56.

Pekkarinen, Tuomas, Roope Uusitalo, and Sari Kerr. 2009. School tracking and intergenerational income mobility: Evidence from the Finnish comprehensive school reform. *Journal of Public Economics* 93 (7–8): 965–73.

Petty, Sir William. [1676] 1899. Political arithmetic. In *The Economic Writings of Sir William Petty*, ed. Charles Henry Hull. Cambridge, UK: Cambridge University Press: 233–313.

Piopiunik, Marc. 2014. The effects of early tracking on student performance: Evidence from a school reform in Bavaria. *Economics of Education Review* 22: 12–33.

Podgursky, Michael J., and Matthew G. Springer. 2007. Teacher performance pay: A review. *Journal of Policy Analysis and Management* 26 (4): 909–49.

Pritchett, Lant. 2001. Where has all the education gone? *World Bank Economic Review* 15 (3): 367–91.

Pritchett, Lant. 2004. Access to education. In *Global Crises, Global Solutions*, ed. Björn Lomborg, 175–234. Cambridge: Cambridge University Press.

Pritchett, Lant. 2006. Does learning to add up add up? The returns to schooling in aggregate data. In *Handbook of the Economics of Education*, ed. Eric A. Hanushek and Finis Welch, 635–95. Amsterdam: North Holland.

Pritchett, Lant. 2013. *The Rebirth of Education: Schooling Ain't Learning*. Washington, DC: Center for Global Development.

Pritchett, Lant, and Amanda Beatty. 2012. The negative consequences of overambitious curricula in developing countries. CGD Working Paper 293. Washington, DC: Center for Global Development (April).

Pritchett, Lant, and Justin Sandefur. 2013. Context matters for size: Why external validity claims and development practice don't mix. CGD Working Paper 336. Washington, DC: Center for Global Development (August).

Psacharopoulos, George, and Harry A. Patrinos. 2004. Returns to investment in education: A further update. *Education Economics* 12 (2): 111–34.

Ram, Rati. 2007. IQ and economic growth: Further augmentation of Mankiw–Romer–Weil model. *Economics Letters* 94 (1): 7–11.

Ramirez, Francisco, Xiaowei Luo, Evan Schofer, and John Meyer. 2006. Student achievement and national economic growth. *American Journal of Education* 113 (1): 1–29.

Riley, John G. 2001. Silver signals: Twenty-five years of screening and signaling. *Journal of Economic Literature* 39 (2): 432–78.

Ripley, Amanda. 2013. *The Smartest Kids in the World and How They Got That Way*. New York: Simon Schuster.

Rivkin, Steven G., Eric A. Hanushek, and John F. Kain. 2005. Teachers, schools, and academic achievement. *Econometrica* 73 (2): 417–58.

Rockoff, Jonah E. 2004. The impact of individual teachers on student achievement: Evidence from panel data. *American Economic Review* 94 (2): 247–52.

Rockoff, Jonah E., Brian A. Jacob, Thomas J. Kane, and Douglas O. Staiger. 2011. Can you recognize an effective teacher when you recruit one? *Education Finance and Policy* 6 (1): 43–74.

Romer, Paul. 1990a. Endogenous technological change. *Journal of Political Economy* 99 (5, pt. 2): S71–S102.

Romer, Paul. 1990b. Human capital and growth: Theory and evidence. *Carnegie-Rochester Conference Series on Public Policy* 32:251–86.

Rose, Steven. 2009. Should scientists study race and IQ? No: Science and society do not benefit. *Nature* 457 (February 12): 787–88.

Rotberg, Iris C. 1995. Myths about test score comparisons. *Science* 270 (December 1): 1446–48.

Rothstein, Jesse. 2007. Does competition among public schools benefit students and taxpayers? Comment. *American Economic Review* 97 (5): 2026–37.

Rouse, Cecilia Elena. 1998. Private school vouchers and student achievement: An evaluation of the Milwaukee Parental Choice Program. *Quarterly Journal of Economics* 113 (2): 553–602.

Ryan, Paul. 2001. The school-to-work transition: A cross-national perspective. *Journal of Economic Literature* 39 (1): 34–92.

Sachs, Jeffrey D., and Andrew M. Warner. 1995. Economic reform and the process of global integration. *Brookings Papers on Economic Activity* (1): 1–96.

Sala-i-Martin, Xavier, Gernot Doppelhofer, and Ronald I. Miller. 2004. Determinants of long-term growth: A Bayesian averaging of classical estimates (BACE) approach. *American Economic Review* 94 (4): 813–35.

Sandström, F. Mikael, and Fredrik Bergström. 2005. School vouchers in practice: Competition will not hurt you. *Journal of Public Economics* 89 (2–3): 351–80.

Schoellman, Todd. 2012. Education quality and development accounting. *Review of Economic Studies* 79 (1): 388–417.

Schuetz, Gabriela. 2009. Does the quality of pre-primary education pay off in secondary school? An international comparison using PISA 2003. Ifo Working Paper 68. Munich: ifo Institute for Economic Research at the University of Munich.

Schuetz, Gabriela, Heinrich W. Ursprung, and Ludger Woessmann. 2008. Education policy and equality of opportunity. *Kyklos* 61 (2): 279–308.

Schultz, Theodore W. 1961. Investment in human capital. *American Economic Review* 51 (1): 1–17.

Schultz, Theodore W. 1975. The value of the ability to deal with disequilibria. *Journal of Economic Literature* 13 (3): 827–46.

Schumpeter, Joseph A. [1912] 2006. *Theorie der wirtschaftlichen Entwicklung.* Berlin: Duncker Humblot (English translation: The Theory of Economic Development).

Schwerdt, Guido, and Amelie C. Wuppermann. 2011. Is traditional teaching really all that bad? A within-student between-subject approach. *Economics of Education Review* 30 (2): 365–79.

Sianesi, Barbara, and John Van Reenen. 2003. The returns to education: Macroeconomics. *Journal of Economic Surveys* 17 (2): 157–200.

Slater, Helen, Neil M. Davies, and Simon Burgess. 2012. Do teachers matter? Measuring the variation in teacher effectiveness in England. *Oxford Bulletin of Economics and Statistics* 74 (5): 629–45.

Smith, Adam. [1776]1979. *An Inquiry into the Nature and Causes of the Wealth of Nations.* Oxford: Clarendon Press.

Solow, Robert M. 1956. A contribution to the theory of economic growth. *Quarterly Journal of Economics* 70 (1): 65–94.

Spence, A. Michael. 1973. Job market signalling. *Quarterly Journal of Economics* 87 (3): 355–74.

Spence, A. Michael, and Danny Leipziger, eds. 2010. *Globalization and Growth: Implications for a Post-crisis World.* Washington, DC: World Bank.

Stern, Nicholas. 2007. *The Economics of Climate Change: The Stern Review.* Cambridge, UK: Cambridge University Press.

Temple, Jonathan. 2001. Growth effects of education and social capital in the OECD countries. *OECD Economic Studies* 33:57–101.

Temple, Jonathan, and Ludger Woessmann. 2006. Dualism and cross-country growth regressions. *Journal of Economic Growth* 11 (3): 187–228.

Tol, Richard S. J., and Gary W. Yohe. 2006. A review of the Stern Review. *World Economy* 7 (4): 233–50.

Tooley, James. 2009. *The Beautiful Tree: A Personal Journey into How the World's Poorest People Are Educating Themselves.* Washington, DC: Cato Institute.

Tooley, James, and Pauline Dixon. 2005. *Private Education Is Good for the Poor: A Study of Private Schools Serving the Poor in Low-Income Countries.* Washington, DC: Cato Institute.

Topel, Robert. 1999. Labor markets and economic growth. In *Handbook of Labor Economics*, ed. Orley Ashenfelter and David Card, 2943–84. Amsterdam: Elsevier.

Turkheimer, Eric, Andreana Haley, Mary Waldron, Brian D'Onofrio, and Irving I. Gottesman. 2003. Socioeconomic status modifies heritability of IQ in young children. *Psychological Science* 14 (6): 623–28.

Tyler, John H., Eric S. Taylor, Thomas J. Kane, and Amy L. Wooten. 2010. Using student performance data to identify effective classroom practices. *American Economic Review* 100 (2): 256–60.

U.S. Department of Education, Institute of Education Sciences. 2008. *National Assessment of Educational Progress—The Nation's Report Card*: Website: http://nces.ed.gov/nationsreportcard/aboutnaep.asp.

UNESCO. 1998. *World Education Report, 1998: Teachers and Teaching in a Changing World*. Paris: UNESCO.

UNESCO. 2014. *Teaching and Learning: Achieving Quality for All—EFA Global Monitoring Report 2013/4*. Paris: UNESCO.

van Elk, Roel, Marc van der Steeg, and Dinand Webbink. 2011. Does the timing of tracking affect higher education completion? *Economics of Education Review* 30 (5): 1009–21.

Vandenbussche, Jérôme, Philippe Aghion, and Costas Meghir. 2006. Growth, distance to frontier and composition of human capital. *Journal of Economic Growth* 11 (2): 97–127.

Venn, Danielle. 2009. Legislation, collective bargaining and enforcement: Updating the OECD employment protection indicators. OECD Social, Employment and Migration Working Paper 89. Paris: OECD.

Wayne, Andrew J., and Peter Youngs. 2003. Teacher characteristics and student achievement gains: A review. *Review of Educational Research* 73 (1): 89–122.

Weber, Sylvain. 2014. Human capital depreciation and education. *International Journal of Manpower* 35 (5): 613–642.

Weede, Erich, and Sebastian Kämpf. 2002. The impact of intelligence and institutional improvements on economic growth. *Kyklos* 55 (3): 361–80.

Weiss, Andrew. 1995. Human capital vs. signalling explanations of wages. *Journal of Economic Perspectives* 9 (4): 133–54.

Welch, Finis. 1970. Education in production. *Journal of Political Economy* 78 (1): 35–59.

West, Martin R., and Paul E. Peterson. 2006. The efficacy of choice threats within school accountability systems: Results from legislatively-induced experiments. *Economic Journal* 116 (510): C46–C62.

West, Martin R., and Ludger Woessmann. 2010. "Every Catholic child in a Catholic school": Historical resistance to state schooling, contemporary private competition and student achievement across countries. *Economic Journal* 120 (546): F229–F255.

Woessmann, Ludger. 2003a. Schooling resources, educational institutions, and student performance: The international evidence. *Oxford Bulletin of Economics and Statistics* 65 (2): 117–70.

Woessmann, Ludger. 2003b. Specifying human capital. *Journal of Economic Surveys* 17 (3): 239–70.

Woessmann, Ludger. 2004. Access to education: Perspective paper. In *Global crises, Global solutions*, ed. Björn Lomborg, 241–50. Cambridge: Cambridge University Press.

Woessmann, Ludger. 2005. The effect heterogeneity of central exams: Evidence from TIMSS, TIMSS-Repeat and PISA. *Education Economics* 13 (2): 143–69.

Woessmann, Ludger. 2007a. International evidence on expenditure and class size: A review. In *Brookings Papers on Education Policy 2006/2007*, 245–72. Washington, DC: Brookings.

Woessmann, Ludger. 2007b. International evidence on school competition, autonomy and accountability: A review. *Peabody Journal of Education* 82 (2–3): 473–97.

Woessmann, Ludger. 2009a. International evidence on school tracking: A review. *CESifo DICE Report—Journal for Institutional Comparisons* 7 (1): 26–34.

Woessmann, Ludger. 2009b. Public-private partnerships and student achievement: A cross-country analysis. In *School Choice International: Exploring Public-Private Partnerships*, ed. Rajashri Chakrabarti and Paul E. Peterson, 13–45. Cambridge: MIT Press.

Woessmann, Ludger. 2010. Institutional determinants of school efficiency and equity: German states as a microcosm for OECD countries. *Jahrbücher für Nationalökonomie und Statistik/Journal of Economics and Statistics* 230 (2): 234–70.

Woessmann, Ludger. 2011. Cross-country evidence on teacher performance pay. *Economics of Education Review* 30 (3): 404–18.

Woessmann, Ludger, Elke Luedemann, Gabriela Schuetz, and Martin R. West. 2009. *School Accountability, Autonomy, and Choice around the World*. Cheltenham, UK: Edward Elgar.

Wolf, Patrick, Babette Gutmann, Michael Puma, Brian Kisida, Lou Rizzo, Nada Eissa, and Matthew Carr. 2010. *Evaluation of the DC Opportunity Scholarship Program: Final Report*. Washington, DC: Institute for Education Sciences (June).

Wölfl, Anita, Isabelle Wanner, Tomasz Kozluk, and Giuseppe Nicoletti. 2009. Ten years of product market reform in OECD countries: Insights from a revised PMR indicator. OECD Economics Department Working Paper 695. Paris: OECD.

Wolter, Stefan C., and Paul Ryan. 2011. Apprenticeship. In *Handbook of the Economics of Education*, vol. 3, ed. Eric A. Hanushek, Stephen Machin, and Ludger Woessmann, 521–76. Amsterdam: North Holland.

World Bank. 1993. *The East Asian Miracle: Economic Growth and Public Policy*. New York: Oxford University Press.

World Bank. 2013. *Using Low-Cost Private Schools to Fill the Education Gap: An Impact Evaluation of a Program in Pakistan. From Evidence to Policy*. Washington, DC: Human Development Network, World Bank (September).

World Bank Independent Evaluation Group. 2006. *From Schooling Access to Learning Outcomes: An Unfinished Agenda*. Washington, DC: World Bank.

Index

Printed in the United States
by Baker & Taylor Publisher Services